After the End of History

Evolving Values for a Capitalist World

In most of the world today, the issue is not whether or how to embrace capitalism, but how to make the best of it. The currently dominant capitalist values include competitive individualism, instrumental rationality, and material success. The series explores questions such as: Will these values suffice as a basis for social organizations that can meet human and environmental needs in the twenty-first century? What would it mean for capitalist systems to evolve toward an emphasis on other values, such as cooperation, altruism, responsibility, and concern for the future?

After the End of History

THE CURIOUS FATE of AMERICAN MATERIALISM

Robert E. Lane

The Spinach Pie Papers
Someone had planned to take half of his or her spinach pie (spanako-pita) home but, as usual, had left it on the restaurant table. Wrapped around the pie was a thick folio of typed manuscript, containing, as it turned out, a mostly legible dialogue between an economist and a philosopher–social scientist. Uncertain of their value, the publishers nevertheless have published them for whatever audience is curious about the future of market economies.

THE UNIVERSITY OF MICHIGAN PRESS
ANN ARBOR

Copyright © by the University of Michigan 2006
Published in the United States of America by
The University of Michigan Press
Manufactured in the United States of America
♾ Printed on acid-free paper

2009   2008   2007   2006   4   3   2   1

A CIP catalog record for this book is available from the British Library.

Library of Congress Cataloging-in-Publication Data

Lane, Robert Edwards.
    After the end of history : the curious fate of American
materialism / Robert E. Lane.
        p.   cm.
    Includes bibliographical references.
    ISBN-13: 978-0-472-09915-3 (cloth : alk. paper)
    ISBN-10: 0-472-09915-9 (cloth : alk. paper)
    ISBN-13: 978-0-472-06915-6 (pbk. : alk. paper)
    ISBN-10: 0-472-06915-2 (pbk. : alk. paper)
        1. Quality of life—United States.   2. Materialism—United States.
    3. Interpersonal relations—United States.   4. Contentment.
    5. Humanistic ethics.   I. Title.

HN60.L36   2005
306'.0973—dc22   2005012047

Contents

After the End of History
Foreword by Neva Goodwin

This is an extraordinary book. For anyone—scholar, student, casual reader—it is extraordinary to learn so much in such an entertaining manner. For the scholar, the footnotes and bibliography provide an unsurpassed summary of the newly developing fields of studies that explore the causes and the meanings of quality of life, or happiness, or well-being. For other readers, the book is a witty dialogue that reveals two amusing characters as they probe questions of the greatest interest:

> What causes happiness?
> Why do life circumstances, such as riches or achievement, not necessarily bring about the happiness that might be expected?
> Do people generally know what to do to promote their quality of life?
> Is our society developing toward—or away from—an increase in human well-being?

It is interesting to raise these questions. What makes this book really exciting is the fact that Robert Lane also goes a good way toward answering them.

And who better than he to do so? Over his long career at Yale University, Lane has earned a worldwide reputation as both a leader and a synthesizer in exploring what the social sciences say about how our states of mind are related to what we do, have, and are. With a broad command of the behavioral sciences, Lane has brought solid data and theory to bear on such perpetual questions as "Under what circumstances does money buy happiness?" "Are friends an adequate substitute for money?" and "Do the answers to these questions differ in rich countries and poor countries?" Building on the data in his recent books, *The Market Experience* (1991) and *The Loss of Happiness in Market Democracies* (2000), Lane now extends his findings and their application to broader questions of a possible shift from materialism to humanism, the problems of transition for developing and advanced countries alike—and the obstacles in materialist societies to such a transition.

No one has read more widely or thought more deeply about the human condition in modern times than Robert Lane. In this book he makes his discoveries available in a delightful form to readers inside and outside of academia. It is the sort of book that is bread and music to a bright and eager mind and that the friends and relatives of such people will discover joyfully as the ideal gift.

One protagonist of the book is an economist, Adam, who is convinced that he knows what matters—material wealth—and (in principle, at least) how to get it. The other character is a humanist, Dessie, who feels passionately that the economists are still fighting the last war—the war to get enough to stay alive—and that, for the parts of the world where that war has essentially been won, there are more pressing concerns. Dessie sets out to persuade Adam that the materialist emphasis is passé for most of the industrialized world and that social scientists should be thinking about other, more direct routes to well-being. Many readers will be especially interested in the implication that differences between left and right are also losing relevance as compared with the humanist/materialist spectrum.

Surveying the world's literature, Dessie lines up the philosophers' conclusions on what really matters in a human being's life. He also exposes Adam (who is far from being a helpless or passive player in this drama) to what can be learned from anthropology and primatology about where we should turn our efforts when we have gone beyond the problem of scarcity. The economist is reluctantly lured away from his discipline's reduction of all goals to the "maximization of utility," which gets translated into a simple search for satisfaction of wishes (with the assumption that satisfied desires are equal to happiness). Early on, Dessie lays out a major issue by saying, "I see this friendly quarrel as a conflict between the dominant materialism of our time, of which you are a high priest, and an alternative vision that, for want of a better term, I shall call a humanist vision. As it happens, you have recorded history on your side, and I have the future on my side—a future fortified with research on the quality of life and human development." Adam replies, "I've never argued with a visionary before. It will be a new experience, but not one I care to mention to my colleagues."

Adam's reluctance to reexamine his assumptions and his desire to win any argument are counterbalanced by an intellectual honesty that can be found with a little digging and by a real friendship between the two quite different men. He accepts, with a struggle, the idea that happiness is not the only thing that counts, and he is willing to consider other goals, including justice and various kinds of human development—cognitive, emotional, and moral. The reader, watching the balls that are served, returned, lobbed, and lost between the two academics, gets a comprehensible introduction to the ideas of Piaget, the brilliant theorist of childhood learning whose writings are unreadable for most people (whether in the original French or in translation), as well as to recent work on emotional intelligence and moral development.

With the ultimate goals set out more clearly and acceptance that material possessions beyond survival needs are important only as they serve these ultimate goals, the heroes of Lane's story continue their discussions over spinach pie and crackers (or sometimes eggs) in their favorite New Haven hash house. In the final chapters of the book they debate how societies should develop to promote human well-being. Should poor countries follow the trajectory of the rich countries, bending most efforts to material achievement before worrying about what else there is? And what is the evidence that the rich countries have gone beyond materialism?

Adam and Dessie are quite evenly matched. Dessie knows more of the relevant literature, but even Adam can occasionally surprise us by quoting a philosopher or a poet, and he does not let Dessie get away with confusing what (he thinks) should be with what is. Both men are, of course, smart and learned. We are privileged to listen in to their conversations, related by the author with a wry amusement at human vanity and academic games, and we learn much about what is possible in a good society. Dessie would like to persuade his colleague that the world is moving along a path toward a better future. Adam is unpersuaded. But we are left with a vision of that future. We can make of it what we will.

Acknowledgments

Dessie wishes to thank, and Adam to acknowledge, those who facilitated previous exposures of the ideas expressed in this book. Chapter 3, "What's Wrong with Materialism?" had a selective viewing in *PAE News*, no. 15, September 4, 2002. Chapter 4, "Humanism: The Value of Persons," borrows heavily from Robert Lane's talk at a conference in County Clare, Ireland, in 2000, published as "Putting People at the Centre of Things" in *Redefining Roles and Relationships,* ed. Harry Bohan and Gerard Kennedy (Dublin: Veritas, 2001), 131–62. Chapter 6, "Diminishing Returns to Happiness," borrows from Robert Lane, "Diminishing Returns to Income, Companionship—and Happiness," *Journal of Happiness Studies* 1 (2000): 103–19. And Chapter 8, "Getting Rich the Right Way," borrows from Robert Lane's talk on "Third World Transition: Through Materialism to Humanism," presented at the Conference on Consumption and Society," University of Costa Rica, March 12–13, 2002.

Both Dessie and Adam are deeply grateful for the skill and generosity of Neva Goodwin, economist and codirector of the Global Development and Environment Institute, Tufts University. She transcended the limits of her discipline and enhanced the coherence of this book. She is a truly great humanist.

Three institutions gave shelter and stimulation to the author while he wrote this little book: Yale's Institution for Social and Policy Studies; Nuffield College, Oxford; and the Whitney Center, Hamden, Connecticut.

Although Adam has reservations, Dessie would like to thank his namesake for the license to pursue serious matters in a lighthearted manner. He says,

> I saw how ordinary men were corrupted by opinions of the most foolish kind in every walk of life. I longed to find a remedy more than I hoped for success. And then I believed I had found a means whereby I could insinuate myself into those over-indulged souls and cure them by giving them pleasure. I had often observed how a gay and amusing form of advice like this had happy results in many cases.
>
> (Desiderius Erasmus, "Letter to Dorp" (1515)
> on the publication of *In Praise of Folly*)

Spanakopita One

Prologue

*A*dam, a tall, angular economist with a high forehead and a low threshold for foolishness, confidently entered Clark's, the local Greek hash house, and seated himself at one of the red leatherette booths by the window. He looked around for his friend, Dessie (named after Desiderius Erasmus), and sighed. What nonsense would this paraphilosopher and semi–social scientist offer today? It was hard to say what discipline Dessie represented: he taught in the political science department, but *what* he taught was some combination of political psychology and philosophy in his own idiosyncratic mix: a humanist social scientist? Whoever heard of such an animal? But that's what Adam liked about him: his irreverence for what was "known" and reverence for the humanly possible—or what Dessie thought was possible. And in return, Dessie cherished Adam for his strong-minded realism, his good sense penetrating both Dessie's illusions and (sometimes) the silly superstructure of his own discipline.

Then Adam spotted Dessie, puffing his bundled-up way in from the cold while allowing the icy wind to sweep by Adam's legs.

"Sorry I'm late," said the portly Dessie, adding in a confidential whisper, "I think I know the answer."

"As Gertrude Stein said 'What is the question?'" asked Adam with a sober face.

"Well," said Dessie, "Given the recent pronouncements about the 'End of History,'[1] the silly term referring to the endless reproduction of our market and democratic systems—that is, the status quo—I have been wondering what happens when, like everything else, the status quo actually comes to an end. Now I think I know." Dessie paused to give a theatrical effect to his revelation. "If things go well and the constellation of forces is in our favor, we will have a society that puts people, rather than God or money, at the center of things. In a word, it will be the New Humanism." He smiled as though he were the angel reporting the Annunciation.

"Is that all?" said Adam, disappointed.

"Don't you see?" said Dessie, "Under the new circumstances, we must drop the pilot who brought us into the harbor and find another. You economist chaps have done a wonderful job, but perhaps, like so many others in the labor markets you somehow justify, you have worked yourselves out of a job. To put it most simply," he smiled in an embarrassed way, as though explaining to an adolescent how babies are made, "the materialist world of which you are an interpreter and priest is no longer satisfying. When people realize the cause of their hunger, they will turn to other interpreters and priests." He beamed his benign smile at Adam and everyone else within sight.

"Are you prepared to officiate?" asked Adam without a trace of priestly jealousy.

"Not yet," said Dessie, "but when called, I will be ready." He paused and went on with his conception of "post-end" societies. "I have been wondering if this civilization is devoting its very considerable resources and talents to what is most fulfilling and enriching. A text on consumer behavior imagines Rip Van Winkle's observations on waking from his very long sleep: he would, says the text, 'come to the conclusion that selling, buying, and consuming lie at the very core of life in most of the developed countries of the world.'[2] An anthropologist calls this preoccupation a 'rage to consume' and attributes it to an outgrown 'logic of scarcity,' the 'logic' that converts yesterday's concept of plenty into today's scarcity.[3] Calling modern humans *Homo consumens*, Erich Fromm claims that 'we, as human beings, have no aim except producing and consuming more and more.'[4] I dabble a little in philosophical and historical concepts of the right and the good, and I must say that this preoccupation with buying and selling and with material commodities has no resonance with that literature."

" 'Getting and spending, we lay waste our powers,' " muttered Adam. "Don't tell me you see Proteus rising from Lake Whitney and hear old Triton blow his horn on Whitney Avenue." He paused to listen for Triton and, not hearing him, went on. "Not only Wordsworth (1770–1850) but also Tocqueville (1805–59): 'It is strange to see with what feverish ardor the Americans pursue their own welfare. . . . A native of the United States clings to this world's goods as if he were certain never to die; and he is so hasty in grasping at all within his reach that one would suppose he was constantly afraid of not living long enough to enjoy them.'[5] This alarm over consumption is hardly new," continued Adam. "Recall that both of these authors were writing about primarily agricultural societies, and their alarms may say more about human sensibilities than market societies."

"An English nature poet and a French aristocrat —" Dessie left the sentence unfinished. "It is not easy for people living in a period of transition to diagnose it accurately," he continued plaintively, "but I sense a possible transition from a 'creed outworn' to something new. I have been reading some of the 'posts' (postindustrialism, postmaterialism, postmodernism, posthistoricism), and although I reject much of their content, I accept their belief that we are on the threshold of a major transformation marked by a rapid change in communication technology and information overload (the cybernetic revolution); the collapse of what many thought was the main alternative to market democracies, communism (the Marxist God that failed); the struggle with Islamic fundamentalism in the Middle East and Christian fundamentalism in the American and Italian South; the whimpering end of Freud's human tragedy where the big red libido and the remorseless superego hammer mercilessly on that fragile little ego crouching in the middle of the ring. In academia, the sporadic popularity of depersonalizing, cultic theories of human behavior, such as learning theory and rational choice, diminish the human personality. Nietzsche's death of God came to life when Sartre translated this as confrontation with 'nothingness.'[6] One unhappy prophet of the 1960s found that 'people are dejected and disheartened by a vast meaninglessness that seems to have insinuated itself into their lives, a lack of purpose, irrelevancy. . . . We reach out and no one is there, turn inward and find nothing inside. There is a sense of nightmare, and there is real madness.'[7] Okay, that's self-pitying hyperbole, but it is hard to falsify President Carter's sense that there was (and is) a sense of malaise abroad in the land. What Carter couldn't know is that the approved goals of American society—getting richer and having more things—were no longer satisfying. The job of social scientists is, as it always has been, to make articulate the inarticulate grievances people have. Perhaps the surge in discussion of well-being means that social scientists are finally doing their job."

Adam smiled, recalling the anti-intellectual hysteria of the children of the 1960s and 1970s. He wondered what their contribution to GNP had been but was wise enough not to ask. "You want to find a watershed in history so you can guide the waters to the promised land. But the periodization of history always seems different in retrospect, so perhaps we are going through what has become normal change in a technological age,[8] or perhaps, as you suspect, we experience only the small waves on some larger cycle that we cannot now understand. Or," he smiled again, "perhaps you are merely experiencing the disappointment of continuity as we face that 'end of history' you mentioned. Does Fukuyama distress you? The worldwide convergence in basic institutions around liberal democracy and market economics forces us to confront the question of whether we have reached an 'end of history.'[9] I know you never expected the wrenching 'closing chapter of the prehistoric stage of human society' that Marx predicted,[10] but you are an idealist and inevitably discontented with the benefits of a commercial society that satisfies so many others."

"A better historian puts it this way," said Dessie, trying to disguise his contempt for the silly phrases about history having an end. "Like communism, 'capitalism will someday pass from the stage of history, as feudalism did earlier.'[11] This is not the day (*der tag!*), however, and my so-called idealism has nothing to do with it. From many sources—some in quality-of-life research (such as the long-term shift in what people find satisfying), some in the conflict within your discipline,[12] some from assorted environmental and anticonsumption organizations and publications[13]—I sense a cultural shift that future historians might refer to as the struggle between the materialist's view of the world and the humanist's view of the world. We did not live through the earlier struggles between feudal and industrial societies or the late-nineteenth-century battle between science and religion, but most of us have seen the struggle between capitalism and communism now whispering its extreme unction. That battle is over. What takes its place? Certainly not the end of ideology; rather, I think, the struggle between the materialist and humanist visions follows the ideological fault line of this cultural shift—though humanism is hardly yet an organized force. Permit me to call this period, still in utero struggling to be born, the New Humanism." Dessie paused for a moment and continued. "Whether or not we stand on the shoulders of giants,[14] our job is to see farther than others, isn't it?"

"You are an alarmist. Your giants should be ashamed of you," said Adam. "From where I sit slurping my soup in Clark's"—he looked around at the slurping and munching secretaries and professors—"I do not see this malaise; indeed, I see no evidence of major cultural shifts whatsoever."

Dessie looked at Adam with concern. "Here is a pair of glasses provided by a playwright turned president of a small middle European country, Vaclev Havel: 'We all know that civilization is in danger: population explosion, greenhouse effect, holes in the ozone, . . . the expansion of commercial television culture. . . . What is needed is something different, something larger. Man's attitude to the world must be radically changed.'[15] Is what is visible from Prague not visible from where you sit?" asked Dessie.

Adam paused to digest his food and thoughts. "Thirty years ago," he said, "the Club of Rome saw world devastation by the end of the twentieth century.[16] Do you feel devastated—I mean, more than normally devastated?" he asked. "Anyway," he added, "we have markets and democracies to correct our faults."

"Confidence in self-correcting processes for societies has historically been misplaced," said Dessie. "For example, among the natives of Dobu, an island in the western Pacific, belief in sorcery created such mutual suspicion that those friendly relations that in other societies make people happier and life more rewarding were missing.[17] Dysfunctional societies abound in history.[18] There seems to have been no set of endogenous forces to bring these societies around to a more felicitous way of doing things. I fear," said Dessie with a sigh, "that our market-dominated, consumer-oriented society is similarly bereft of restorative forces."

Adam saw his opportunity. "Given that we live in an age marked by unprecedented feedback, an information glut demanding interpretation at every stage, we are not quite in the same position as other civilizations whose mainsprings weakened without anyone being aware of what was happening—societies such as ancient Alexandria, fourth-century Rome, or the Soviet Union in the 1980s.[19] Information-rich societies are blessed in this respect. And part of the globalization that exercises so many people is exactly the globalization of this information revolution."

"There is no more information-rich segment of our society than the economic sector, especially the Wall Street region of that sector," said Dessie in sharp rebuttal. "With all that information and talent, how does your profession fare at predicting the changes in the business cycle and the stock market? Or, longer term, in the midst of Japanese prosperity, did you see the signs of a decades-long depression on the horizon?" Dessie paused long enough to see that Adam was missing the main point. "Anyway," Dessie added, "any reliance on the feedback system of the market will fail to correct the problems I'm talking about because the changes are not changes among market goods; the goods I refer to are not priced. In this case, the market is not the cybernetic device that we count on. You and I are that device: *we* and our colleagues are the feedback information system."

The contrast startled Adam. Comparing the elegant, worldwide, lawful market system to this speculative conversation between two friends in a Greek hash house seemed grotesque. He went back to Dessie's earlier point. "I am not making any prophecies or predictions about sharp changes in the cultural values of our society; you are," he said. Then, seeing his exposure, he added, "In any event, my implicit prediction is continuity or persistence forecasting, meaning that the next decade will be very like this one."

"The end of history," muttered Dessie under his breath; then, more forcefully, he said, "I went to a conference in County Clare, Ireland, not long ago, where, observing the frantic—and successful—economic development of the Celtic Tiger, a certain Father Harry Bohun asked, 'Are we forgetting something?' He meant what is left out when attention is devoted almost exclusively to a people's economic transformation." Injudiciously, Dessie paused—and lost the floor.

"I am a little skeptical of any line of thinking that implies that people, in all their wonderful manifestations, are not better off because of economic growth," said Adam. "The United Nations Development Programme *Reports* certainly tell that story in graphic detail: higher literacy, lower infant mortality, longer life, and so forth.[20] But, because you are my friend and because we economists are eager to learn whatever you humanist–social scientists think you can teach us (I guess), I'm willing to listen to what you have to say—whatever that may be." Adam's smile was slightly patronizing, but his tone was calculated to suggest that he believed that he was talking to an equal.

Dessie caught the tone and braced himself. Perhaps, after all, tennis was better than discussion for maintaining friendship. Nevertheless, he was a man with a mission. "Let us avoid argument and engage in dialogue," he said.

"My impression of the Socratic dialogues," said Adam, "is that Socrates has all the good lines and his companion is reduced to saying 'How true!' And I don't believe I've been cast as Socrates."

"Nonsense," said Dessie. "Whoever heard of anyone winning an argument with an economist? I sadly fear that you may actually win the dialogue—if a dialogue, like a debate, is winnable. It's every man for himself, and nothing is decided until the very end. As I said, I see this friendly quarrel as a conflict between the dominant materialism of our time, of which you are a high priest, and an alternative vision that, for want of a better term, I shall call a humanist vision. As it happens, you have recorded history on your side, and I have the future on my side— a future fortified with research on the quality of life and human development."

"I've never argued with a visionary before," said Adam. "It will be a new experience, but not one I care to mention to my colleagues."

"What is the correct term for a point of view that assumes perfect knowledge, perfect markets, and perfect rationality?" asked Dessie with an ingenuous smile.

"Tell me about your humanist vision," said Adam, all innocent and wide-eyed. "Can one see it from Clark's?"

"You can see it from any place except Economica, which is located on the Dead Sea," said Dessie. "Indeed, I think for everybody else, the basic elements of my 'vision' lie in plain sight, as I may explain when we meet again. What the vision says is that after having achieved a certain level of economic welfare, one at which the basic needs and certain (changing) amenities are secure, people want other kinds of goods. As I mentioned, for the most part these are not goods that are offered in the market; rather, they are goods such as companionship, intrinsic work enjoyment, aesthetic supplies, self- and social esteem, a sense of accomplishment and of contribution to one's society.[21] Perhaps, people want something like the Stoic (and Confucian) ideal: harmony with nature and with other people."

"The test of what people want is what people seek in a free society," said Adam slipping his comment into a steady flow of exposition. "Propositions are not true by fiat but are made valid (not quite the same as 'true') by correct inference from the evidence."

"Truth is more complex," said Dessie in a minatory tone. "Evidence must be interpreted in the light of a theory. For example, good economists have always believed that the bundle of goods people demand changes as their income levels rise: for example, a smaller proportion of their income is spent on food and shelter and a larger proportion on travel and entertainment and education—and saving. The only thing that economists, except for Tibor Scitovsky,[22] have not already noticed is that the goods people now want—or at least the goods that make them happy—are those that are not to be purchased in the market."

"Why is that a vision of 'the good' or the promised land or whatever you want to call it?" asked Adam. "Why is your dinner a lesser good than your ideas or your friendships?"

"We can't compare them until we know whether or not you have had your dinner," said Dessie. "Your namesake, Adam Smith, assumed it was dinnertime when he talked about material self-interest,[23] and for many people in the eighteenth century dinnertime came more often than did dinner. I am only reciting somewhat obvious and stale economics, but for once it makes sense. In capsule form: if you are hungry, dinner has a higher priority; if (after dinner), you are lonely, friendships are more desirable." By comparison, he thought, explaining that two and two make four would be a deep exercise.

"All right," said Adam, somewhat mortified, "but you're not talking simply about a change in the goods people prefer; you're talking about a systematic shift in values. What do you call your new system? The New Humanism? And you want to contrast this new system with an old one, one that the public calls capitalism, economists call a market economy, and you call, much less precisely, materialism. Aside from substituting a preference for people over commodities, as you might say, what's the difference between the two systems?"

On the Threshold of a New Humanism?

Dessie wrapped himself in his prophetic mantle, spreading a dangling piece of spinach pie onto his lap as he did so. "I am guessing," he said, that advanced countries are on the threshold of a promising historical period when the values that made them so rich no longer reflect their most urgent needs or their understandings of the sources of well-being, a period fundamentally different from the industrial age that extended our lives and educated so many of us—and, incidentally, a period when your discipline ossif—crystallized. As I mentioned, this new era seems to be 'posteverything': 'postindustrial'[24] because of the shift in jobs from the industrial to the service sector; 'postmaterial' because of the rise of humanist values;[25] 'postmodern'[26] because of the shift from material, scarcity values to quality-of-life values; and, if one were to take 'the end of history' seriously, even 'posthistorical.'[27] Pointing to these changes, two of the most sober psychologists I know have asked for a 'new paradigm.' They comment, 'As the world enters a new era of material abundance, a new paradigm is needed in which greater emphasis is placed on fulfilling work that benefits society, and on preventing the involuntary poverty that is associated with a higher risk of unhappiness."[28] The 'post' terms address the point of departure; I call the new period the 'New Humanism' because, as I said, it promises to put humans and human encounters at the center of things. The transition to the New Humanism involves some poignant shifts in priorities:

> from priority of goods and services to priority of companionship;[29]
> from materialism to postmaterialism;[30]
> from avarice to enjoyment of the arts of life;[31]

from a fight against nature to games among people;[32]
from commodities stimuli to relational stimuli;[33]
from exclusiveness (ethnic, sexual orientation, gender) to inclusiveness, transcending inbred preferences for the familiar and the similar;[34]
from physical capital to human capital[35]—to human capabilities;[36]
from material welfare and survival to quality of life;[37]
from economic development to human development.[38]

And, if we call human engagements where money changes hands *transactions* and engagements where it does not *encounters,* then I would add

from primacy of transactions to primacy of encounters."

"That's all very well," said Adam, "but you seem to believe that the prosperity that sustains these changed priorities will continue without any attention to or, indeed, motivation for material well-being. You go beyond what you call 'my people' (by which you seem to mean economists) in assuming the automaticity of increased productivity and general equilibrium of a market economy. Do you realize that it takes at least a 2.5 percent growth rate in the United States just to maintain full employment—well, more or less full? Instead of facilitating the pursuit of happiness, you risk facilitating guaranteed pain." Because he had never thought about a society where the market was not the central, indispensable institution, Adam spoke with conviction.

"There is a lot going on in society other than buyers and sellers seeking to match their respective offers," said Dessie. "Of course, the market is an essential institution and must be nourished (as well as regulated); unless some people want to make money producing goods and services and others want to buy those goods and services, the market society will not thrive. But you must agree that there is more to life than that." He looked out on bustling Whitney Avenue and then back at Adam, who was eating his crackers with evident pleasure.

"Dear Adam," he pleaded, "look up and see the world: it is not just a world of transactions or even the detritus of transactions past and the ghost of transactions future. Those are people, not just customers, hurrying in their self-preoccupied way along Whitney Avenue."

Adam knew all this and thought Dessie was dramatizing his argument in an unfair way. What had this to do with the shift from materialist to humanist values? "All right," he said, "tell me how poetry and character will thrive when we become a developing country again."

"Realists need not be depressives," said Dessie with something approaching a smile. "Assume a market run by materialists who devote themselves to making money and, in the process, enlist the invisible hand to make the rest of us rich enough to become affluent consumers. If that is the subject matter of life, it is not very attractive. But we do not change our societies because their social roles are unattractive. Something else must move us, something I will explain later. It is subterranean. I think advanced economies are, quite unconsciously, engaged in a silent struggle to cross the threshold to the New Humanism, held back by a paradoxical need simultaneously to retain and to discard elements of the old economistic order. As Freud said of the cosmic struggle in the 1930s between civilization and the forces of death—at a time when it seemed that Thanatos was winning—'And now it can be expected that the other of the two "heavenly forces," eternal Eros, will put forth his strength so as to maintain himself alongside of his equally immortal adversary.'"[39] Dessie had been carried away by Freud's poetic language and belatedly realized that he had cast humanistic, self-correcting social science as Eros!

"Are you implying that the economics that has extended life to so many people is death and that social science is sexy or erotic?" asked Adam, reading Dessie's thoughts. "I know it seems rude to brush the 'heavenly forces' away from this earthly hash house, but going beyond cosmic struggles, may I come back to the from/to travel agenda you outlined a minute ago? I assume that one side represents the departure from a market economy—perhaps the departure from 'death's pale kingdom'—and on the other side, the arrival at the New Humanism?" He said "New Humanism" as though it tasted bad.

"You are wrong about my departure and arrival schedule," said Dessie with some heat. "In the New Humanism, we do not forsake money and material things, living like orchids on air (but, like orchids, entangled parasitically with some material host). Rather, it is a matter of emphasis: we become as concerned about our human encounters as we are about our transactions and take just as many pains to make them reciprocally successful (as, indeed, we often do now, without admitting it). In short, we shift our emphasis from money and commodities to an emphasis on human well-being and development. Economists are the philosophers of money and commodities, and we will always need them—or at least some of them."

"This is the first time I have been called a philosopher," said Adam, more annoyed than pleased. "Tell me more about this materialism that, as you said, has given us a society wealthy enough so that we can talk about directions alternative to those that brought us here." And under his breath, he added, "So you can bite the hand that feeds you."

"I will, but before we get to that or even to a description of humanism," said Dessie, "I wonder if it wouldn't be a good idea to see what all the fuss in our disciplines is fundamentally about: What are we trying to do with our market and governmental institutions? Indeed, what should we be doing?"

"Sounds soft and deep, like a pillow," said Adam, as though depth were something to be avoided by honest workaday scholars. "But you called me a philosopher, so I guess I must wrap myself in a philosopher's cloak, like Machiavelli, and make like a philosopher." He sounded reluctant, but he had not yet confronted a problem that did not yield to the tools acquired along with his Ph.D.: preference and indifference curves, production functions, equilibrium analyses, and the one he liked best, the kinky oligopoly curve.

"Fine," said Dessie. "I have always thought that a central problem characterizing both economics and political theory was their mistaking means, like wealth and freedom, for ends. This leads to all kinds of errors, like limiting the idea of efficiency to material efficiency or making a fetish of choice. So, if you are agreeable and are interested in examining what we should be doing, we'll start with ideas about the right and the good."

Adam was restless; he knew forbidden territory when he saw it. "You mean you intend to say which preferences are better than others?" he asked in the tone of a Christian asked which god he worshiped.

"Of course," said Dessie, with blithe insouciance. "You do that, too, whenever you talk about efficiency. I am just taking it one step further: What should we be efficient in doing? The only reason rational choice works to the pitiful degree that it does is because it is applied only to the means for maximizing utility. But neither God nor Aristotle ever said that happiness (neither of them used the vulgar word *utility*) was the only good. If it makes you feel more comfortable, instead of saying that the subject of our next session will be the 'nature of the good,' we can just say we will devote our next session to asking, 'Efficiency for what?' Or, to put it differently, 'What should we be doing?' " Dessie couldn't help feeling that this was an inspired way of enticing Adam into a discussion of things quite beyond equilibrium analysis.

"I know what you're up to," said Adam, looking askance at his partner. "I could short-circuit the whole damned discursive deliberation by saying flat out, 'It is because human beings cannot be exchanged that they have a special value, one that Kant calls dignity.[40] Wealth is a means that serves the ultimate purposes that you will designate.' Okay?" Now it was Adam's turn to smile a self-satisfied smile. Had he short-circuited the whole damned deliberation? Well, no. Dessie was not turned off so easily. No person with a vision ever is.

"We must be concerned with the implications of the statement of the good that you've just bravely announced," he said blandly. "What does it imply for the way we create and tend our institutions? Have you, with this statement of the good, just degraded economics to the status of a minor discipline? (Keynes once said he thought economists should be treated as dentists!)[41] What happens when we accept the statement and ignore its implications? If it is implausible that *every-thing* about human beings is so valuable, what aspects of human beings are and are not valuable? Kant's statement tells us nothing (beyond benevolence) about how to nurture 'dignity' and especially how to nur-ture it without lapsing into the paternalistic state of affairs that alarmed him. If humans are an end, must they also be a cause? And how can we make humans the cause of their own fates without blaming the victims of this world for their victimhood[42] or giving fundamentally erroneous historical explanations?"[43] Dessie was wound up, but Adam, who was trying to fit indifference curves to the situations described, failed to notice.

"Aha," said Adam as he started to draw some curves on his crumpled napkin, "I think I know how the preferences you're talking about can be mapped. Look at this."

"Dear Adam," said Dessie ignoring the crumpled napkin thrust across the table between them, "I am not talking about preferences or choices but about principles and their causes and consequences. We will not solve it by climbing the utility mountain but rather by thinking through a complex situation, philosophically in the ethical domain, con-sequentially in the cause and consequences domains."

"In my opinion, the utility mountain is more promising than your 'city set on an hill,'" said Adam. "But you were going to tell me about the domain where I am a 'philosopher,' the material or, as you would say, 'materialist' world whose 'philosophy' is my business."

Materialism

"Okay," said Dessie, "although as its interpreter, you should be telling me. As the guiding philosophy of 'economic man' (a chap who was, for-tunately, stillborn), materialism prowls the corridors of our minds the way Weber said that the 'idea of duty to one's calling prowls about in our lives like the ghost of dead religious beliefs.'[44] As I shall explain in some subsequent meeting, *materialism* is many things to many people, but now we can measure one aspect of it, giving it a scientific character, avoiding long sessions on its meaning. I will use the term both in a broader sense, to mean a focus on goods and services rather than on people or beauty or spirituality, and in a narrower sense, to mean the attitudes and beliefs measured by the 'Materialism Scale'—that is, the importance of acquiring things, the belief that commodities are the main source of happiness, and admiration for those who have those commodities.[45] You said earlier that I called the market economy a materialist economy; compared, say, to the Kula Rings of the South Pacific, it is. Market economics, bounded as it is by the 'measuring rod of money,'[46] is also materialist. As a general theory of choice, however, economics is not materialist but is simply a psychologically uninformed theory of how people choose."

Adam nodded his head. Meanings were not much discussed in economics. For Adam, declarative sentences, indicative mood, and denotative definitions were home territory. His mind was a steel trap, but he had a tin ear.

Humanism

"I think it only fair," said Dessie with all the charm and candor of a door-to-door salesman, "to discuss the meaning of *humanism* so that you can have a clear target for your fantasy-driven realism."

"I thought you did that earlier when you talked about your 'vision thing,'" said Adam, smiling tolerantly at his friend.

"Oh, that was just the beginning," said Dessie. "We can define *materialism* from a set of common usages and measures; *humanism,* however, has a much more diffuse set of meanings and no measure whatsoever. Its origin is the Greek *paedeia,* or 'aimed at the many sided development of man's faculties and the creation of the highest excellence of which he is capable.'[47] It has a Roman version, a medieval version, and of course a Renaissance version, but, as I mentioned, I will define it as a philosophy or ideology that places at the center of concern human beings rather than wealth (like you), or piety or God (like Augustine), or duty (like the Japanese),[48] or even happiness (like the utilitarians). Much flows from that focus, and I warn you, its implications are not favorable to economists. Thus, we shall have to see what it means to put human beings at the center of things, how that might affect our institutions developed in a materialist age, on what grounds we give priority to people and what about people is worth this centrality."

"I anticipate a discussion filled with high thinking and little evidence or theory," said Adam, puckering his lips and gritting his teeth at the same time.

"You remind me," said Dessie, "of Galbraith's dismissal of happiness as a goal on the grounds that it was too vague for use by economists and citing as proof Bertrand Russell's definition of *happiness:* 'a profound instinctive union with the stream of life.'[49] Galbraith's writing mostly predated the quality-of-life research and its more precise (if still a little vague) references. He wanted to substitute *material production* for *happiness*.[50] Things have changed since Russell and especially since the Enlightenment's discussion of the perfectibility of humans, a concept to which I shall try to give some empirical precision."

Adam thought if lefty Dessie could attack lefty Galbraith, something useful might come out of the discussion after all. Although Adam cherished the concept of preferences, he had a horror of preference-driven discussion. "Okay," he said, "so we must explore what you call meanings and implications at some goddamned ultimate level; then the materialism for which I am a spokesman ('philosopher,' you said); and then this humanist vision of which you are a spokesman (or do I mean evangelist?). Does that wrap it up?"

Happiness

"Good heavens, no," said Dessie. "Let us suppose that happiness turns out to be one of the ultimate goods: you and your colleagues, with a little sleight of tongue, have converted this to 'utility' and built a towering, if shaky, edifice on what you call 'utility theory,' whereas my people have built a rival edifice on quality-of-life research. You wouldn't want to leave people wondering which building to enter, would you?"

"Yes," said Adam, "it's their choice."

Human Development

"So that represents something we have to clarify. But beyond that, there is this matter of human development left over from the Enlightenment discussion of human perfectibility. This is very dear to my heart."

What was dear to Dessie's heart was a matter of only moderate concern to Adam, but he was well brought up and tried, with only moderate success, not to be rude.

"As you know, I believe people are individually responsible for what they become. It has always seemed to me that our responsibility as social scientists"—he nearly choked on that term—"is to arrange things to give people the resources and opportunities to become what they want to and can become. Full stop. The rest is pure paternalism."

"Do you claim that the market teaches people nothing?" asked Dessie with a rising inflection.

"Of course it teaches people prudence, to take care of themselves, to look ahead and save for their own futures—'deferred gratification,' in your language. It is one of the great teachers of self-reliance," said Adam, hardly realizing the contradiction.

"You believe that this teaching market is like nature—it's just there! But we have learned to make nature do our bidding and serve humankind in ways that we consciously specify. 'Prudence,' 'self-reliance,' 'deferred gratification' are exactly the types of qualities that I had in mind when I spoke of human perfectibility. So you must agree that we should assess how our institutions help or hinder the cause of human development, a term that can have more specific meaning when it is broken into cognitive, emotional, and moral dimensions." The trap had caught its rabbit, and Adam was condemned, one way or another, to participate in or partake of rabbit stew.

Justice Deferred

"Thank you for avoiding the relative claims for 'justice' and 'morality' in this clash of materialist and humanist philosophies that you are setting up," said Adam, clothing himself in a philosopher's cloak with a newly minted silver lining. "It is not that I oppose justice or morality but that the world has had a little experience with ethical economics, first with the Christian economics that impoverished the Middle Ages, then with the egalitarian vision of the late communist countries, and continuing with the kibbutzim in Israel, now losing their members to the inegalitarian Israeli market economy."[51]

"Sorry," said Dessie, without the slightest trace of sorrow in his voice, "but the fact is that one cannot talk about the merits of a philosophy without reference to its implications both for who should get what—that is, welfare economics—and such virtues as you mentioned. Indeed, the whole point of talking about justice and morality in materialist and humanist philosophies and practices is to do just that: What are the moral costs of materialism? What are the material efficiency costs of humanism?"

"You smell of the moralist to me," said Adam somewhat rudely. "But if you are willing to see, with Mandeville, that luxury and inequality may be the small moral costs, if that is what they are, that protect us against the much larger immoralities of poverty and joblessness, we might—dare I say it?—be in business."

"Great," said Dessie. "We are doing the business we are supposed to do: clarify the choices (a word you love) between two ways of looking at and evaluating the world." He looked quite irrelevantly at his watch. "The fact is," he said, "that, as usual, we won't have time for justice. It is too big a subject, and again as usual, justice will have to wait."

Through Materialism to Humanism

"But justice has many faces," continued Dessie, "one of which is proper attention to the poor. Thus, there is the matter of what the developing countries should do. They must, of course, get richer so they can afford the humanist way of looking at things, but they have to get richer in the right way."

"Getting richer has its own way of happening. Interfere at your peril," said Adam.

"Getting richer has two ways of happening," said Dessie more positively than he felt, "one way for the developing countries, when, as Keynes said, avarice is useful, and another way for advanced economies, where they can afford to cultivate, again as Keynes said, 'the arts of life.'"[52]

"There's a quite competent economic growth center here on the campus," said Adam, aghast. "Are you going to second-guess those guys?"

"I doubt if they take up the central question I have in mind: Is it necessary to go through materialism to get to humanism?" said Dessie, who already knew and liked the fellows of the growth center.

"All right," said Adam doubtfully. "Are you about to say that we in the United States have arrived at the point where we need no further growth?"

"Of course not," said Dessie doubtfully, for he feared an extension of this line of thought. He returned to his vision of the great transformation confronting the advanced countries of the world.

After the End of History

Dessie went on: "The 'Great Transformation' that Polanyi described was the rise of capitalism: the industrial revolution plus the development of markets for labor, land, and capital.[53] Capitalism emerged slowly in the late modern period in Britain, driven by desire for material gain and informed by technological developments and a social organization that made gain possible. While accompanied by great pain, as Marx and Dickens made clear, even during the worst of the transition period, say from the 1760s to 1830, the actual diets of the members of the working class improved.[54] The configuration of forces at the time made its success inevitable."

"So far, so good," said Adam, a little bored by this recital.

"We are not as lucky," continued Dessie. "The second great transformation may or may not occur in our lifetimes; the configuration of forces"—he spoke as though he referred to the configuration of the heavenly spheres in the Age of Aquarius—"is not as favorable. What is good for mankind is clear enough to me and to many others, but what mankind—sorry, I mean humankind—situated as it is in the midst of the Age of Materialism, wants or even demands is not clear."

"Your shift from *mankind* to *humankind* did not go unnoticed," Adam said, pursuing a line of thought that marked him off in his department. "Although I think your New Humanism is economically indefensible, as I listen with my other ear"—did he mean the ear tutored by his feminist wife?—"I see it as a society more congenial to women, the other half of the population. I suspect that women are less materialistic than men[55] and more tuned to the interpersonal relations[56] you think are important. That ear cheers you—if you will allow a synesthesia of sense organs in this manner. But I suspect that increased poverty will affect both halves of the population in the same unfortunate way."

"What we have to work out is a kind of cost-benefit assessment of the materialist vision and the humanist vision along with an assessment of the configuration of forces on each side," said Dessie, a little deaf in his feminine ear.

Adam, somewhat disturbed, interrupted him. "Are you saying that human preferences are not to guide us in this transformation?"

"They must be taken into account," said Dessie patiently. "It's just that when economic growth stops providing further utility, we all will want to pause and think of how to improve the well-being of our fellow human beings." He looked quizzically at Adam. "Won't we?"

Well, Adam knew that economics had somehow gotten itself into a situation where utility theory based on revealed preferences served to justify much that economists did, and he wasn't about to let the beautiful structure, so painfully designed and defended, be undermined or savaged by amateurs from outer space. Figuratively speaking, he stood up and, with an air of a man whose honor has been challenged, said in mock indignation, "I warn you, sir, you have gone too far. Be advised that people's preferences are sovereign in any decent society."

"Sir, I will not retract what I have said," said Dessie calmly. "Seven o'clock next Wednesday at Clark's. Scrambled eggs at fifty paces."

Adam looked bleakly at Dessie. "Hard-boiled," he said. Then, calming down, he added, "I think I need a more detailed view of this promised land you say we may be about to enter."

"As it happens," said Dessie, I have a diagram in my head, but I acknowledge it is a bit short on details: inside toilets, of course, and Internet connections in every room. It hasn't been lived in yet and, for all I know, has a leaky roof. But," he added, "those are only material things."

"Stay dry," said Adam. "Next week at Clark's—but I am allergic to eggs."

Spanakopita Two

What Should We Be Doing?

*I*t was another Wednesday, and Adam seated himself by the window waiting for his all-too-substantial friend to join him in the red leatherette booth. Idly, he wondered if in a wrestling match he could pin Dessie to the mat and concluded that he could not. It would not be difficult to fell him with a sudden unexpected header to the stomach, but it would be impossible to keep this slippery adversary down long enough to pin both shoulders flat on the mat. Just at that moment, Dessie appeared in the doorway, blinking his way toward the booth they usually shared.

"You preceded me again. What's happening?" he asked as he caught his breath.

"There is no strategic advantage in being first," said Adam. "It is only God's Boolean order—that's Boolean, not Boola Boola. Did you know that there is a crumb cake called 'Ultimate?'"

"Crumbs, I know about; cake is something else," said Dessie. "I thought you were shy about the ultimates of this world. But since you brought it up, are we agreed that happiness and human development are ultimate goods?" Dessie had hardly settled into the booth before he launched into his missionary work.

Adam smiled. There was old Dessie at it again. But why not; it was as much fun talking about the ends of life as about his colleagues—well, almost as much fun. "Last time you said we would talk about what we should be doing, what is worth doing. I thought last time that this topic had a noble ring, but I confess I fear talk about 'love thy neighbor,' agape, and that punctual friend of yours whom I quoted last time, Immanuel Kant. I would like to say one more thing about your friend Kant: It is really pretty empty to say that the dignity of humans is the end toward which we should strive, for it tells us nothing about how to go about it. Every day I have a choice between seeing more students and finishing my article on utility maximization in the professions. So, if I act as though my act were embodied in a universal law, either I treat my students as the means of getting a livelihood while I seek glory in some obscure economic journal, or I treat the members of my 'invisible college' as a means of getting tenure so I can teach my students. Throw a high-sounding word such as *dignity* at you guys and you'll gnaw on it for centuries." Adam never minded mixing metaphors.

"You mean we concern ourselves with eternal problems," said Dessie with a trace of irritation. "Would it be better if we dealt only with ephemeral problems? I doubt if you can even ask, let alone answer, questions about what we should be doing without referring to some such concepts as 'the good.'"

"I've been thinking about the hidden meanings of the word *good*," said Adam. "What was it that Charles Stevenson said about moral words? They are 'aha' expressions designed to give an affective glow to people who use them—something like that.[1] I fear the easy use of *good*."

"You can't avoid it, even if you talk only about the means to some end. For one thing, evaluation is built into our systems. For example, the good-bad dimension is the first in a factor analysis of the connotative meanings of words and comes easily to the mind as well as the tongue.[2] Also, whatever may be the implications of rational choice, the first evaluations that come to mind are largely emotive; only later, if at all, do cognitive judgments supersede them."[3] Dessie paused for a moment to consider where the trouble lay. "You know," he continued, "I think your problem is special to your discipline. Political theory deals with the philosophical implications of political practice; sociology treats concepts of the good society without embarrassment; and in psychology, the least well integrated of the social sciences, there is a fairly substantial attention given to mental health and to the development of effective, moral people.[4] Welfare economics, however, accepts the narrower limits of positive economics. Tjalling Koopmans says that 'in defining normative economics, we say that we seek clarification as to what are, according to some suitable criterion, best ways of satisfying human wants, starting from a given state of knowledge and experience,'[5] but he does not mean such wants as companionship, self-esteem, and intrinsic enjoyment of work—the wants whose satisfaction make life an enjoyable and fruitful enterprise. The point is that every discipline needs a normative and philosophical branch, but the economic branch takes the ends of economics as given and does not explore beyond these limits."

"Our advantage," said Adam, defending his discipline, "is that the good we offer is a fungible, universally valued currency that permits people to satisfy their wants without our specifying in detail what it is that they do or should want. This protects their autonomy and choice in a way that your buddy Kant would envy."

Dessie was not going to let Adam ignore his comment about the narrow exclusiveness of Koopmans' kind of wants. "Harrod defined the wants that economics deals with somewhat better than Koopmans," he said. "'Economics,' said Harrod, is 'concerned only with the goods and services of which the constituent items can be made alternatively available to one or [an]other of different persons. Thus goods like friendship and mystical experiences are excluded.'⁶ Given that we are social animals whose bonding is essential both for survival and reproduction and that, by one estimate, most civilizations have given religious values primacy over economic values,⁷ the wants economics serves are really a pretty narrow slice of what people want. For this reason, searching for the kinds of goals that have stronger yields of beneficence than materialist goals is a valuable, even necessary, enterprise."

Adam did not want to appear to be a narrow specialist interested only in the material side of life. Insofar as he understood it, he believed he had a broader philosophy that had a set of moral claims that had survived many years of criticism: that philosophy was utilitarianism. "With qualifications regarding its egalitarianism, I am a utilitarian," he said, "with a belief that the greatest happiness of the greatest number is an appropriate moral end, even though I know that there are ambiguities about the implied distribution that have to be clarified."

"Do you mean happiness, as your discipline originally claimed, or do you mean preference satisfaction, as it now claims, in spite of some rather trenchant criticisms of this change in the meaning of the word *utility*?"⁸ asked Dessie, a little like the grand inquisitor.

Adam knew the problem and fudged. "Inasmuch as preference satisfaction is the best route to happiness, I mean both," he said. "The defense against that nine-headed Hydra (even when reduced to only two or three heads) has to come in several parts, the main part being postponed until we address that siren, utilitarianism." He realized he was creating a veritable pantheon of Greek she-devils and wondered if he couldn't somehow add Pandora and Medusa to the indictment. At the same time, Adam was wondering why Athena had been omitted. "But to take up the 'preference satisfaction equals happiness' thesis now, do you mean to imply that people never make mistakes or choose unwisely?" he asked in his bittersweet manner.

"Do you know any psychological doctrine of choice that holds true under all circumstances without exception?" countered Adam, more bitter than sweet.

"So, in the pursuit of satisfying one's preferences, one's 'rational expectations' could be wrong about the ensuing yield in happiness—what? Half the time? Every tenth time? Most of the time?"[9] Dessie was enjoying this quiz.

"People learn," explained Adam. "First purchases are less likely to pan out than later or repeated purchases."

"Maybe," said Dessie. "Second marriages are more likely to break up than first marriages. And what people learn from their first jobs are the values inherent in those jobs so that most people do not know anything about the values in another type of career that might better suit their temperament. Furthermore, I know economists like to ignore sunk costs, but most people pay a lot of attention to them. Finally, even in the market, about a fifth of the purchases are reported to be unsatisfactory.[10] But these are only one set of reasons why preferences do not always lead to happiness."

"If all you are saying is that people often make mistakes, I cannot disagree with you," said Adam, trying to cut short the obvious.

"So why not just say *happiness* rather than *preference satisfaction,* as I. M. D. Little suggested more than a quarter of a century ago?[11] But that's not all I want to say on this subject, for there is now new evidence that wanting and liking are two different emotions and occur separately in the brain. They cannot be treated as identical: even when people get what they want, they may not like it."[12]

"So, welfare economics is too narrow; utilitarianism and guidance by the sovereign masters of pain and pleasure won't do for reasons you have yet to give me; preferences are misleading and their satisfaction does not lead to happiness. Anything else?" asked Adam, half in disbelief and half in scorn.

"Yes," said Dessie with the self-assured humility of someone reciting the Lord's Prayer. "That fungible currency you propose may buy the things people want, but it won't buy the things that will make them happy because those things are not market goods."

"All of this just to clear the way so you can recite *your* list of what you want to call 'the good,'" said Adam with traces of disgust. "Moreover, you want me to take your discounting of happiness on credit and of preferences and money on two-sentence dismissals!" This was so preposterous that Adam was now amused. "I'll give you infinite credit on your person, but on your arguments I'll give you 50 percent credit, as though you were flipping a coin, a generous proposition since actually you are rolling dice. What do you call a person who is a too easy source of credit? Credulous?"

"I'll be back," said Dessie, reassuringly. Or so he thought. "But in the meantime, I want to tell you why I have scanned philosophy and social science for things that could be called 'ultimate'—" He looked at Adam's darkening face. "Don't worry, I do not plan a recital over spinach pie today, but if you will put up with me, I would like to suggest a way of clustering these items to make the list manageable."

Adam visibly brightened. "I see," he said, "It's like a tour of the heavens for a poor earthbound materialist. But we will look at galaxies rather than individual stars."

A Program of Weight Reduction for Ultimate Goods

While he appreciated Adam's poetry, Dessie went on ruthlessly. "Here," he said, "are some of the ends that philosophers and religions have thought were ultimate in the sense of being the final criteria for what is valuable, for things worth pursuing over a lifetime. Happiness and freedom (your preference ordering in a more noble dress) make the list, but note how much more capacious the heavens are. And, please, don't plead parsimony yet—you'll get your chance." Dessie then handed Adam a sheet of paper with the following items scribbled on it:

Concepts of the Ultimate

Religion
> Union with the infinite (generic)
> Gift of grace, salvation (Christian); mercy of Allah (Islamic)
> Withdrawal from stimuli, care, emotion in Nirvana (Hindu, Buddhist)
> Love of the father "as a good man . . . in whom is reflected the image of the supreme mind which alone they call the *summum bonum*"[13] (Erasmus)

Philosophy
> Thinking philosophically (Plato, Aristotle); "reflective equilibrium" (Rawls)
> Virtue: as morality (Spinoza); as craft of life (Aristotle)

Benevolence (Kant; "charity" in the trinity of faith, hope, and charity)

Harmony with nature and with oneself (Stoics, Buddhists)

Friendship (G. E. Moore, Stoics, Yeats)[14]

Appreciation of beauty (G. E. Moore, Freud)[15]

Social esteem and its derivatives: honor (military, chivalric code); reputation (in professions)

Self-esteem: as dignity (Kant), as self-respect (Rawls), as amour propre (Rousseau)

Happiness (Bentham); deserved happiness (W. D. Ross, N. Rescher)

Doing one's duty (Confucius, Asian codes generally)

Justice (Rawls, Barry)

Autonomy and freedom (Kant, J. S. Mill, T. H. Greene)

Toward perfectibility of humans (Condorcet, Marx and Engels,[16] Maslow)

"Human flourishing";[17] development of "essentialist functions"[18]

Mental health: as a condition for effective pursuit of all goods, as relief from pain, as part of the perfectibility of humans, and as good in itself

True knowledge (Plato, W. D. Ross)

Integrity: as keeping promises, as fidelity to others, as reliability, etc.

Adam looked at the list and experienced two incompatible emotions. The first was a kind of distress that his discipline had so little to say about these wonderful things, so rosy in their hopeful attitudes toward the human species. The second was relief that he did not have to cope with them and could go back to the simplicity of preferences, utility, and welfare that Dessie had trashed a few minutes ago. Corresponding to these two emotions, Adam said with what could be interpreted as appreciation (emotion no. 1) or sarcasm (emotion no. 2), "Very pretty."

"You can think of these things as preferences if you want," said Dessie, ignoring the possible sarcasm, "but, as Albert Hirschman once said, values are really different from items on a shopping list[19] because they govern a much wider range of behavior. Perhaps we don't need ultimates, but we do need to have priorities or we lose our way pursuing subordinate goals such as consumption. If you have a chain of priorities, you can call the top of the chain anything you want, but as soon as you defend it by citing some subordinate good, it ceases to be at the top of your chain."

Adam paused as he digested his friend's whirlwind tour of the final, even sacred, things that people thought of as ultimate goods. It wasn't a model; it failed to specify how these goods related to each other, and because there was no way to attach prices or some other metric to the goods, the list made resolving conflicts very difficult. If it were a list of preferences, what was the value of listing various philosophers' preferences without being able to order them transitively or knowing anything about who shared them—that is, the demand for the values mentioned? Furthermore he suspected (correctly)[20] that people's values were somewhat inchoate and would sort themselves out only in conversation. But he knew that economists graded goods according to the "utilities" they yielded, so he decided to take another tack.

" 'I fear thee, ancient Mariner'," said Adam with a smile. "Any effort to establish overarching goals suggests first a degree of centralized planning and then coercion to implement those goals, a coercion that frightens me."

"Is it not true that economics has as its overarching goal, the maximization of utility? You even said your own philosophy was for the overarching goal of 'the greatest happiness for the greatest number,' mutatis mutandis. Why not, say, 'human flourishing' as an extended and more satisfying version of your pinched utilitarian philosophy? Your fear of other people's goals is pure ideology."

Adam could see an important difference between a set of goals for individuals to strive for and a set of goals for society to 'enact' and then enforce, but he had other quarrels with Dessie's list.

"Two more points," said Adam. "First, isn't it odd that survival, or life itself, isn't on this list, as though the nourishment and shelter of mankind were irrelevant. As Schumpeter said, 'the unending rhythm of economic wants and satisfaction'[21] shapes our goals as well as our ways of thinking."

"Sorry," said Dessie, "I should have thought of that. Indeed, a current hierarchical ordering of 'needs' puts the 'physiological needs' first, as a condition for achieving all the others,[22] although there are causes for which people will sacrifice their lives. But of course Hobbes makes the point about survival and Marx about the priority of eating in the eating-thinking sequence." He was going to say academia reversed that sequence, but, given his indulgence in spinach pie, he let it go.

"Second, and relatedly, I find it curious that the one thing everybody wants, wealth, is not on your list," said Adam. "Nor, come to think of it, is sexual or sensual gratification. Perhaps wealth and sex are excluded from what you call 'the good' because they *are* wanted. There is an ascetic quality to this list of concepts of the good that I think says more about the listers than about what people pursue as good."

"You must understand, even if Aristotle did not, the fundamental distinction between the *desired* and the *desirable*," said Dessie. "Only the desirable counts as 'the good.' Going from the desired to the desirable is a variant form of the proscribed going from *is* to *ought*. Anyway, wealth is universally thought of as a means—to power, popularity, and so forth. In your cosmology, it is a means to happiness—a mistaken theory, as I shall explain later. Economics offers a better theory of important but selective sources of welfare (especially relief from hunger and homelessness), but it certainly has no theory of the good and has nothing to do with the intrinsic—that is, anything that is good in itself." He paused before he presented the idea that he believed might place his preferred goods, happiness, human development, and justice at the top of the familiar philosophical canon.

Economics in the Presence of Ultimates

*A*dam was not only restless but disturbed. He was proud of his discipline and certainly believed that it had done more for humankind than develop a science of wealth. He agreed with Marshall, who, about a century ago, had said that the economist "does not ignore the spiritual side of life. On the contrary, even for the narrower uses of economic studies, it is important to know whether the desires which prevail are such as will help to build up a strong and righteous character [and are concerned] with the *ultimate aims of man*."[23] There they were, the things Dessie was talking about: human development and the "ultimate aims of man." But how had economics trained Adam to cope with questions of human development, let alone harmony with nature, friendship, beauty, autonomy, freedom, "the spiritual side of life," and "the ultimate aims of man"? If he followed Ludwig von Mises, he knew that "all action was economic,"[24] but the economics of appreciation of beauty and especially of harmony with (not dominance over) nature escaped him. If he followed Tjalling Koopmans, he might get a better notion of how economics dealt with these strange but important problems. As economists, reported Koopmans, "we say that we study the satisfaction of wants in human society" and the specification of welfare economics mentioned earlier.[25] All these

philosophical chaps had spent their lives trying to figure out the basic
wants and needs of human beings: knowledge? virtue? benevolence?
companionship? Adam ransacked his brain for clues as to how economics studied the satisfaction of these wants or clarified the best ways of satisfying them. Finally, if he followed Milton Friedman, he knew that market economies were a condition for freedom and that the "kind of
economic organization that provides economic freedom directly, namely
competitive capitalism, also promotes political freedom."[26] Adam certainly agreed that maximizing freedom and thus maximizing choice was
a good thing, but Dessie was saying that one had to do more than mention such glow words as *freedom;* one had to defend them against other
glow words, other concepts of the good. Ah well, one could not expect
any single discipline, even economics, to prepare a person for all arguments. Still, Adam was distressed to find that once out of the sphere of
priced objects, Marshall was wrong: economics did not have any good
answers.

There was a fallback position that he did not much like but that might
impress Dessie: "You know, of course, that John Stuart Mill defended
the view 'that the energies of mankind should be kept in employment by
the struggle for riches as they were formerly by the struggle for war, until
the better minds succeed in educating the others into better things,'" he
said.[27] "Also, Hume and Keynes, in their separate versions, defended the
pursuit of riches as ways to keep people out of mischief."[28]

"Humph!" said Dessie. "The whole point of my thesis is to go beyond
and to bury such nonsense."

Adam saw that he had walked into that trap and changed the subject.
"You said you wanted to subsume those peachy values people should
pursue," he said.

The Latent Trinity

*W*hat do all these good things have in common?" asked Dessie rhetorically. "Except for the religious goals, they are interpretations of how to
please, instruct, save, elevate human beings. One might say that they all
bear testimony that human beings are the center of value."

"You already said that," said Adam, relieved that no more powerful
argument was lurking in the bushes but wondering how Dessie would
explicitly address the "second sex."

"More than that," said Dessie, "I believe that they all include answers
to the three questions one should ask about any experience: (1) Did the

experience make you happier, more contented, more satisfied with your life? (2) Did you learn something you value or at least that you find useful; did it help you develop cognitive, emotional, or moral skills? And (3) was the outcome fair, both to the parties engaged and to others? You will notice that the questions Did it give you what you wanted? and especially Did it make you richer? are not included."

"My mother always asked me when I came home from school, 'Whom did you help today?'" said Adam. "Your set of questions is hopelessly self-focused and self-serving."

Dessie thought for a moment. Adam was right. Dessie felt quite strongly that his trinity of goods was right but saw that his questions did not capture the idea, included in utilitarian thought, that insofar as each person's experiences affected others, the same good should apply to them as to the self. But, of course! Erik Erikson's golden rule was the answer; it was, indeed, an integral part of the second question: "The Rule would say that it is best to do to another what will strengthen you even as it will strengthen him—that is, what will develop his best potentials as it develops your own."[29]

"I hate to sound like the perpetual groundling in your ethereal world," said Adam with annoyance. "Why isn't one of the fundamental questions 'Did you have the resources necessary to pursue your vision of the good?' Or 'How were these resources produced and distributed and at what cost?' If there is a moral issue here—and you always seem to find one—it is covered by the little slogan moralists use, 'ought implies can.' As you may have guessed, I do not spend much time thinking about the great world of ultimates, but I am constantly worried about how these ultimates, whatever they are, can survive without a material (or materialist) base."

"I'll come back to that," said Dessie, who had the mind of a juggernaut (without the Hindu obscenities but quite willing to crush even his own followers under his wheels). "First I want to give a bit of a rationale to the way I subsumed the ultimates of all my greatest predecessors into three qualities. The first, you recall, was happiness or positive affect, on the grounds that no good (or bad) thing gets done without the doer anticipating some kind of positive (or negative) affect. It is not true that virtue is its own reward; rather, a good conscience is the reward for virtue. Nor is it true that to see the good is to desire it, or at least it is not true that when people see the good, they feel they must act to achieve it. There must be something more, some payoff, whether, as I said, a good conscience or, more likely, a good reputation. In that sense, 'positive affect' (happiness) is involved in all pursuits of the good. Your utility theory says the same thing but tends—unnecessarily I think—to make the pay-off in the currency of the market. I think you will agree that all versions of ultimate goods include a hedonic dimension." The humanist in Dessie felt a little soiled in making these statements about payoffs, but the social scientist in him was reinforced by a treatment of "hidden costs" he had once read[30] in which *intrinsic* enjoyment was demystified by attributing it to the pleasure in exercising one's autonomous faculties—in essence, an enjoyment of self-expression.[31]

"So far, I understand you to be identifying what you call 'the good' with utility theory." Adam was amused at this long way round to what seemed obvious to him.

"Second," said Dessie, concentrating on his own thoughts rather than Adam's response, "each of the concepts of the good that we unearthed implies human development in the sense that in all actions people learn something, something good or bad. That learning could be of some disposition, a skill, a thought, an attitude—whatever. That is where answers to the question What did you learn? come in. Of course, it is not true that all learning implies something we would call human development; one might achieve an ersatz Nirvana by learning to smoke pot or develop a skill in burglary. So learning is only a stand-in for more explicit concepts of the kind of learning we might agree is genuine human development."

Adam had no trouble with this either, though he feared that Dessie would use it to justify some birdbrained scheme to substitute the making of "better people" for the making of products. "Okay," he said, "but don't forget that we know the production functions of widgets but not of better people."

"And third," said Dessie, "as I mentioned earlier, part of the human tendency to evaluate includes the fairness dimension: fairness is caught up in the evaluation implicit in language[32] and the tendency of our brains to respond first with an emotional evaluation.[33] Moreover, 'there is considerable evidence from systematic observation that, in fact, the most singularly *desired resource* is that people have what they deserve.' "[34]

Adam paused to break open the crackers that came with the soup. "All right," he said, "assume that indeed there are common elements to most concepts of the good; it would be surprising if there weren't. And equally surprising if they were exactly three in number (and that you have them right)," the latter clause sotto voce. "What should we do about it?" By *we* Adam really meant economists, but he included others as a courtesy.

"Modesty is becoming in a discipline that has just lost its claim to authorship of the good," said Dessie. "Walk humbly with thy god, who might himself be feeling low because he has just lost his supremacy. But let us all treat the god of prosperity—Plutus, isn't it? (or Mammon)— with respect. He presides over the circumstances that make other goods possible or at least easier to achieve."

"Mammon thanks you, if you will allow me to speak on his behalf."

"As I said, the point is to show that there are hidden or implicit meanings in traditional concepts, meanings that support my modest (or hubristic, if you prefer) trilogy."

For Adam, the notion that there were "hidden meanings" in words was slightly irritating. He thought with nostalgia of allusions in law and literary criticism to "the plain meaning of the text." If that were not enough, however, a meaning could be specified by the operation showing whether something was present or absent and, ideally, the degree to which it was present. (As a sophomore. Adam had read Bridgman on operationalizing concepts,[35] and the lesson stuck.) But, come to think of it, he and his colleagues used their mathematical models precisely to search for hidden relationships. "Okay," he said. "Your effort seems a bit tendentious to me, but I see what drives you to search for philosophical precedent. Go on."

Then Dessie remembered that he had promised to respond to Adam's comments about the importance of a material base for all the good things in the philosophical armory of ultimate values.

The Economic Basis of the Good

But you were saying," Dessie said, "that, like everything else, ultimates need nourishment. You are right: as David Ross, the author of *The Right and the Good,* observed after expounding his ideas of ultimate goods, 'The existence of a material universe may . . . be a necessary condition for the existence of many things that are good in themselves.' He then went on to suggest the material base of knowledge and pleasure and even said, 'Virtue owes many of its opportunities to the existence of material conditions of good and material hindrances of good.' But then he ended by saying, 'But the value of material things appears to be merely instrumental, not intrinsic.'[36] Of course, this reference to material bases does not help very much because it seems to apply as much to physics and biology as it does to economics and, in any event, as Ross notes, the material bases can hinder as well as promote the achievement of the good."

"I am glad to find a 'fellow philosopher' agreeing with me," said Adam, "and I am not disturbed that economists share with biologists and physicists the honor of his attention. But think of it practically: economics is about (1) what goods shall be produced, (2) how these goods shall be produced, and (3) for whom these goods shall be produced.[37] If the creation of beauty requires artists and working materials, then, whatever else it may be, the support of these artists and the provision (and prices) of their materials is an economic problem. If fostering human development requires schools, then the financing of education is an economic problem. Calling these 'merely instrumental, not intrinsic' doesn't change their importance in the least. Ross is only exhibiting the philosopher's snobbishness disguised in such terms as *intrinsic,* whatever that may be."

"Then we are agreed," said Dessie, a little disappointed that harmony should break out in this argument. "The kind of wants (or ultimate values?) that Koopmans has in mind are only those for which material resources are required—not appreciation of beauty or artistic inspiration but that minor aspect, artists' supplies, not friendly conversation over a spinach pie but only the pie that the friends are eating. I'm sorry, but you cannot make ultimate goods of these commodities. I do not mean to savage your discipline, Adam," said Dessie disingenuously, for that was exactly what he did mean to do.

"As a discipline, we're doing all right," said Adam, slightly amused that Dessie thought that great edifice of economics might be upset by this terrier barking at its doorstep. "The notion that the problems of making and distributing the material goods that made these so-called ultimates prosper are 'merely means' or 'merely extrinsic' and therefore trivial is a parochial view of the world." You could almost hear Adam say "Ha! Take that, you old philosophical windbag."

"Means are important, of course," said the philosophical windbag, "and not just because they are discussed by philosophers. Like others, some philosophers acknowledge that all means have intrinsic satisfaction or dissatisfactions and are, therefore, proximate ends in themselves[38] (the hedonic function I mentioned earlier). Moreover, people will not pursue ends for which the means are distasteful.[39] If I had to dissect a frog to get a degree in biology, I would shift to botany. It is, in part, a practical matter. But more importantly, the availability of resources often determines which of several ends a person pursues: only the wealthy collect first editions, only the educated (human capitalists?) prefer Proust to Stephen King, and—essential to my thesis—only the economically secure and educated are 'free' to assume that their material needs will be taken care of and that they can, therefore, pursue the humanistic values I espouse. I am building my castle not on sand—which, incidentally, is a better foundation than ordinary soil—but on the prosperous terrain you guys helped to create." Dessie liked this feeling of seeming to yield territory while expanding his turf.

"You're claiming jurisdiction over the kingdom of ends and leaving me, as the treasurer and accountant of your better world, to provide the means. You say what we should be doing, and I decide the scale of the enterprise. Is that it?" asked Adam, not sure whether he could tell his economist friends that they were, in the end, merely the accountants of this world—though, come to think of it, that was at least as good as Keynes's concept of economists as dentists.

Now Dessie sought to reclaim even more of the small acreage he had yielded to his friend. But he knew he had to proceed diplomatically. "Let's go back to your disguised quotation from Samuelson and his heirs: 'What goods shall be produced?' If the market is responsive to demand, doesn't that imply that economics offers a science of the formation of tastes that shape demand?" Dessie smiled like a cat who has just had too much catnip.

"No," said Adam, "unless you happen to think, along with some economists, that the market shapes taste through an endogenous learning process[40]—which, of course it does to a minor extent. But I agree with Kenneth Boulding that 'our main contribution as economists is in the description of what is learned,' not in explaining the learning process or taste-formation process itself."[41]

"I see," said Dessie, "and I gather that if you do not study taste formation, a fortiori you do not study value formation either. How do you decide 'What goods shall be produced?'"

Adam snorted. "*We* don't decide; *they* decide," he said with scorn. "Dear Dessie, if you could learn the first lesson of economics, you would be better off. That lesson is that demand (and supply) are autonomous, governed by people's calculations of what they want and can afford. Your basic way of thinking violates minute by minute the idea that people can do things for themselves. If there ever was a place where popular sovereignty—for which you must have some reverence—works, it is in the market. Moreover, at least since the Enlightenment, the values of autonomy, of 'thinking for ourselves,' of self-reliance and individualism have enjoyed the respect of both philosophers[42] and others."

"Your emphasis on individual autonomy resonates with the great traditions of philosophy, including the preferences of Kant, Mill, Greene, and Stuart Hampshire,"[43] said Dessie, assuming his philosophical hat. Then, using the same hat but sneaking social science into the discussion, he said, "But so stated, we are dealing with a causeless phenomenon. As Isaiah Berlin said, 'Kant's free individual is a transcendent being, beyond the realm of natural causality.'[44] Nothing short of a flexible intelligence, of the kind of cognitive complexity and emotional stability that permits a person to absent himself from felicity awhile, to abstract the self from the objects of study and hold preference in abeyance, will provide the rationality often demanded by economists and philosophers. But these demands are inevitably frustrated by cognitive overload, the boundedness of rationality, and the natural tendencies of the 'cognitive miser' to conserve his small hoard of intelligence.[45] Moreover, not only do people have limited access to their own internal processes (the limbic system is like the autonomic nervous system in this respect), but people's limited cognitive ability also interferes with their self-knowledge, a matter that would bother Plato more than it does some contemporary psychologists.[46] In a kind of answer to Kant, psychology has now produced important evidence showing that people interpret, by a process of social induction, not only the causes of their own behavior but what they actually feel. They ask, 'What would a person following the norms of my society do and feel in this situation?' "[47]

"Very interesting," said Adam. "So your interpretation of what you are thinking and feeling has nothing to do with what you are actually thinking and feeling but rather is an extrapolation of what you think others would think and feel when talking about how people think and feel while eating a spinach pie." He laughed out loud, frightening the baby in the adjoining booth.

"Different situations and acts evoke different strategies," said Dessie, not amused. "At the moment of tipping, I will be governed by the norms of tipping, another way of saying I will unconsciously follow the patterns I think others would follow in my place. For unconventional, perhaps even unique, types of behavior, this other-directedness is of no help. How many professors do you know working on the problems of autonomy, mixing psychology with philosophy and called on to explain the limits of autonomy—with or without a forkful of spinach pie in their mouths? If the answer is one, then, it is indeed true that I refer to that relevant 'group' to see what I think." Dessie had the feeling that this was pretty hokey, but since to ask the person citing a study whether he was bound by that study would neither confirm nor disconfirm it, he felt no disgrace.

Adam got the point. "Okay," he said. "The general point is that demand in the market and opinions on other matters are derived not so much from consulting one's own values and tastes as from social induction.[48] The venerated autonomy disappears in a miasma of imitation and group pressure. That is almost certainly too strong a statement."

He glanced at Dessie, who was nodding in reluctant agreement but who could not let go unchallenged the idea that the market was the paragon of popular sovereignty and the epitome of uncoerced choice. "Hang on," he said. "In the first place, there are the arguments that the market is characterized not by consumer sovereignty but by producer sovereignty. Your free, autonomous chooser is bullied into buying what producers—or at least advertisers—want her to.[49] But perhaps the argument is badly phrased and the consumer's contribution to the variance in purchases is greater than Galbraith thinks."

"I think you are back to a prescientific version of explanation. Most people in your profession, whatever that is, concede that *interaction* between stimulus and a perceiving organism carries the greatest freight,"[50] said Adam, treading on Dessie's turf. "I carelessly spill my soup in your lap; you, out of character, call me a 'clumsy oaf'; I spill a little coffee in pursuit of the soup. Even in the most humanist of societies, our reciprocal responses can be explained only by the interaction of temperament with situation."

"If you had been eating spinach pie, you would have saved us both a lot of trouble," said Dessie looking down to see if the imaginary soup had stained his very real trousers. Then, back to business, he went on: "Unless advertisers are irrational, they must believe that their stimuli are persuasive—and not just to keep up with rivals. But the main point I wanted to make is not that technical one; rather, it is the larger one dealing with this free spirit you say inhabits the markets. Back to values: values are cognitive representations of emotions and motives.[51] Wouldn't you agree that the essence of autonomy is the ability to choose one's own values—a faculty, incidentally, that Harry Frankfurt says distinguishes humans from beasts?[52] Could you explain how the market facilitates the choices among, say, the values of benevolence, harmony with nature, duty, and freedom? No? Well, what about the daily choices among pity, anger, fear, love, grief, and relief, emotions that a cross-cultural study says are prompted largely by interpersonal relations?"[53]

"You don't choose emotions," said Adam, "they choose you according to the demands of a presenting situation."

"A drunken prostitute gets syphilis. Blame or pity?" asked Dessie.

Adam knew that societies graced with religions originating in the Middle East blamed the women who sold sex much more than the men who bought it, but he wasn't going to raise that question now. "Really, Dessie," he said with exasperation, "you can't expect the market to be nurse and tutor to its participants. Isn't it enough that the market offers them free choices over a very large range of the things they actually do want?"

"A large range of commodities, of course, although even here it seems that what a buyer experiences as choice is often determined by invariant personality traits.[54] But, if you will forgive me, only an economist would think that a large range of commodities— well, and jobs, where there is a choice—is a large range of the things that a person wants from life. How could it be if most of the major emotions are products of interpersonal relations wherever these occur?"

Adam began to think this beautiful edifice of economics was not a marble hall, after all, but a more modest office building occupied by a lot of very bright technicians. High ground! He would go to higher ground. "But you have not answered my point about whose ultimate values these are," he said, about to invoke freedom values. "If the values you treated with such reverence are held by people, they will be like utility values in economics and your scheme will preserve their choices. If they are values held by philosopher-kings—God forbid—they are likely to lead to coercion, as in Plato's *Republic*." Adam was rather proud of those classical references and smiled quietly to himself so as not to disturb the baby in the next booth.

"The origins of values are complex,"[55] said Dessie with his usual academic (and evasive) seriousness. "But one thing is certain: values change within any population as experiences change and as varied interpretations are offered and then selected by the people if the interpretations offer a better fit with experience. I am not legislating from Clark's Greek Pizzeria but rather trying to hammer out a better interpretation of the public's changing experiences. Isn't that what we should be doing?"

This was "taste formation" again, and Adam had no handle on it. He had to move to even higher ground! "True to academic training," he said, trying to be friendly by avoiding any reference to disciplines, "you want to talk about verbal expressions, values, while the important things that are taking place in people's lives go unobserved. Only a few hundred years ago, people's occupational choices were regulated by both the tradition that they follow their father's trade or by actual legal restriction on who could do what. Although the early labor market has a bad name, at the same time that it confined the freedom of individuals on the job it created opportunities for occupational choice that never existed before. Marian, our waitress, is choosing to work so she can help put her daughter through college."

"Every so-called choice takes place within a set of constraints," said Dessie, long bothered by the economists' blithe assumptions about the benefits of choice. "If you listen to Susan Okin[56] and other feminist authors, you would realize that the choice to work as a waitress was, after all, the product of a system that limited Marian's education and options but did not limit her brother—or at least not to the same degree."

Pleased as he was that Dessie's feminist ear had been tuned to reality, Adam wanted to defend the idea that markets were the emancipating instrument for occupational choices. "Earlier," he continued, "as Lewis Coser points out, it was the rise of labor markets that freed people from the continuing feudal indenture in great families.[57] Your friend Karl Polanyi gives a pretty fair account of how the rise of the market in land broke the bonds of entailment.[58] And freeing commodity markets from rules against regrating and 'fair prices' opened up trade to give choices to people who had never had them. In fact, to revert to what you said a minute ago, *that* was the moment of change from producer to consumer sovereignty."

Now it was Dessie's turn to feel that he had overstated his argument. If the market was not a facilitator of choice, what was it? "I only meant to say that the answers to what we should be doing with our lives were not to be found in the market," he said mildly.

But Adam was wound up. "If you are looking for a forum to discuss ultimate values, you will not find it in the market," he said. "But the fact is that the market has opened up more choices to more people than any other institution, including democracy. The cognitive and social limits on choice apply everywhere. All acts of thinking, including academic discussions such as this one, are constrained by the limited capacities of and social influences on the thinkers. You can account for the variance of an act or a thought by the history of the individuals concerned, the social milieu in which they grew up, special hormonal influences on their brains, their ignorance of probable consequences, and so forth,[59] but you cannot abolish people's sense that they are deciding for themselves. Nor would you wish to."

Autonomy and Empowering People

"What should we be doing?" Dessie asked himself. One thing that was central to the humanist agenda was empowering people to control their own destinies, an Enlightenment-Millian agenda. But how to do that and at the same time facilitate human development, which was often only a minor part of most people's agendas? Dessie knew that Adam was partially right but also knew that turning things over to the market no longer was the solution to enlarging people's sense of subjective well-being and certainly did not serve the purpose of human development. Well, he could not deal with all of this at once, but he felt he must confront, if not solve, the implications of that ancient slogan, "power to the people."

· "All right," he said, "we have marketized the world; people are free to buy anything that is priced and that they can afford and in that way to control their destinies. Having done that, we continue with no handle on happiness (or utility), involuntary unemployment, environmental disasters, a rising tide of clinical depression, inadequate preparation for the responsibilities of marriage, untrained and unregulated emotions, a working class characterized as 'incomplete adults'[60]—but a wealth of commodities. What kind of autonomy or empowerment is that?"

Adam was slightly fazed but was ready with a counterattack. "Okay," he said, "You have established emotional training in the schools (at the sacrifice of math and literacy), you have enough marriage counselors to fill a large bureaucracy, you have a WPA program to take up the slack in employment but at the cost of heavy deficit financing, and your free clinics for the depressed are working overtime. At the same time, the public resources for these programs are depleted by the inhibitions to growth these 'reforms' impose on the national economy. What kind of autonomy or empowerment is that?"

Dessie saw that they had reached a stalemate for three reasons:

(1) They disagreed about the priorities in a cybernetic system: (a) attend to the economy and let the humanist agenda prosper, as it may, with the new wealth, or (b) attend to the humanist agenda and let the enlarged human capital contribute, as it may, to such economic growth as may be needed to support the humanist agenda.

(2) Correspondingly, they disagreed about the relative social worth of the two kinds of products, material wealth to facilitate certain limited choices, a limited good in itself, versus human development, a larger good in itself.

(3) Consequently, they disagreed on what intellectuals should be doing about happiness and human development: acceptance of laissez faire (or everyone for themselves) versus some more (but unspecified) dirigiste approach.

"As Herbert Simon explained in 'The Architecture of Complexity,'"[61] said Dessie, trying to be more lucid than usual, "we can't solve everything at once. Let's take one goal that we both agree on, helping people to decide for themselves the issues that affect their lives. You say, 'Turn them loose in the market.' I say, '(1) Train them in the belief that they *can* decide matters for themselves, (2) provide them with information and cognitive and emotional skills for these decisions, and (3) structure several different forums for deciding issues other than what jobs and what commodities they want. Okay?"

Adam thought Dessie was loading the question in his favor, but so far Dessie's characterization of Adam's position represented what he had said and what he thought. "Okay," he said.

"As we shall see later,"[62] said Dessie, looking far ahead, "the way to learn self-attribution (the belief that one can control one's own fate) is through exercising it, a thoroughly Aristotelian concept. What you say about the market helps, but there is an awful lot of 'learned helplessness'[63] in market societies, and the effect of markets on those with little money can hardly be to learn their own effectiveness. Good parenting would be even more helpful—hence the need for training parents—a bit of the dirigisme that you fear.

Adam grunted.

"Second," said Dessie, "the skills needed to decide what career or 'lifestyles' (ugh) include deferred gratification, emotional control, socio-centricity,[64] and other matters of which markets and their students are studiously ignorant. Nor is autonomy the simple matter of willpower that Kant thought it was."

Adam was restive. "That's very nice," he said in a somewhat nasty way, "but if these properties are to be taught by some kind of training or experience, you have not specified what they are."

This was a hard question for Dessie, since it meant that he would have to get into the mechanics of facilitating human development. Oh well, there was no shortage of spinach pies. But was Adam "credulous" enough to extend Dessie credit for a few weeks? "Will you believe me if I say there is a lot of research I want to tell you about on these matters but can't do it now?" he asked.

"No," said Adam with a smile.

"Good," said Dessie. "Then let me get your opinion on a delicate moral problem that confronts all people who are trying to empower others.

The "Noble Lie"

Adam was not accustomed to being consulted on moral problems and was pleased in spite of himself. "Moral philosophy is second nature to us economists," he said, tongue displacing the crackers in his cheek.

"Thank God," said Dessie. "Here is the problem: We want all people to believe that they are the masters of their own fates because of its beneficial effects on enterprise and self-esteem, as I shall explain later.[65] But it really isn't true—that is, most of the variance in explaining behavior is accounted for by circumstances, not dispositions.[66] What should one do with a concept that is both useful and generally false? We exaggerate the intermittent control we have over our own lives because we *want* to have control, we are programmed biologically to believe in such control, and we grasp at illusions—the 'illusion of control.'"[67] Dessie feared that he was not getting anywhere—and Adam confirmed it.

"You worry too much about motives and what you call 'dispositions,'" said Adam slyly. "I have thought of an answer. Why not assume that people autonomously want more of what pleases them, or more of any fungible asset that permits them to get more, and that the variance lies in their circumstances, such as their budgets and the prevailing prices. If you assume autonomy without inquiring too deeply into it, you get its advantages at no analytical cost."

Dessie was horrified and said so: "God save us from the utopianism of the world of *assumed* reality," he said. "Science is the inquiry into our world of assumptions: the flatness of the earth and the effectiveness of the élan vital and the 'humors.' I am ashamed of you."

"So what do you propose?" asked a chastened Adam.

"I have told you that belief in one's own efficacy is a healthy belief, at least if one is successful," said Dessie, not quite certain how he would end this answer. "As 'internal locus of control,' it helps people to thrive and to develop themselves. Consider Henley: he said that the 'fell clutch of circumstance' had him in its grip but that he was not going to let that get him down:

> It matters not how strait the gate,
> How charged with punishments the scroll,
> I am the master of my fate:
> I am the captain of my soul.[68]

Admiring Henley and eager to endow people with these humanly fruitful qualities of internal attribution, why should we not encourage everyone to believe that he (or she) is also 'the master of my fate, the captain of my soul'? Conservatives, who give 'character' more explanatory weight than do social democrats, might take a pragmatic attitude toward truth: if it works and helps people to do well, it is 'true.' Like another conservative, Plato, people might say that if it is a lie, it is a 'noble lie' that is good for society (even though Plato's noble lie held the opposite premise: people are born to be either leaders or humble followers)."

"We cannot do that," said Adam sententiously, "because as economists and social scientists, we have an overarching commitment to truth. When truth conflicts with usefulness, it is our calling to defend truth. Dessie, I am ashamed of you"—the last phrase said with great satisfaction in restoring the shame equilibrium

Of course, Adam was right, so Dessie elided with practiced skill into a related topic: "There is another reason, a moral one, for limiting the scope of dispositional, internal explanations such as autonomy. The idea that people are the masters of their own fates is only a different way of saying that people get what they deserve, that victims bring their misfortunes on themselves, that this is, in the end, a *just world*.[69] This belief says that the son of a heroin addict growing up in the ghetto is as responsible for his fate (perhaps prison or death by firearms) as is the suburban white son of a doctor. The callous white wife of a president can blame the ghetto dweller's character (he was too weak to follow her injunction to 'just say no') but her dispositional explanation is wrong and her casual injunction is cruel. The lie is not so noble after all."

"Truth is what works the way you want it to work," said Adam, taking the high ground again. "Scratch a humanist and you find a person with a practiced skill in manipulating his conscience. I've got to meet a class."

Spanakopita Three

What's Wrong with Materialism?

Adam entered the restaurant angry. He had been thinking about Dessie's high moral tone in attacking materialism, as though he was dealing with an ethical norm, like virtue, that could or should be justified as its own reward. "Materialism must be judged by its consequences," he said, "and not as a virtue or a vice in itself. It's not just your dinner that's at stake but the whole market system that has brought us so far." He sighed. "Capitalism without a profit motive?" he asked in a state of self-propelled indignation.

"We'll get to that," said Dessie, who had entered through the back door. "In a profound sense, neither of us knows what materialism means. I have a friend, Ed Lindblom, who won't talk to me about materialism because he says it's too vague a topic."

"Smart fellow, that Lindblom," said Adam, "even though he is not wholly sound on neoclassical economics."

"So when confronted by a vague concept, you don't just abandon it; you clarify the meaning of the concept. If necessary you assert yourself against the word, as Humpty Dumpty suggested."

"You'll get egg on your face," muttered Adam.

"Definitions are useful only when they shed light on what you want to do or talk about," said Dessie pompously. "Although I mentioned last time the cosmic battle between materialism and humanism, we are not really battling over spiritualism or the dominance of the senses[1] or evolution as a materialist system or the mind-body problem and its increasingly important brain-mind aspects." Dessie paused to change perspective. "By the way, even the mind-body problem has a left-right dimension. "'Scientific psychology,' said Lenin, must 'set about making a direct study of the material substratum of psychical events—the nervous system.' He claimed that any mentalistic emphasis represented a 'confused idealist position.'"[2]

"You do know that E. O. Wilson, the creator of sociobiology,[3] was attacked by lefties as a rightist social Darwinist," said Adam with an amused air of scorn at this social science nonsense.

Dessie let it go. "In a minor way, I suppose we are talking about the moving forces of history—dialectical materialism and all that—but only tangentially. Do you agree that the interesting problems on the table, along with the soup and spinach pie, are the values that people hold and the motives that drive them?

Adam had not been thinking about the agenda for today's discussion, so he promptly agreed. It was only just the other day that he had come to think of economists as "materialists," though he was willing to accept that term as long as it was not loaded with either metaphysical nonsense or implications of uncivilized vulgarity.

"This is only tentative," said Dessie, feeling his way, "but I think materialist or idealistic interpretations of history are more or less irrelevant to the interpretation of the motives and values of participants in history, don't you? I mean, materialist interpretations of history do not require avaricious actors but do require changes in the productive system of the society, just as idealistic interpretations do not require deep thinkers—only powerful thoughts that fit the changing cultures of the time."

"I agree," said Adam, relieved that Dessie was not going to psychologize history.

"Mental sets (cultures) do influence which of the many environmental changes people will see and respond to; in that sense, I am an idealist. But the stimulus to change is more likely to be circumstantial. As Marx and Engels said, 'Does it require deep intuition, to comprehend that man's ideas, views and conceptions, in one word, man's consciousness, changes with every change in the conditions of his material existence, in his social relations and in his social life?'[4] In a way, that is the very basis of my belief in the immanence of the New Humanism. But when you reverse that and make economic motives of the public the moving force of economics, you have vulgar Marxism."

"That's only a phrase—and not even Marx's phrase," said Adam. "For example, I found persuasive John Hicks's economic history showing the way in which the search for economic security caused civilizations to change their institutions and adapt to new situations.[5] Who needs the dialectic under these plainly understood, straightforward conditions? I am not saying that economic man is the only actor on the stage of history, but he has been around a long time. As Joseph Schumpeter says, 'Pre-capitalist man is in fact no less "grabbing" than capitalist man.'"[6]

"It is very hard to argue that the nature of humanity, including material desires and needs, explains the world's gloriously multivalent histories," said Dessie. "You cannot explain variation with a constant. Anyway, a strictly materialist explanation of history is a silly theory that Marx and Marxists have never been able to follow[7] and that ignores the fact that material changes are the products of invention, technology, and science, all of which are in some degree independent of the forces of production. In Marx's term, they are 'phantoms of the brain.'[8] We'll come to the problems of historical change later, but for now can we agree that historical explanation and everyday motives in economic life are different issues? For our purposes, materialism is a set of values, beliefs, and motives that must, I think, be replaced by another set of values. Okay?"

Materialism as a Set of Beliefs, Values, and Motives

*B*rought up to believe in economic man as an active agent, at least in market matters, Adam had no difficulty with Dessie's broad characterization of that individual. "Okay," Adam said, "but I don't think he is replaceable. We need him—or at least his cousin with a little more polish to him. Those fellows with the 'rage to consume'[9] whom you mentioned in our first encounter over spinach pie lack polish."

"If we define materialism as a set of beliefs, values, and motives that informs people's search for a better life for themselves and their children, you may think this leads straight to the profit motive or to the only two mental properties modern economists allow, greed and rationality. But you will be mistaken."

"Oh, Mammon!" exclaimed Adam, "or do I mean 'Oh, Plutus?' What proliferation of meanings of materialism must we now suffer through?"

"Three," said Dessie, and remembering Lindblom's reluctance to talk about the undefined, Dessie excused himself: "Specifying meanings has the advantage that when we then use a term, we are more likely to be talking about the same thing. First, as a mental set, materialism sometimes means *thing-mindedness*—that is, the very reverse of the natural tropism toward people and people perception I am proposing.[10] Second, and very close to this idea, is an unusually strong attachment to one's *possessions*. The evidence I have seen suggests that this can be normal, even wholesome, as it may be for a homeowner who loves the things in her home.[11] But if it is a substitute for attachment to people, it is mischievous.[12]

"Are you saying that if a materialist is also a humanist, he earns credits in your golden book?" asked Adam with a kind of wide-eyed innocence. "Would it be equally true that if a humanist is also a materialist, he earns added credit or, indeed, that unless a person is both, he is in some degree an incomplete person?" He smiled his Cheshire grin again.

Dessie felt that things were not going well for him today and hastened on to the meanings of materialism, where he had more data. "The third set of meanings," he said, avoiding the issue of whether a well-rounded humanist must also enjoy possessions (why couldn't an ascetic be a good humanist?), "is a measure of materialist attitudes in a consumer society. We are not pioneers, creating our own maps of unexplored terrain. Others have been here before us. For example, Marsha Richins and Scott Dawson have developed a measure of materialism that deals with three aspects of the concept: (1) acquisition centrality, meaning that 'materialists place possessions and their acquisition at the center of their lives'; (2) acquisition and possession of things as the central route to happiness—that is, materialists 'see possessions and acquisition as essential to their satisfaction and well-being'; and (3) success is defined in terms of material things: 'Materialists tend to judge their own and others' success by the number and quality of possessions accumulated.' Technically, these three elements represent three independent factors in Richins and Dawson's factor analysis of a broad range of relevant questions. To measure the first factor, they ask whether the following is generally true for the respondent: 'Buying things gives me a lot of pleasure.' To measure the happiness dimension, they invite responses to 'It sometimes bothers me quite a bit that I can't afford to buy all the things I'd like.' And to test the third dimension, dealing with success, they ask agreement or disagreement with the proposition 'Some of the most important achievements in life include acquiring material possessions.'[13] Whereas Richins and Dawson focus on values, there is another, somewhat similar, measure of materialism that focuses on such personality traits as envy, nongenerosity, and possessiveness.[14] The two are closely correlated,[15] and we will focus on the Richins and Dawson measure."

"You're stacking the deck by your definitions—a formal rhetorical error," said Adam. "Here is young Albert starting out in life; he is married and has two small children; he has to pay for shelter, food, clothing, and medical care for his family; he should save something lest his job fail and, in any event, for his children's education and to supplement Social Security for the increasingly long years of retirement. Because he cares a lot about money, you call him a materialist and put him down. It isn't fair." Adam seemed to suffer vicariously for Albert.

"We are not talking about the priority of needs,"[16] said Dessie. "I agree with you and, as it happens, with Marx, who said someplace, 'We must eat before we think.' But that is true of people with a variety of motives and points of view. It will be more fruitful if we focus on Richins and Dawson's conceptualization of materialist beliefs and motives."

"Richins and Dawson offer a neat device for their and your purposes," said Adam, sorry that they were getting into issues of psychological measurement. "But this is all attitudinal stuff. How do we know that these so-called materialists actually behave that way—that is, when confronted by choices between material gain and spiritual gain, whatever that may be, how do we know that they choose material gain?"

"Dear Adam," said Dessie, imitating his friend's intimate style, "we are talking about attitudes and properties internal to the mind. Although incentives are more or less objective, motives are subjective and must be inferred, usually from asking people questions. But you have a point. Perhaps it will not persuade you, but those who score high on this measure of materialism place 'financial security' ahead of 'self-respect,' ahead of 'warm relations with others,' and ahead of 'a sense of accomplishment.' At least their other attitudes are consistent with their materialism. If it helps, this is what de Saussure says is the way to think of meaning."[17]

"All right," said Adam, almost resigned to what he had been taught was a violation of scientific method—that is, reliance on self-reports—but quite uncomfortable with French linguistic philosophy. "I still don't see what's wrong with emphasizing material acquisitions. Albert, our young father just starting out, did. And what's wrong with agreeing with the vast majority of Americans that those who 'make it' financially have indeed succeeded?"

"As a matter of fact," said Dessie, wearing his social science hat, "what Americans think of when they think of materialism is: 'status display'; seeking 'wealth for its own sake'; and people who are 'predisposed toward money, wealth, innovations, and the possessions of others.'[18] So Albert and the rest of us working stiffs may or may not be materialists, but an interest in earning a living is neither here nor there." Dessie felt that things were going better.

"So now you have a definition and a measure: how does this help us understand why we must give up the attitudes and values that have made us rich?" asked Adam, weary of distinctions in what had always seemed like a straightforward natural preference for a fungible currency that bought so many pleasures. He worried for a moment that Dessie would catch him for saying that it was a psychological propensity that made us rich, not just the material resources and means of production. He need not have worried; Dessie was off on another tack.

The Dark Side of Materialism

First, materialists are less generous than others," said Dessie, counting on his fingers. "Richins and Dawson offered their subjects a hypothetical twenty thousand dollar windfall and asked them how they would spend it. As it turned out, 'materialists would spend three times as much on themselves, would contribute less to charity or church, give less than half as much to friends and family.' Materialism scores were negatively correlated with support for a specific environmental charity. Compared to others, materialists also reported that they do not like to lend things to their friends and that they do not like to have guests in their homes."[19]

"Second, materialists are more invidious than others, especially but not exclusively when they compare themselves with those who are richer than they are.[20] 'Materialists tend to judge their own and others' success by the number and quality of possessions accumulated.' They value these things more than they value their relationships to other people.[21] This may be because of lack of interest in people, a matter of taste, or because of the lack of social skills that haunts these thing-minded people."

"Third, materialists seem to be more difficult to satisfy; they report that they need higher incomes than those low in materialism.[22] They are insatiable and, more than others, dissatisfied with their lives. As Durkheim prophesied,[23] empirical studies find that 'although materialists expect acquisition to make them happy, . . . the lust for goods can be insatiable: the pleasures of a new acquisition are quickly forgotten and replaced with a desire for more.'[24] One excellent economist calls this 'luxury fever.'"[25]

"The consequence of all this," said Dessie, using his hands to wield his fork instead of to count the points he was making, "is that materialists are significantly less happy than are nonmaterialists: in the Richins and Dawson study, materialism was negatively related 'to satisfaction in all the aspects of life measured': amount of fun being had, income and standard of living, friends, and even (modestly) with satisfaction with family life.[26] These findings are not idiosyncratic; another study including young people drawn from outside college life found the same thing.[27] And yet another study found that average happiness was lower in countries whose people valued happiness more than love.[28] 'One of the most important findings with regard to materialism is the consistent relationship between high levels of materialism and low levels of life satisfaction.' "[29]

"The invisible hand is thumbing its nose at you, Dessie," said Adam in a jocular tone. "As you might have guessed, it isn't the fact that people want money but *why* they want it that influences their happiness. From a study of business students, we know that motives include security in old age, current family support, charity (!), and personal motives such as relieving self-doubt. Those who sought money for its own sake or because of pride and vanity were, as you might expect, unhappier than others. Those who sought money for such purposes as family support and charity were as happy as anybody else—normally happy.[30] I just can't believe," he continued, "that the hardworking people who brought us this wealth" (he looked around at the restaurant's imitation leather and Coca-Cola clock—and looked away) "can have created so much prosperity while suffering the pains of the materialism you describe."

"Remember," said Dessie, "that we are not talking about Frank Knight's 'most noble and sensitive characters,' condemned 'to lead unhappy and futile lives'[31] because they are nonmaterialists; we are talking about the unhappiness of perfect fits: materialists in a material civilization."

"If this is true, why are people in more prosperous countries happier than those in poorer countries?" asked Adam.[32]

Dessie was wound up. "We'll come to that," he said. "Fifth, and by a quite different study with a similar but different measure, 'placing money high in the rank ordering [of personal goals] was associated with less vitality, more depression and more anxiety.' For adolescents, 'high ratings of the importance of financial success were related to lower global functioning, lower social productivity, and more behavior problems.'[33] As Durkheim would have predicted, materialism is related to anomie— that is, one measure of anomie (ends justify the means, friends cannot be trusted, people do not help each other) also includes the item 'I must admit I put a pretty high value on material things.' "[34]

"You sound as though Andrew Carnegie, J. P. Morgan, and Bill Gates were all sick personalities," said Adam, shaking his head with disbelief.

"According to your friend Schumpeter, the great entrepreneurs are not materialists," said Dessie, mobilizing one economist against another. It is not the material gain that attracts them but the creation of 'private kingdoms'[35] or fiefdoms where they are the revered leader—a quite different matter. For the rest of us, however, it seems that symptoms of early acquisitiveness in childhood predict failure to adapt to the problems of social relations in adulthood.[36] But I do not think of materialists as 'sick' as much as undeveloped—on an ego-development scale, the pronounced 'love of nice things' is a mark of stunted development."[37]

"Are you sure you're not letting your distaste for economic man (or is it economist men?) bias your account of materialism?" asked Adam, who was used to criticisms of the market on ethical grounds but never on hedonic or pathological grounds. He couldn't help wondering if, like God, psychologists were not making the model of the healthy person in their own image. He wanted to question the validity of the studies but the fact that several studies seemed to confirm each other made him hesitate. "Being less happy, or out of tune with American materialism, or even a little less charitable than others can't explain why materialism is derogated by philosophers and, as you pointed out, by the general public as well. If the materialists have brought prosperity to the world, why do they have such a bad name?" asked Adam in something as close to a plaintive tone as a proud economist could assume.

Why Does Materialism Have Such a Bad Name?

Dessie smiled as though he had just won a debating point, which of course, he had not yet done. He leaned back: "One reason is that materialists are more envious," he said. "Tocqueville said of the Americans, 'I never met in America any citizen so poor as not to cast a glance of hope and *envy* on the enjoyments of the rich or whose imagination did not possess itself by anticipation of those good things that fate still obstinately withheld from him.'[38] Of course, Tocqueville thought that envy was the inevitable consequence of American egalitarianism, a suggestion in line with the tendency of people to compare themselves only with similar others and to follow the cultural norms telling them whom they should be as good as.[39] But contemporary studies stress that not all measures of materialism are associated with envy. In extended interviews with working-class men in Eastport in 1957, Lane found that most of them agreed with the plumber who said, 'If Rockefeller can make it, more power to him.' They were resentful not of the rich but rather of the members of the underclass down the road who were on welfare.[40] Downward comparisons are more gratifying.[41] Moreover, few people admit to envying the rich (only 17 percent in a 1990 Gallup poll, while 82 percent denied it),[42] but we are talking not about the general public but about materialists, and at least three studies find a higher level of envy among materialists than among nonmaterialists.[43] Notice that it is the materialists who are envious, not the rest of the public who are judging materialists."

Adam was not persuaded. "I don't see why a materialist's envy of those who are richer should be so much more despised than an athlete's envy of those who win prizes that he wishes he had won or of a teenager's envy of a rival in the endless high school popularity comparisons. In any field of comparison, those who care about the rewards in that field are going to be more envious of the winners than those who don't."

"Okay," said Dessie. "Try another name for the love of money, *avarice,* which the dictionary says means 'inordinate desire for wealth,' implying 'both miserliness and greed.' Throughout history, most people, including Keynes,[44] have criticized avarice. Do you see anything wrong with that?"

"'Inordinate' anything is bad," said Adam. "Indeed, the seven cardinal sins are mostly about ordinary appetites taken to excess: gluttony, lust, and so forth. Even moral acts beyond the normal ethical requirements (actually, beyond what is necessary for salvation) have a bad name: supererogation. Anyway," he continued, "since you have adopted Keynes and we are switching heroes, recall that David Hume thought the love of gain was an advance over the love of pleasure."[45]

Dessie wondered how Adam would defend gluttony and lust (but, of course, like any self-respecting economist, he would detest sloth) but let it go. "It is not true that 'the road of excess leads to the palace of wisdom,'" Dessie said with a flourish. "I am no partisan of the middle way or of the golden mean, but the term *excess* means that something has been carried too far for some implicit purpose or norm. You have not defended avarice by saying it is simply excessive love of gain."

Adam felt that he was being trapped by semantics. "Call it 'avarice' and you get adverse reactions; call it 'ambition' and you get favorable ones. What's in a name?" he asked, glad to quote Shakespeare to his humanist friend.

"Unlike roses, greed and ambition do smell different," said Dessie, brushing aside the point Adam had made.

Adam saw his chance. "Remember Emerson," he said. "'Money, which is the prose of life, and which is hardly spoken of in parlors, without an apology, is, in its effects and laws, as beautiful as roses. Property

keeps the accounts of the world, and is always moral.' "[46] Adam smiled
benignly on his friend.

"Emerson also believed that the proof of self-reliance was the ability
to resist an appeal for charity from a friend.[47] He was not the kindly and
humane essayist you think he was," said Dessie, but he felt this was going
nowhere. "Getting back to the subject: context makes a lot of difference,
too; 'ambition' in Caesar smelled bad. But one consequence of what
seems to be materialists' insatiable desire for more money is that it can
never be fulfilled; their ambition is fed by comparisons with movie stars
and other 'heroes of consumption,' putting their goals always out of
reach.[48] Satisfaction has an uncertain philosophical and hedonic status,
but chronically dissatisfied people are thought to be complainers and
tend to be disliked. As a great American kitsch poet, Ella Wheeler
Wilcox, said, 'Laugh and the world laughs with you, / Weep and you
weep alone.' She was right: happy people have more friends than
unhappy people."[49]

"I believe this is the first time that kitsch poetry has been cited to
advance an economic argument," said Adam with a sour expression.

"All right," said Dessie. "You defend selfishness on the grounds that
it provides us with our dinners; you think that the materialist's envy is an
artifact of the way the fields of interest are defined, that avarice is simply
another name for an exaggerated passion like any other—a normal
excess—and that dissatisfaction and complaining are trivial. In fact, you
have revealed a saintly tolerance of human defects that is unbecoming in
a secular realist. I believe, however, that there is a further quality associated with materialism that is not so easily dismissed."

Having been called a philosopher in an earlier session, Adam found
he had now been promoted to saint. "Go ahead," he said with a beatific
smile.

"Because, as I have said before, the way we treat each other is of particular interest to me, and only partly because it is the source of our most
important moods,[50] what would you say to the fact that materialism provides people with the schemas or concepts for assessing others: 'materialists not only perceive people in terms of possessions, but they use these
criteria' in their treatment of others.[51] There is a default value for the
terms *rich* and *poor* that leads people to ascribe good things to the rich—
or at least to middle-class people—and bad things to the poor.[52] And like
African-American children who prefer white- over dark-skinned dolls,
compared to materialist middle-class teenagers, working-class teenagers
form more favorable impressions of those who are described as owning a
lot of possessions.[53] Thus, materialism creates identities for self and oth-

ers that are detrimental to the poor and for everyone obscure other, more personal qualities. Materialists are deaf to the appeals of the equality of humankind and, worse, are deprived of access to people's inner lives that is necessary for true friendship."

"A British anthropologist, Geoffrey Gorer, said of Americans, 'Until you know the income bracket of a stranger, and he knows yours, your mutual relationship is unsatisfactory and incomplete,'"[54] said Adam. "It doesn't seem to prevent friendship; indeed, Gorer thought it was a condition for friendship." "I aced Dessie," he said to himself, but he wasn't quite sure whether he was playing tennis or cards.

"It's more complicated than that," said Dessie, yielding ground gracefully. "It's probably true that economic equals are more likely to be friends than those whose income differences create lifestyles that separate them, but after they use that income information to extract something from their friends, like teenagers just learning about friendship, they lose their friends.[55] In any event, we are talking about how materialists stereotype people by income brackets, which is a different matter from finding out how much money your fellow passenger earns."

"You always want to make economic relations into a game of interpersonal relations," said Adam with a hint that this made the nice clean analysis of interests somehow less clean. "Most relations during a day are with people we don't know very well."

"Friendship is one of the dimensions of the way we treat each other," said Dessie, ominously clearing his throat. Adam interrupted.

"I am reminded," said Adam, "of what we said in our very first spanakopita about women's lower ratings on materialism and their higher ratings on responsiveness to people.[56] If the New Humanism seeks feminist goals, then one reason why materialism has a bad name may be the feminist movement that seeks to equalize the treatment of the sexes in this male-dominated society. And this would be especially true if, as you say, materialism tends to inhibit attention to other people—a major female skill and interest."[57]

Because of Dessie's tin ear on feminism, he proceeded as though he had not been interrupted. "In addition to friendship, there is that relation to strangers that is sometimes called social trust—that is, feelings that other people can be trusted or that one must be wary in dealing with them. It is a central feature of the social capital that is being treated as a 'God-term' these days because it has been shown to be a foundation of democracy[58] and—hold on to your hat—central to economic development.[59] Why is materialism important for social trust? Because, recent research shows 'how materialistic values, in particular, have seriously eroded young Americans' levels of social trust.' Historically, when materialist values increase, social trust decreases, and individually, materialists are less trusting than others.[60] And, dear Adam, once you get on the wrong side of this trust argument, you are in deep trouble these days."

"Isn't it the case that social trust increases with economic development?[61] How can you be sure that it isn't economic development that promotes social trust?" asked Adam with the sweetest smile he could muster. Then, reflectively, he continued. "You are saying that people who are particularly interested in making money want it mostly for themselves, are envious of others who have more of it than they do, use money as a clue to their own and others' identities, and use money as a default value in judging others. I do not say that you are right, but I would like to know whether materialism actually interferes with what you might call a higher or more ethical level of personality or whether, out of the pool of ordinary people in the population, the 'lower' types you describe (who will always be there) are those drawn to productive enterprise. Does the market simply recruit people with the unpleasant qualities you describe, or does it shape people in these unhappy ways?" Adam thought of how Deirdre McCloskey had found that economic students were more Hobbesian (selfish) than others only after they began to study economics: as she said, "It is not the case that selfish people want to be economists."[62]

"It shapes them," said Dessie, "as we know from research by economists from what might be called the Zurich school."[63]

Does Materialism Crowd Out Moral and Intrinsic Motives?

*A*dam had been braced for an assault on the market on ethical grounds but not on hedonic grounds, which, he had thought, represented the market's strength. In an effort to get the discussion back to the ethical issues for which he thought he had answers, he said, "I always thought materialism was the butt of criticisms by moralizers, not hedonists. For example, Frederick Lange thinks that the idea of a division between the legitimate exercise of self-interest in the market and of ethics and spirit in other domains of life 'leads to censure of charitableness or of public service without recompense and depreciates religion.'[64] Contemporary moralist Robert Goodin makes somewhat the same point in his criticism of 'moral pollution' by the market. His solution is to further segregate what is moral or priceless from what is materialistic or priced.[65] The moral dimension of market materialism is what gives it a bad name. But I should remind you that moral economics in its incarnation as Christian economics did not rescue the developing countries of Europe from their poverty and, well, their 'backwardness' in the Middle Ages."

"Morality is multidimensional," said Dessie, with a little of his name-sake's superior moral tone. "As I said, the experimental evidence shows that materialists are more selfish and greedy than others,[66] but is it true that materialism crowds out religion, as poor old ambivalent Lange suggests? I think not, at least not in Baxter's and Wesley's England or Cotton Mather's American colonies. And today in this land of materialistic fervor (if Tocqueville and more recently Brogan[67] are right), it seems that religion flourishes, with piety holding up rather well, at least for the 1970s and 1980s, when the proportion of the population claiming a strong or somewhat strong religious faith increased from 51 percent to 55 percent.[68] Although Catholic theologian Jacques Maritain believed that "material-ism gives all human action a truly diabolical direction: because the end of all this delirium is to prevent man from remembering God,'[69] I don't think the American evidence supports him."

"As a *secular* humanist, you don't seem much distressed by this compatibility of God and Mammon," said Adam, smiling.

"That is a nineteenth-century battle; I am concerned with the twenty-first-century battle between materialism and humanism." He had just thought of a way to show the power of materialism. "Will you agree that if people's material self-interest dominates choices in the presence of monetary appeals and wanes when community service or other charitable appeals are made salient, materialism can be said to 'crowd out' non-material, often moral appeals?"

"We are back to Stigler's proposition that in any test, material self-interest will win over nonmaterial appeals,"[70] said Adam. "I smell another one of your behavioral studies coming up. It does not smell of roses."

"Aha! But this time the research is by economists!" said Dessie triumphantly. "Consider why people pay taxes under circumstances where the chance of being caught cheating is trivial. Will you agree that the only plausible explanation is that they are responsive to community ethical norms—that is, that ethical norms dominate material self-interest in these circumstances?"[71]

"Economists have never claimed that material self-interest dominates *all* other interests, such as maternal love, under *all* circumstances. They are talking about financial situations," said Adam, slightly annoyed.

"Do you mean that the extraction of taxes by governments is immune from material self-interest?" asked Dessie incredulously.

"Well, no, but the main application is in market situations," said Adam defensively.

Dessie thought this was evasive and probably circular. If the market was defined by exchange of money for services, that seemed to include the tax situation even though the services to be received were not specified. When material self-interest dominates other interests, we have a market situation, and we know we have a market situation when material self-interest is dominant? Sounded circular to him, but he did not want to get into the definition of exchange, so he let it pass.

Similarly, Adam thought of saying that material self-interest was more likely to be the dominant motive in the absence of the coercive power of the state, but the example had defined this away by saying there was only a trivial chance of being caught. "Go on," he said, not quite sure how many of these exceptions he would be forced to make.

"Consider the case of attitudes toward depositing nuclear waste in a person's own canton in Switzerland: When *not* offered a collective payment, a majority supported it as a civic duty even though they knew the hazards in such waste in their own backyards. But when offered a subsidy, far fewer people accepted the risk. This was not because the offer of money changed the perception of the risk.[72] Perhaps again you will say that when a civic sacrifice is presented as a case of material exchange— accepting risk in exchange for money—it changes from a civic duty to a market exchange. And again I must remind you that this is an evasion of the issue: the redefinition of the situation is the way material interests are allowed to crowd out moral considerations. Incidentally, this redefinition of the situation has been found to occur in individual cases in the United States as well: experiments find that people are more likely to volunteer to give blood if they are *not* paid than if a payment is offered."[73]

"Okay, so ethics and identification with community may sometimes crowd out material motives, and material motives can crowd out ethical and intrinsic motives," said Adam, hoping to limit the damage to a few extraordinary situations. "What does that prove?"

"Well," said Dessie, "you asked whether materialism was the source of the selfishness, envy, and unhappiness associated with it or whether the market recruited selfish, envious, and unhappy people to do its materialist work. This Zurich crowding-out research certainly suggests that as a dominant gestalt, materialism shapes motives and values and crowds out competing ones wherever the competition from other motives is less forceful—that is, altruism and the appeal of community service compete with materialism for people's souls. If you will allow me to personify and dramatize, I see an eternal struggle between THE MATERIALIST, who is much more than a biological creature seeking gratification of various acquisitive wants, and THE HUMANIST, seeking competing gratification of a different set of wants." In spite of his corporal excesses, Dessie, like Freud, was something of a poet and had granted himself wide poetic license on this issue. "Who arbitrates this struggle?" he asked in a final flourish. "Shall we personify the norms of a society specifying material self-interest[74] and call this image MATERIALIST CULTURE? In a relatively unrelieved materialist culture, it is not surprising that MATERIALISM wins. We stack the cards in its favor." In spite of the hopelessly mixed metaphors, Dessie was happy with his poetic outburst.

Self-Interest: Material and Other

*Y*ou know," said Adam, "when my namesake said it was not benevolence but self-interest that prompted the butcher, the brewer, and the baker to provide us with our dinner,[75] he never said that was the only thing that self-interest did. Also, although he was not specific, when he elsewhere reported that 'it is chiefly from this regard to the sentiments of mankind that we pursue riches and avoid poverty,'[76] he did not say that this was any less an example of self-interest. It is you humanists who add the adjective *material* in front of *self-interest*. Behind every altruistic motive and intrinsic enjoyment, there is a rich array of various kinds of self-interest. I think we are comparing different kinds of self-interest, different selfishnesses wearing different masks."

"Remember the Richins and Dawson experiments, where when the subjects were offered a hypothetical windfall of twenty thousand dollars, the materialists kept more of it for themselves and the nonmaterialists gave more to charity, presumably because this gave them more pleasure?" asked Dessie. "Do you want to erase the difference by claiming that each group was self-interested but only in a different way? Do you want to equate Midas with St. Francis?"

"No," said Adam. "Do you want to claim that the altruistic group got less pleasure from their gifts than the selfish group got from their appropriation of the money for their own delight?"

"Right," said Dessie. "it's an old problem. One way to go is to ask cui bono. If only the self benefits, the act is selfish; if others benefit, the act is not selfish. But intention is a better way of sorting out these attributions: if the act was intended to benefit only the self, it was selfish; if it was intended to benefit others as well (benevolence), it was not selfish."

"You are not facing the problem," said Adam. "If a person gets more marginal pleasure from benefiting others than from only benefiting the self, he is still selfish. Only his tastes are different."

"Let's try a different language. Who actually benefits is irrelevant for the use of the word *selfish;* what counts is intention. Only benevolence, intending to benefit others, is not selfish. Whether and in what way the self also benefits, materially or through internal workings of conscience, is a matter of 'self-interest.'"

"A lot of beneficence gets lost in this focus on intention, including the good that the butcher, brewer, and baker do," said Adam, puzzled. "I don't really see how markets can handle benevolence, although I believe Robert Frank,[77] Herbert Margolis,[78] and others have shown ways of handling beneficence."

Dessie thought he saw a breakthrough in an impenetrable fortification of interlocking defenses. If economics could not handle intentions, it might handle justice questions or perhaps could not handle moral questions at all. Perhaps this was why the idea of self-interest was so indissolubly connected to material interests. Adam's desire to make gratification of conscience just another case of self-interest was now understandable. Dessie thought it might be useful to be more concrete.

"Two studies might clarify this issue. First is a study of volunteering for community help. By the test of cui bono, that help certainly included the impoverished members of the community (who were grateful)—but it also included the volunteers themselves. Asked why they volunteered, 'Really enjoy it,' said 72 percent of one sample; 'Enjoy seeing results,' said another 67 percent; 'Meet people and make friends' (48 percent); 'Gives me a sense of personal achievement' (47 percent); 'It is part of my religious belief or philosophy of life to give help' (44 percent).[79] But notice that it is not material benefits to the helpers that gives them pleasure; it is something else. Thus (1) self-interest that is not material has a special, although not necessarily meritorious, standing (as where the benefits to helpers are in pride and boasting), and (2) the fact that the volunteers enjoyed the work probably *added* to the benefits to the community. In consequential terms, that is, there were two sets of beneficiaries, not just one. Poor old economic man; he is indifferent to the fates of others because their utilities are not included in his calculations. So he cannot qualify as benevolent no matter how much good he does in the world. No wonder he has been reported dead so often—but then, he always was dead." Dessie positively beamed.

"You said there were *two* points. Did I miss something?" asked Adam, wishing to steer the discussion away from Stigler's failed proposition.

"Oh yes," said Dessie. "The answer to the question of how to sort out authentic interest in another person (benevolence) and *apparent* interest in another based primarily on self-gratification is given in a clever experiment designed for this purpose. An apparently lonely person expressed to one group the desire to be helped and to another group the desire to work through her problems by herself. Those whose helping motives were self-oriented became intrusive in the 'work-it-through-myself' condition while those whose motives were genuinely compassionate and other-oriented were willing to respect the woman's desire to help herself."[80] Put differently, acts of 'altruism' can but need not be purely selfish." Was this answer germane to the larger question of materialism versus humanism? Well, yes, he thought, because it helped to show that humanistic benevolence was really something different from selfishness, materialist or otherwise.

"Okay, okay," said Adam, with growing exasperation. "Your humanist man is human, whereas economic man is not. Is that what you want me to say?" He thought about Marshall's reference to economists' 'interest in man's highest nature and affections' and wondered what had happened to economics in the past hundred years.[81] But, although angry, he wanted to shoot the other arrow in his quiver—and not a cupid's arrow, either. "Tell me about the benevolence of intrinsic work enjoyment," he said as sweetly as his anger permitted. "Isn't that the darling of the humanists?"

Intrinsic Work Enjoyment

And each for the joy of the working,
And each in his separate star,
Shall paint the thing as he sees it
For the God of things as they are.

Dessie quoted from Kipling almost automatically. "It bears on Marshall's—and all economists'—belief that the 'desire for pay is the steadiest motive in ordinary business work.' A lot of research suggests that except for the most routine kinds of work, the intrinsic interest in the task (the actual enjoyment of performing it) is often another 'steady' motive.[82] And since we were talking earlier about how material self-interest 'crowds out' other motives, we should at least point to the 'hidden cost' research, which shows, in some detail, that when a task has some interesting, challenging features, a person will work on it voluntarily without pay in his spare time. Offer that person pay and the worker reinterprets her attitude toward the task and says, in effect, 'If I am paid for this, I must be doing it for pay, and if that is the reason I am doing it, I must not enjoy it.' That is, pay crowds out intrinsic enjoyment.[83] This is a fascinating counterintuitive theory supported by an impressive body of research, but it applies only to tasks that offer some intrinsic enjoyment."

"Fine," said Adam. "Intrinsic work enjoyment is nonmaterial, but I don't see how it is 'other-oriented' or benevolent in any way. I gather that exclusively self-interested motives are acceptable as long as they are, so to speak, noneconomic. I think you are losing your moral halo," said Adam, feeling avenged in a small way.

Dessie was not a suicide bomber, but he had indeed been hoist by his own petard. "Look, lets share the honors," he said. "I'll take benevolence and the benefits of intrinsic work satisfaction, which turn out to be the joy of self-expression and feelings of personal control.[84] You take the genuine benefits of material rewards. And we will share the satisfaction from producing wealth, however unintentional (the invisible hand) that may be." This was the benevolent Dessie, rising above his claims to the partial victory he thought he had earned. In explanation, he would have said that he did not want to kill economic man (okay, he knew he had called EM dead a minute ago) but only to relegate him to the (shrinking?) sphere where he belonged.

Adam, although no more of a peacemaker than Dessie, was willing to take his chips and go home. He feared that the next step was an inquiry into how much economists had to be paid to publish in the better journals[85] or, worse, whether economic students were more selfish than others (he was familiar with the Marwell and Ames study showing that they were).[86] He decided it was time to leave this topic. "That's all very well," he said vaguely, "but if, like all cultures, humanism needs nourishment, can money buy your cherished humanism?"

Can Money Buy Humanism?

This precise question had been bothering Dessie for many weeks, but he had been afraid to mention it to Adam: Does money buy civilization? Dessie's theory was based partly on the idea that it has indeed done so: society had to be rich enough to afford nonmaterial values, at which point the things that people got most satisfaction from were no longer things that were priced. And he knew that if wealth were a necessary condition for high civilization, it was not a sufficient condition. But how about individuals? Even though unpriced, to what extent were humanist values indirectly for sale? Well, Dessie decided to expose himself and asked Adam.

"One obvious answer," said Adam, "is that the money prize for effort and skill is a fungible reward that can be used for buying a variety of things. You scorn the love of money, but what other good can be converted into so many other sources of satisfaction?" All that Adam had learned about the fungibility of money and money's uses as a means of exchange, a measure of value, and a store of value could not be dissolved by this flurry of studies on quality of life. He remembered a piece he had read on the superiority of money rewards over other attempts to motivate workers, such as participation in decision making, goal setting, and so forth. "Think of the variety of things money buys, of the variety of human needs that money satisfies," he said:

> Money is directly or indirectly relevant to all of man's needs. For example, money can be used to buy tickets to plays and concerts (artistic and aesthetic needs), to take out your spouse (romantic celebration), to go on vacations (leisure needs), to finance your favorite organization (self-actualization needs?). Money can serve to reward you for using your mind effectively and as evidence that you are capable of earning a living and thus related to (though not a cause of) self-esteem.[87]

Dessie thought of the economist's concept of "romantic celebration" without mentioning love or even a kiss, of the poet's aesthetic needs reduced to the purchase of tickets to a play or concert, of the life of the mind restricted to "calculation," as Erich Fromm and Hannah Arendt had caricatured it.[88] He wondered what the opportunity cost of a kiss might be. He sighed, knowing that economists loved their wives as much as did philosophers but that economists' mental grids could not seem to bend to acknowledge what their hearts told them was true. Then, in a flash, he realized that Karl Marx had already answered Adam's (actually, A. E. Locke's) line of thought. Marx came in two installments: "Money is the supreme good," quoted Dessie, "therefore its possessor is good. Money saves me the trouble of being dishonest: I am therefore presumed to be honest. I am *stupid*, but money is the *real mind* of all things and how then should its possessor be stupid? Besides, he can buy more talented people than himself, and is he who has power over the talented not more talented than the talented?"[89] "So," continued Dessie, "what is the solution? What would happen without this 'supreme good' where human

properties governed human relations? This is Marx the humanist's
answer:

> Assume *man* to be *man* and his relationship to the world to be a
> human one: then you can exchange love only for love, trust for
> trust, etc. If you want to enjoy art, you must be an artistically cul-
> tivated person; if you want to exercise influence over other people,
> you must be a person with a stimulating and encouraging effect on
> other people. . . . If you love without evoking love in return—that
> is, if your loving as loving does not produce reciprocal love; if
> through a *living expression* of yourself as a loving person you do
> not make yourself a *loved person,* then your love is impotent—a
> misfortune.[90]

What a pity," thought Dessie, "that Marx went on to write *Das Kapi-
tal.*" Out loud, he said, "Without acknowledging Marx, Tibor Scitovsky
said somewhat the same thing, arguing that in this 'joyless economy,' the
most important sources of pleasure, such as work satisfaction, are not
priced and do not go through the market.[91] Nor are the shadow prices of,
say, companionship and love any kind of reflection of their value.[92] This
point goes to the heart of our difference. Having dislodged the market
from its embedded location in society, as Polanyi said,[93] you economists
now want to substitute the market for society. There is no evidence that
Horatio was an economist, but it is fair to say, 'There are more things in
heaven and earth, Horatio, / Than are dreamt of in your philosophy.' "

"My philosophy embraces human welfare, just as yours does," said
Adam with assurance. "The difference is that my method of getting there
has a pretty good track record and yours has none at all."

"I am trying to make sense of the quality-of-life studies that seem to
be saying that your materialist method's track record refers more to poor
societies than to rich societies. In the age of air travel, you are telling me
of the wonders of the transcontinental railway. Under these circumstances, resting your assurance on the past seems to be misplaced."
Dessie, who was always looking for a "more fundamental level" as a way
of putting down his opponents, thought he saw an opportunity. "Perhaps," he said, "as I mentioned earlier, this materialist orientation stems
from a more basic orientation, one toward any extrinsic goal, such as
fame or popularity or others' appreciation of one's good looks, whose
gift is in the hands of others—as contrasted to an intrinsic enjoyment of
one's friends. Tim Kasser and Richard Ryan think so and report that
those who seek the intrinsic (inherently satisfying) goal of 'meaningful
relations with others' are happier and better adjusted to their lives than

are those seeking the conventional goals in the American success pattern.
They say,

> Thus it appears that the suggestions within American culture that
> well-being and happiness can be found through striving to become
> rich, famous, and attractive may themselves be chimerical.
> Instead, this work provides support for an organismic perspective
> in which persons are viewed as inherently oriented toward being
> active, agentic, and meaningfully related to others.[94]

"Why can't people be 'active, agentic, and meaningfully related to
others' while at the same time devoting themselves wholeheartedly to
earning as good a living as they can?" asked Adam, who was determined
to avoid any suggestion of an 'organismic perspective,' whatever that
might be, in what Dessie had called his philosophy.

But Dessie suddenly saw a connection between Kasser and Ryan and
reports from the happiness archive in Rotterdam. "America is less happy
than its level of income would suggest, judging by the pattern of income
and happiness in other nations,"[95] he said. "What Kasser and Ryan point
out is that this hedonic deficit arises because of, not despite, the power of
the American dream. The extrinsic character of the dream's goals, fame,
popularity, and material success impedes the pursuit of happiness. The
irony will not be lost, except, perhaps, on economists." That was nasty,
and Dessie regretted it.

Adam thought it curious that a member of a backward discipline was
claiming an advantage over market economics and was about to point
out how well Gary Becker had done in pretending that families were just
different kinds of markets,[96] but Adam had, quite illicitly, read some sociological criticism of Becker[97] and decided against it. So, like his friend
Dessie, he turned to poetry. He remembered a wicked little verse aimed
at an English professor by Hicks—not John, but Granville—at Harvard
so long ago:

> When some men achieve a mild success
> They think of spirit more, and matter less.
> And as they wiser grow, wiser and fatter,
> They scold the common herd who worship matter.

"I have satisfied my material needs," he said looking at his empty soup
bowl, "and my friendship needs." He paused as he put his jacket on.
"But intellectually, I need more nourishment."

Spanakopita Four

Humanism: The Value of Persons

Although the academic at lunch is not a pretty sight, this did not bother Dessie today, even their picking up their asparagus in their fingers, like the British, because today he had to expose his delicate concept of the humanist society to Adam's withering comment. Last week he could attack Adam's materialism, feeling himself a spokesman for a substantial group, the antimaterialists. But this week he spoke mostly for himself—there was no coherent coterie of humanists at Clark's (the English professors all lunched at the Yorkside) or in that frightening larger world outside of New Haven eating places or even outside of New Haven altogether. "Very well, then. Alone!" he said to himself, striking a Churchillian pose in the red leatherette booth—awkward, at best.

"What are you muttering?" asked Adam, sitting down.

"*Homo sum; humani nil a me alieanum puto,*" said Dessie.

"Oh, I thought you were going to have spinach pie," said Adam with a smile.

Dessie leaned forward in the booth, a bad sign, indicating a longer disquisition than strictly necessary. "In Edgar Allen Poe's mystery story," he said, "there is a map in which is hidden the main clue to the mystery. Searching for this clue, the amateur detectives got out their magnifying glasses and pored over the fine detail on the map for the answer to the mystery. As everyone knows, the clue was written in large type across the map so that no detailed search could spot the obvious. So is it with the clues for what to put in the place of the material goals that have served us so well for most of history but now seem insufficient to sustain our morale. If society is humanity writ large (which is true only in a misleading metaphoric sense), the large type has eluded our sophisticated social science magnifying glasses."

"Very pretty," said Adam with a sigh. He knew about graphs and models, but the size of the type on a map seemed extraneous to any problem he had ever tackled before. "What are we supposed to make of your mystery story reading?"

"Only this," said Dessie (stifling the completion of Poe's poetic phrase "and nothing more"). "It is a query: What measuring rods are people using when they discard the one Protagoras claimed: 'Man is the measure of all things?'"

Adam looked at Dessie quizzically, thinking that if, as he had heard it said, his mind was like a steel trap, then Dessie's mind was like a dry sponge, absorbing literary references and dripping them out one by one at odd moments. A similar dripping reference popped into his head, Pigou's "measuring rod of money,"[1] but he suppressed it. "Are you forgetting, or rejecting, the pluralism of this land of plenty?" he asked. "I don't know what Protagoras meant by his eloquent but obscurantist phrase, but last week you offered a whole lot of criteria which must, for their authors, have implied measuring rods other than Protagoras's. Is 'Man,' in his ignorance, the measure of verifiable knowledge or of the cosmic beginnings long before he arrived?"

"It's a metaphor," Dessie said with a patronizing air. "Protagoras's 'measure of all things' refers to all the contribution to the welfare and well-being and development of the human species." He paused to rehearse his extemporaneous views.

"Remember our discussion two weeks ago," said Dessie, bracing himself for the inevitable. "Well, now I have to make good on my promise to give an account of the humanist values I espouse. As I said then, humanism has had a history of various definitions. For my namesake and others in the late medieval period, it meant a return to the classics (especially the Roman classics). But in some ways, it is best conceived as an opposition to something else: for Erasmus, a reaction against high church doctrine; for Alexander Pope (1773, echoing Pierre Charron), 'Know then thyself, presume not God to scan, / The proper study of mankind is man'—also a reaction against theologizing and a typical Enlightenment sentiment (whose members, however, never used the term *humanism*). As the dominance of the priesthood and the church waned, humanism came to be regarded as a worldview somewhat opposed to science or even the scientific method in literary and historical matters. For example, Marcel Proust said that the academician Brichot 'was out of sympathy with the modern Sorbonne, where ideas of scientific exactitude, after the German model, were beginning to prevail over humanism.'[2] That meaning continues in the term *humanities*. Today," added Dessie with a sly glance at Adam, "the opposition has shifted from religion and science to materialism, of which economics is the formal expression." Dessie paused for a minute. "Humanism is *for* something, as well," he said. "It is for the well-being and development of humanity."

The Materialist-Humanist Axis

*T*oo vague," said Adam with a teacher's righteousness. "In what way does your new humanism oppose market economics, whether or not economics is the formal expression of a materialist ideology?"

"Well," said Dessie, "in one way it does not so much oppose as extend it. As I mentioned last time, humanists recognize the validity of the economist's concept of declining marginal utility and simply extend it to that universal commodity, money. We'll get into that later, but in this sense we are, among other things, weak utilitarians, maximizing happiness like you, but more scientifically and only as part of our broader agenda."

Adam snorted. *Humanistic science* was an oxymoron, like *smart idiot*. "Go on," he said, with an amused look slightly tinged with irritation that one of his analytical devices should be used against him.

"If, as Boulding said, 'Economics is mostly interested in the behavior of commodities,'[3] humanism is mostly interested in the behavior of people—their behavior in all contexts, not just market contexts."

"Do you think of demand and supply as something independent of people?" asked Adam, knowing that economists treated these two lords of the ring as impersonal forces without much inquiry into the emotions or even the calculations that informed decisions to buy and sell. But, of course, Dessie was right about the market contexts.

"If *transactions* are interpersonal engagements where money changes hands and *encounters* are the much larger set of engagements where the exchange is of such things as bonhomie and camaraderie and mateyness and good (or bad) feelings, materialist economics focuses on the first and humanism on the second. Not only is the world of encounters much larger than the world of transactions, it is the major source of people's emotional life."[4] And to himself, Adam added, "and therefore of utility."

"Encounters don't feed the world as transactions do—except the cannibal world," said Adam, wondering, if vegetarians eat vegetables, what do humanitarians eat?

"What is left out of accounts of the market journey," said Dessie, "is, so to speak, the fun of getting there, the utility derived from the processes of production and distribution—the process benefits.[5] Your silly colleagues treat work as a disutility for which pay is the compensation when actually, for much the population, work offers many intrinsic pleasures. In reporting what they like doing, regardless of consequences, many people report that what they do at their jobs gives them more pleasure than watching television or reading the newspaper! Grocery shopping is one of the most disliked activities.[6] For many people, though not teenage girls, the utility of the goods they buy is net of the process of shopping for them. The humanist vision embraces process benefits—the joy and pain of activities in and out of the market—while the materialist vision focuses on the value of the products bought and sold."

Adam knew why he worked for a professor's salary when he could get a much higher salary as an economic consultant for a Wall Street firm: he enjoyed his work as a professor. But introspection was not one of the approved tools of his trade, so he kept quiet.

"But the main reason why the humanist vision is superior to the utilitarian-economist-materialist vision," continued Dessie, "is because it emphasizes human development. People, in all their glory and ugliness—and not just their happiness—are of concern to us. Remember the Roman philosopher Terrence: 'I am a man. I count nothing human foreign to me.'" Dessie smiled because he doubted that Adam had understood when Dessie quoted the same phrase in Latin earlier that day.

"You're repeating yourself," said Adam. "Furthermore, you talk as though economists had no concept of the value of the human person. We do, and it is reasonably well worked out."

"Tell me," said Dessie with a baited smile.

People as Producer and Consumer Goods

Adam drew a deep breath. "In economic terms," he said, "humans have two kinds of value: as *producer goods*, their value may be measured by their lifetime net economic product, which, in a perfect market, is the same as their lifetime earnings. As *consumer goods*, they must yield utility or satisfaction to someone directly, with the level of satisfaction measured by what someone is willing to pay for their company or perhaps just for their being."

"I see," said Dessie, "How much would anyone pay to ransom a person? Is one allowed to bid for one's own ransom?"

"There is good news on the producer-goods front," said Adam. "As Nobel laureate economist Theodore Schultz reports, people are worth more today than ever before.[7] This outcome, says Schultz, occurs because the returns to human capital are now larger than the returns to physical capital in both advanced and developing countries. However one calculates the economic value of people—according to their contribution to economic productivity, according to their earning power, or according to the investment in their training—people are economically more valuable today. Here, indeed, is progress."

'I see," said Dessie again. "Because of the greater investment in my education, I am more valuable than my father, who, in turn was more valuable than his father. Poor old Granddad! Do you know Michael Young's *The Rise of the Meritocracy*, where people's pay varied with their IQs? It was rather hard on the older meritocrats whose IQs declined with age."[8]

Adam pretended that he was amused and went on. "People are also more valuable by measures of their replacement value—the life insurance they hold. In current dollars in 1980 in the United States, the per-household dollar value of life insurance was $41,900; in 1993, that per-household value was $111,600. Allowing for inflation, the value of people had about doubled over the period." Adam again looked pleased.

"What a pity!" said Dessie, "By this measure, my namesake, Erasmus (1460–1536), was not worth much when he died, for he had no insurance whatsoever."

"I would like to say that longevity has increased the value of people, but I can't, because they do not work any longer than they used to," said Adam, partly in jest but partly seriously. "In one sense, longevity reduces the value of human beings because the period of their lives when they consume more than they produce is extended. It is for this reason that I cannot see how Gary Becker can estimate that the remarkable increase in longevity in the twentieth century has added as much as 2 percent per year to our GNP."[9]

Dessie was amused at this reversal in priorities. "The value of increased longevity lies in its effect on GNP, and not vice versa." He sighed in mock melancholy. "But I am haunted by the fear that the marginal product of any book I might publish in my retirement would not justify my pension—but perhaps I have already become more expensive than I am worth."

"Never mind," said Adam, "as my friend you continue to have consumer value, the direct yield of utilities to me and others and, indeed, to yourself. I hate to say this, but with present company excepted, by these consumer utility standards, the value of people has probably not increased over the generations."

"I am beginning to understand how to value human beings," said Dessie. "At any one time, the more friends a person has (and the fewer enemies she has), the more valuable she is. But with no market mechanism, how do you manage your assessments of value? Perhaps you imagine an auction whereby people could bid for a person's friendship: if she happened to have rich friends, she might turn out to be a very valuable person even if she was not a rich or productive person herself. Cultivating rich friends for this imaginary auction would certainly be the rational course for the person concerned about his or her value. What about the value of children?"

With a kind of self-destructive determination, Adam carried on. "The productive value of an infant is the projected lifetime earnings less the cost of rearing and educating that growing infant to maturity—"

"Excuse me," interrupted Dessie. "Would you say that Swift's 'modest proposal' enhanced the value of infants who otherwise had only negative value?"

Adam did not miss a beat. "You may recall that Adam Smith speaks admiringly of the economic value of children in North America, where, referring to their producer values, he said, 'The labor of each child, before it can leave [its parents' house], is computed to be worth a hundred pounds clear gain to them,' with the added virtue that this value promotes marriage of widows, for 'the value of children is the greatest of all encouragements to marriage.'[10] But in postmodern society, children are primarily expensive consumer goods that must yield much higher direct utilities to their parents to justify their existence."

"Actually," said Dessie, "there is mixed evidence on the value of children to their parents. On the one hand it is clear that couples are generally happier before the children are born and after they leave the nest,[11] but, on the other hand, of the things that people report they like doing best, playing with their own children ranks very high, much higher than watching television or sports.[12] A clever economist like you might take care of these mixed findings by providing a rent-a-child program, but I don't think it would work: the same study that found that playing with one's own children was a delight found that taking care of other people's children ranked at the very bottom of the list of things people enjoyed doing."

Adam felt that he was losing ground and that it might be more fun to talk about the problems of assigning intrinsic value to people. "Okay, I get your point," he said. But to no avail.

"On the whole," continued Dessie, "it seems, sadly, that the value of children has declined in postindustrial society, partly because they are no longer producer goods, partly because the same welfare state that raised the value of older persons makes unnecessary the support of these pensioners by their children, and partly, perhaps, because a materialist society makes child care less 'profitable' than does market work by mothers. Hence, fewer children are produced in advanced societies, which are no longer reproducing themselves. It is a paradox: the countries that have had the best history of growth produce the least children . What happened to the laws of supply and demand?" Dessie paused and asked, "What would you say about the value of women?"

Adam sighed. This monomaniac would not let up. "Women," he said, "are more valuable now than when they did not do so much market work."

"Thank God," said Dessie. "But of course this changed valuation is an artifact of the way GNP has been calculated: for example, if a mother neglects her small child to work as a secretary, she becomes more valuable than if she stayed home to care for her toddler. In this kind of case, it may be said that the toddlers of this world pay for the rise in GNP in all countries."

"You are not up to speed on modern ethical thought," said Adam with some hubris. "Why assume that women are the necessary caretakers of toddlers? As Susan Okin says, the only physiologically prescribed phase of birth and socialization is actual pregnancy and giving birth; the rest can reasonably be taken on by men or professionalized in child care centers whose caregivers can be of either sex."[13]

"If not quite a male chauvinist pig, I am gendercentric and regret it," said Dessie with genuine contrition. "But I would like to add that I find slightly offensive both Schultz's notion that women's value is changed by their entry into the market and Okin's implication that the capacity to give birth is a consideration in a person's ultimate value."

"Don't forget," said Adam, gracefully accepting Dessie's apology, "that the same Ted Schultz who found the value of human populations to be increasing argues that the education of women is the best investment in developing countries because educated women are better mothers; they talk to their children and monitor their health care better than uneducated mothers. Women are more valuable both because they represent greater investments, which gives them value both at home and in the market, and because the demand for their paid services has increased."

*A*dam thought this discussion had not gone well, though he wasn't sure whose fault it was. Perhaps the direct value of people to each other as friends would be a better, even more humanistic, approach. "There is a difference between use value and exchange value," he said with the appearance of friendship. "I would not exchange our friendship for the world, but it does have use value," and under his breath, "I think."

"Use value?" murmured Dessie, wondering who was using whom for what purpose. But true to form, he had to trot out another behavioral study from his overcrowded stable. "It is good relations with others, especially in marriage, rather than money that contributes most to measured happiness.[14] Both of the two major, early studies of subjective well-being (SWB) in the United States found that among all aspects of life, marital felicity was the first- or second-largest contributor to well-being, contributing substantially more to happiness or life satisfaction than did level of income or satisfaction with one's standard of living.[15] But friendship makes a strong contribution: the number of friends people have predicts happiness better than the number of dollars they possess.[16] Cross-nationally as well, happiness in one's marriage is the best predictor of SWB, and those who are married are almost universally happier than those who are not.[17] In another cross-national study, this time of more than thirteen thousand college students, satisfaction with friends was found to be more closely related to happiness than was satisfaction with finances.[18] Other people, not money, contribute the most to a person's happiness." Dessie braced himself for comments about the friendship market, but Adam took another tack.

"I don't see why consumer utilities don't fail your Kantian test," said Adam. "After all, they imply using other people as a means to one's own happiness. It makes the value of people contingent on their capacity to yield companionship, something not everyone can do. If you impose these philosophical bans on materialism, you must also apply them to your so-called humanistic values."

"Fair enough," said Dessie in a fit of good sportsmanship. "I have three answers to that line of criticism: (1) As I hope to show when I get to my second spinach pie, there is a default value that we must employ when the instrumental values have been exhausted. That is, people have a residual value even if they have no friends. (2) The contribution of friends to human development, the second of my sacred trinity, has been well documented both as a source of mental health and as a source of information and an aid to fruitful learning.[19] And (3) the fear of instrumentalizing friendship can be handled by universalizing the companionship argument so that it corresponds to the golden rule (and not so incidentally, to Kant's categorical imperative): In *Candide* (act 1), Shaw puts it this way: 'We have no more right to consume happiness without producing it than to consume wealth without producing it.' Although, as Kant held, empirical evidence cannot alter philosophical arguments,[20] the world has a way of taking care of punishing exploitation of others."[21]

Adam looked quizzically at Dessie. "Is reciprocal use of each other all right, then?" he asked with deceptive innocence.

"Okay," said Dessie, "we can justify friendship by citing authority, which, in this case, is really resorting to a stipulative definition. We simply call companionship an ultimate good, as do the Stoics[22] and philosopher G. E. Moore.[23] In another vein entirely, if the fatherhood of God is an accepted concept, then so must be the brotherhood of man. I will leave the concept of love as agape or Christian love to specialists; it may or may not be related to the friendship and family solidarity on which we have evidence."

Adam had no intention of discussing either agape or Christian or any other kind of love. For one thing, he did not know the production functions of love and would doubt any social scientific explanation that he might suffer through.

"I have had enough and I suspect that you have, too," said Dessie, tired of leading Adam down this weary path. "These conclusions are worse than silly; they are offensive. Why? Because they rely entirely on instrumental arguments: people are valuable because they have certain consequences. Take away these consequences and you leave people valueless. There is no escape: to put people at the center of our value system, they must be endowed with intrinsic value, and the only sources for such value lie in the religious, and humanistic beliefs that people are intrinsically valuable."

Adam saw light at the end of the spinach pie. "However cogent may be your argument for the intrinsic value of human beings, it is no guide for action because it takes no account of important consequences: Shall we save the life of the scientist creating a vaccine for anthrax or the life of the terrorist spreading the virus? The answer is that intrinsic values do not trump consequential values but rather represent a default value, one that is enlisted at the end of the consequentialist chain."

"Great!" said Dessie. "We converge. Without an intrinsic counterweight, economistic formulae destroy the value of all nonproductive people: the old, the sick, and the immature. Adam, old friend, that is not what you want."

"Tell me about the source of this default value, about the intrinsic, if that is the route we must take," said Adam, eager to change topics.

Religious and Humanist Foundations

*T*here are two entities competing for the honor of ultimate and intrinsic value," said Dessie, "divine entities and humans. Although the Greeks started the discussion and Erasmus advanced it, the Enlightenment gave it a modern meaning. These two entities provide us with two ways of establishing the intrinsic value of humans."

"You are a secularist, you paraphilosopher, you! Do we need to go over the three proofs of the existence of God?" asked Adam, hoping to shorten this discussion.

"Not quite that," said Dessie. "But in this field, we will take whatever help we can get. The religious argument is this: because humans were created by God, humans share in his divine and ultimate value. This is not a very good argument, since, according to the same book, God made mosquitoes, which, from a human point of view, certainly do not share in God's goodness and for whose existence we must depend on the inscrutable (or evolution?). There is a bit of a problem, too, with the fact that, from the Western perspective, the Christian God made Buddhists, Hindus, and pagans at the same time (with their differing accounts of human origins), but since they are all endowed with personhood, they are all equally or almost equally sacred in his sight. This universal value is a deeply ethical insight, and it would serve humanity well if people understood it."

"Oh, come now," said Adam. "You know as well as I do that lurking behind the religious argument is something a little less ethical and a little more, well, economic. What Aquinas called the extrinsic value of God is the set of rewards earned if one follows his commands.[24] Similarly, that famous pagan, Aristotle, used something like this argument to defend his choice of philosophy as the essence of the final good: in philosophizing we use the faculties that are most godlike, and the gods will favor us for this compliment.[25] I know there are good hedonic arguments for believing in some religion,[26] but I don't think the cogency of religious arguments for the value of humans adds much."

"The humanist version of the intrinsic worth of humanity is where Kant comes in," said Dessie, hoping Adam would see the point when he was through. " 'Man, . . . any rational being,' he said, 'is an end in itself.' This principle leads to a practical imperative: 'So act as to treat humanity, whether in thine own person or in that of another, in every case as an end withal, never as a means only.' The reasoning behind this assertion and imperative is that the 'value' of things that can be exchanged with one another is less than the 'value' of the one thing that cannot be exchanged, the human person. In this one respect, humans are unique. Kant uses the term *dignity* for this special value of humans, one augmented by the fact that, unlike any other animal or object, humans have wills of their own and are thus capable of autonomy."[27]

"I must say," said Adam, "this is one of the silliest arguments I have ever heard. Uniqueness sometimes is and sometimes is not a source of value. Anyway, we do exchange people; if we did not, there would be no remarriages and more fatherless children. These philosophical chaps are revered not for their cogency but for their prior record of reverential treatment."

The social scientist in Dessie took an illicit pleasure in hearing the unspeakable spoken with such a dangerous candor. But that was a distraction. "The humanist or philosophical element of this debate has another voice," he said, "one that has the unsatisfactory status of giving intrinsic value to humans by default. Henry Sidgewick says, 'If we consider carefully such permanent results as are commonly judged to be good, other than qualities of human beings, we can find nothing that, on reflection, appears to possess this quality of goodness out of relation to human existence, or at least to some consciousness of feeling.'[28] Others have said the same thing.[29]

Adam was enjoying himself; he had found these humanist allusions embarrassing all his life, and now he could get even. "I find this is also pretty weak," he said. "Not finding any nonhuman good, your chaps claim there aren't any. This runs against Popper's claim that you cannot prove a generalization true, only that it is false."[30]

What to do? Dessie thought about self-interest arguments but realized that they had no answer to the person who claimed his or her own value but not the value of others. He decided to face his difficulty. "Perhaps," he said, "this failure to persuade is because we are asking an impossible question: How do you defend an 'ultimate' value when you are forbidden to refer to its origins (genetic fallacy) or its consequences, the latter because once something is defended on the grounds of its benign consequences, it no longer depends on its intrinsic value. In any event, the intrinsic has a kind of ghostly quality about it and, as Kenneth Burke remarked, it is always bleeding off into the extrinsic.[31] As we said in Spanakopita 2, the term *ultimate good* invites the questions: Good for what? Good for whom?"[32]

"So," said Adam, "why not accept my answer to the question, 'Good for what?' A person is valuable to the extent that he or she contributes, by producing something others value, to the welfare of society. It is not necessarily selfish; it is practical and measurable and has borne the test of history."

Are People Worth What They Contribute to Society?

*E*ven philosophers think of something with value as being good for something—as a good knife is good for cutting,"[33] continued Adam. "We might, therefore, defend the selection of human beings as having value for what they can do or be. To do this, we would go to a functional argument: What are humans good *for?* Speaking on the basis of experience in one of the greatest gemeinschaft communities in history, Aristotle outlines what it takes to be an ideal member contributing as much as possible to an ideal community. The *Nicomachean Ethics* is a set of principles guiding the craft of life: temperance, courage, magnificence, and so forth. Just as physicians must know and practice the things used in the art of healing, so good citizens must know and practice the things that make them good members of the good society. You humanistic chaps fairly worship the Greeks; why not allow this same argument for something just as important—economic citizenship, citizens, indeed, of a world economy?"

While the humanist in Dessie boggled at comparing the Athenian citizen with economic man, the social scientist in him accepted the comparison with relish. "This is pure collectivism," he said, "in the sense that the good of the group transcends the good of the individual, a view of life common today in Asia[34] and in *The World We Have Lost*[35] but not acceptable in a modern individualist society[36] because the ultimate worth of the individual cannot be made contingent on something else. Weak as they are, we need the religious or humanist arguments for the intrinsic worth of humans lest those who are thought to contribute less to society be marginalized or rejected. And in the end, the intrinsic is a prophylactic to Mussolini's view: "For the Fascist, everything is in the State, and nothing human or spiritual exists, much less has value, outside the State."[37]

"Good Lord," said Adam, feigning shock. "Are you saying that learning to be a good citizen or even living among good citizens contributes nothing to happiness or human development? Or justice, for that matter? You sound as though you had accepted without reservations Lukes's axiom about individualism—I mean, his moral law that says we must treat the 'individual as an end, society [as] a means. [This idea] has the logical status of a moral . . . axiom which is basic, ultimate, overriding, offering a general principle in moral argument.'[38] Thinking of the worth of a citizen as depending on his or her contribution to the good society certainly violates Lukes's moral law. But," he added reflectively, "if each person's worth depends on her respect for as well as her contribution to other persons' intrinsic worth, maybe we can save Lukes's principle and still embrace a little collectivity—a paradox,"[39] he said with a smile.

"You save Lukes by a little weasel-worded, noncontingent clause—'respect for,'" said Dessie. "I like it as a compromise, but basically I agree with Lukes. The default value must be the intrinsic worth of the individual whether or not she contributes to others."

"You have lived in New Haven too long," said Adam. "The world is not made up of one-way streets. Aristotle's good society certainly was intended to make good people as well as good citizens (a distinction he would not make). Usually, individuals share in group goals and communities benefit from individual successes. Is a person worth what she contributes to her community? Yes, in part. Are communities valued according to their contributions to their members' growth and well-being? Yes. What's the fuss? I think your search for ultimates in the sky has blinded you to the ordinary two-way traffic on the street."

"Did I just hear Lukes's axiom collide with the two-way traffic?" Dessie asked himself. "Or could it be that service vehicles are going one way while ultimates are going the other? That would save Lukes, whom, partly because I like him, I would like to save. But the problem of human value is more complex than a single moral axiom can accommodate." Out loud, he said, "Lukes's moral axiom is less clearly applicable in the collectivist traditions of eastern Asia. At least cross-cultural studies show that its empirical translation, self-esteem, has substantially more effect on life satisfaction in individualist countries than in collectivist (interdependent) countries around the world.[40] This "dignity" or self-esteem that Kant and Lukes found so self-evidently an intrinsic value justifying putting the individual on center stage turns out to be a culture-bound perspective,[41] though that does not make it invalid."

"Anyway," continued Adam, glancing with concern at Dessie's dreamy face, "you will have trouble persuading most of the world of this view that the only criterion available for judging institutions is their contribution to individuals' development: not only those who believe that people exist for the greater glory of God but all the Asian billions who are, in fact, collectivists believing that it is better to pursue social goals at the expense of individual ones than vice versa." Adam paused for a moment and went on to make a related point. "Can I translate that to mean support for that collective good, GNP, but not for individual wealth?" asked Adam, wondering if that meant support for collective goods, such as the Parthenon or I-95, but not individual goods, such as dining out or Gucci shoes.

"To my ear, the collectivist priority sounds ethically superior to the Western 'me first,' said Dessie, who had always thought that the justification for economic growth was in the use of funds for collective goods. But this was quite compatible with Lukes's moral axiom because the value of collective goods could be defended by their contribution to individuals. "I like that," he said, "because it makes contribution to the community a value in the service of individual welfare."

Adam thought for a moment about the question of the worth of individuals measured by their contributions to the community. "Part of the problem," he said with a philosophical air more becoming in Dessie, "is that you keep confounding intention and consequences. They are separate evaluations. In terms of intention, the chap who works in a soup kitchen wins moral credits compared to the local grocer. But in terms of consequences, I cannot get it out of my head that, as I mentioned last week, Adam Smith said you do not count on the grocer's benevolence to produce your dinner; rather, you expect him to do so out of his own self-interest. But I grant you that soup kitchens do not emerge from self-interest, unless one takes that impermissible step of identifying self-interest with the self-rewards of a good conscience. So let us keep two separate accounts of the worth of individuals, one for their intentions, the other for their consequences." He beamed.

"Keeping two sets of books for each account?" asked Dessie, ashamed of the quip in the face of Adam's very good point. Perhaps there was something to this materialist, even economistic, mentality after all. But he feared that if people were appraised separately for their intentions and for their consequences, the consequential appraisal, which affected other people's lives and not just their sense of fairness, would win. In any event, Adam's solution suggested that the worth of people depended either on a (moral) trait or on what they did—contingent worth again. Before closing the books on this lunch, he wanted to clarify one troublesome argument for the centrality of persons.

People as Ends and as Causes

*O*ne distinction that seems important to me in placing people at the center of things," said Dessie, moving the ketchup so that he would not strike it as he gesticulated, "is the difference between honoring humans as the *ends* for which we strive and honoring them as the *causes* of events. The problem is that we want them to be causes—the theme of empowerment that is so popular among sociologists and social philosophers these days—but, as we discussed in Spanakopita 2, in that disastrous attempt to justify the 'noble lie,' people are often the pawns of circumstances and not the origins they want to be."

"Easy," said Adam. "Give them plausible qualities and watch them struggle with variation in circumstances, such as prices and budgets."

"That neither honors them as ends nor gives them any significant roles as causes. As Veblen said, economic man 'is an isolated definite human datum, in stable equilibrium except for the buffets of impinging forces that displace him in one direction or another.'[42] There is little of Kant's autonomy or will in such a creature. Put differently, materialist (or market) theory places emphasis on circumstances (prices), not on people in all their magnificent variety."

"I think you are still wedded to the 'noble lie,' " said Adam, with compassion.

"But it is possible to honor humans as ends without falling into several traps about their roles in causing their own outcomes. Actually, there is no more reason why the object of appraisal, the human ends for which some behavior is taken, needs to be the subject of behavior, the agent of action, than there is for the object of a man's love to be a lover herself. If, to change the metaphor, beauty were one of the ultimate ends of life, we need not say beauty is an effective cause. I know that the Western idea of a developed human being is of a person who thinks of himself as responsible for his own life and the lives and fortunes of his children and others close to him. We *want* him to be a cause, but ends and causes are really very different. If a man's reach is larger than his grasp, and the aphorism says it should be, then that reaching person will often fail to achieve what she reaches for. In short, we are not bound by our desire for people to be the causes of their own outcomes, to believe that they are or will be such causes. Indeed, as we have seen, to give value only to people who are important causes is to make the value of people contingent on their acts—a fundamental moral error."

"Never mind," said Adam, in an effort to console his friend, "the idea that the character of the person or people explains the destiny of individuals and of societies is a view that is far more popular in the United States than in Europe.[43] Moreover," he added, as though Dessie had not disposed of this argument just a minute earlier, "the idea of people deciding for themselves is an implicit and very important assumption in economics."

Dessie sighed. The economist's paradigm was so embedded in the culture that neither he (nor Veblen) would shake it for another hundred years. Well, there was just enough time to give the New Humanism another supporting shot today.

How One Is Treated Versus What One Gets

𝒯he basic idea of the New Humanism is the emphasis on what social scientists, in their colorless language, call 'interpersonal relations,' the way people treat each other,"[44] said Dessie. "In his *Loss of Happiness in Market Democracies,* Robert Lane calls it 'companionship,' but the idea is broader than that, for it includes everyday, glancing relations with strangers and formal relations with authorities as well as relations with friends. Kant's term *dignity* (whatever it may be in German) is too formal; a person who 'stands on his dignity' is an ass."

"I know what you mean," said Adam with some signs of friendliness, "but I think this leads to a spineless society where everyone is nice to everyone else, where authority is veiled in niceness, and where in the interests of niceness nothing gets done. There are niches in society, such as those occupied by police and drill sergeants, where something else is required." He avoided the American cliché that "nice guys finish last."

"Niceness doesn't quite correspond with what I have in mind," said Dessie, wondering how much aggressive, authoritarian behavior Adam would like in his own life. "I think of three things that might be called dignity goods that would be cultivated and distributed in a humanist society: self-respect, sense of personal control over one's own fate, and an understanding of the rules, customs, and procedures in which one is enmeshed. Speaking of the police, for example, the *self-respect* of a driver is threatened when she is stopped for some traffic violation. It is not surprising, therefore, that studies show that when a police officer stops a driver, the most important element in the driver's response is not whether she got a ticket but how the officer treated her.[45] Courtesy is a kind of niceness, but it avoids that sticky sentimentality that you implied, and it is compatible with—indeed, a part of—efficiency."

"Okay," said Adam, "but actually, the support for the dignity good, self-respect, comes more from small, intimate groups than from officials or institutions[46] and particularly from what is called 'reflected appraisal': 'Each to each a looking glass / Reflects the other that doth pass.'[47] We must rely on society, not government, to nurture self-respect. The California Task Force to Promote Self-Esteem was an unhappy failure."[48]

To be reminded by an economist of the force of a society not embraced by markets and governments was a novel experience for Dessie, one he did not cherish. He hurried on. "Giving individuals the sense (or illusion) that they can influence the outcomes of events in their lives is a second way to confer what Lane calls 'dignity goods' on individuals. Lind and Tyler have shown in brilliant detail how plaintiffs and defendants, whether or not they win their cases, are more likely to believe they have had a fair trial if they have a chance to be heard by a judge or jury that seems attentive and concerned."[49]

Adam brightened. "We agreed two weeks ago (didn't we?) that the market is the best institution we have around for teaching contingent responses—that is, getting a response when a person acts so as to elicit it. So the second of your dignity goods, what you call personal control but what others might call self-confidence, is one of the best, if priceless, goods that do go through the market."

Dessie thought of how the poor without funds get rewarded by contingent responses and how the unemployed learn self-confidence from their powerlessness, but he had to agree that for the vast majority in rich nations, the market did work through contingent responses. Knowing that people were aware of this, he had to say so. "In answers to open-ended questions on 'what is good about the U.S. economic system,' more than a third of respondents (36 percent) mentioned opportunity, mobility, the reward of effort; about a fifth (22 percent) mentioned freedom of choice and movement, and only an eighth (12 percent) mentioned a high standard of living or the abundance of goods."[50] Was he yielding too much? "Of course you're right," he said, but he took back this concession with a further question: "I just wasn't sure how you counted this major benefit of confirmed self-attribution in the national income accounts."

Ignoring that barb, Adam went on. "Since you are so generous in your tribute to the consumer market, will you be equally forthcoming on work life in a market economy?"

"Jobs that are nonroutine, relatively less closely supervised, and somewhat complex are known to teach self-direction and the value of self-direction,"[51] said Dessie, with a degree of conviction that was rare, even for him. He paused for a moment to consider whether this was the time to point out the narrow scope of Milton Friedman's defense of the market on the grounds of freedom of choice.[52] He decided it was. "Of all the characteristics of a job—its security, the emotional and physical demands it puts on the worker, the social support that it offers, and so forth—'the one thing that has been found to be associated with the workers' early death is the lack of decision latitude.' One study found that, with all other relevant factors controlled, 'people whose work was mostly routine and passive . . . were 43% more likely to die over a five-year period and 50% more likely to die over a 10-year period' than a comparison group.[53] Any defense of freedom and choice that focuses on consumer choices rather than the choices that are vitally related to well-being and, indeed, to life itself, is a tendentious, ideologically driven argument."

"Are you saying that in your humanistic economy workers will not be supervised?" asked Adam with something approaching a sneer.

"The degree of close supervision or of decision latitude is partly but not wholly technologically given.[54] Producer choices can often be enlarged and are just as important for well-being as consumer choices, as Lane explains in *The Market Experience*,"[55] said Dessie, relishing the incidental attack on Friedman more than the elaboration of the freedoms that count.

"I'm grateful for your acknowledgment that at least the consumer market contributes to people's sense that they control their own lives," said Adam. Smiling, he continued, "I'll take half a loaf if that is all that is on offer. Things come in threes, like your trinity. What was the third so-called dignity good?"

"Oh, yes," said Dessie, as though he had forgotten, "understanding. Without some understanding of what is going on in an experience of any kind, one is inevitably a pawn: one cannot define the situation in other than incoherent and emotional terms. For example, at the simplest level, unless a person understands the customary protocol of restaurant behavior, she will be bewildered by the sequence of waiting for a waiter to come to the table, ordering, waiting for the food to come, eating, paying, and tipping."[56]

Adam wondered how this culture of self-respect, self-confidence, and understanding differed from the concept of "social capital,"[57] about which his more catholic colleagues had been talking, but he didn't know enough about it to say anything intelligent. Rather, he asked, "As the companionable society becomes nicer and poorer at the same time, how long can these amenities last?"

Dessie looked at his watch. "Next time," he said. "The people have had to wait for several centuries; another week won't make that much difference. I have to teach a class."

The Humanist-Materialist Axis

"The world has changed," said the waitress as she came to take Adam's order. "Your chubby friend used to be almost as prompt as you, and now you have been fidgeting here for ten minutes."

"Sorry," said Dessie as he slid tardily into his niche. "A student asked how the market would work the day after the nuclear bombs dropped on Wall Street." He paused to catch his breath. "The world has changed," he said, unconscious of the waitress's observation and giving Adam an eerie feeling that he was missing something that both the waitress and Dessie saw clearly. "Consequently," Dessie continued in a more normal vein, "ideologies, like market economics and other social sciences, must change to address these world changes. The old values guide us to experiences that no longer satisfy. Emergent values nourish experiences that are increasingly satisfying, but because they are somehow unknown to consciousness, we fail to pursue them. There is no 'crisis' but rather a drift from what was a self-evident account of what was worth doing toward something else, something that I regard this conversation with you, Adam, as helping to clarify. Take the first step from your sacred text: Do you agree that people are guided in their behavior by their rationally formed concepts of self-interest and utility?"

"Yes, of course."

"And do you agree that as between two goods, when one good becomes more plentiful with respect to the other one, there is a relative decline in the value of the first good—that is, do you believe the theory of declining marginal utility?"

Adam grunted assent, not too politely, for he suspected a trap.

"Okay," said Dessie, leaning forward. "How then shall we interpret the fact that increased income in poor countries is associated with increased happiness, at least as people report their own feelings, but increased income in rich countries yields no such hedonic gain?[1]

"You mentioned that before, in Spanakopita 2," said Adam.

"Similarly," said Dessie, "although the evidence is less clear, it seems that in collectivist, group-oriented countries, companionship is taken for granted because it is so plentiful, and increased sociability has no effect on happiness, but in advanced individualist societies gains in companionship are associated with substantial increments of happiness or subjective well-being.[2] Thus, with respect to these two goods, income and companionship, in poorer countries but not in richer countries, more money adds what you would call increased utility, whereas in companionship-deficient countries, like individualist market societies, but not in collectivist-oriented societies, more friends and denser social relations do make people happier. Do not these facts suggest and even extend your theory of declining marginal utility—or the general theory of diminishing returns?"

Adam realized that in economics the theory of declining marginal utility had, as Schumpeter said, been more of a logical axiom than an empirically verified theory.[3] In any event, it had always been applied to priced, market goods, and although its logic embraced all goods it had not been applied to the diminishing value of money itself and certainly not to values on this cosmic scale. "What are you getting at?" he asked somewhat querulously.

"I have gone back to our opening discussion of a watershed in circumstances and therefore of values," said Dessie, starting humbly. "The change in values is now limited to the advanced countries, but, like so much else, it will become global as global circumstances change. I would like to propose that the entire axis of argument—the points on which ideologies and cosmologies turn—is changing from something that we vaguely supposed to be a left-right axis to a humanist-materialist axis."

Humanism-Materialism Instead of Left-Right?

*A*re you saying that the materialism-humanism axis has taken or will take over all the left-right axes of the twentieth century?" asked Adam incredulously.

"I think so," said Dessie, with a note of doubt in his voice. "The capitalist-communist axis is certainly dead. When the British Labour Party repealed clause 4 of its charter, I heard the bell toll for the 'nationalization of the means of production.'"

"You will never drive out the terms *left* and *right*," said Adam. "They are embedded in the architecture of parliaments all over the world. Granted, when the Communists became the Right in postcommunist Russia, I lost my lexicographic innocence, but isn't there a constant meaning in the idea that the establishment is right and its challengers are left." Adam thought for a minute. "Except when the Labour Party is in power in Britain and the Social Democrats in Germany," he added with a sheepish smile. "All right, then," he said with finality, "Left and right are relative positions: the more egalitarian of any two parties or persons is more left." He wiped away the sheepish smile and replaced it with a triumphant one.

"Of course, you're right—I mean correct," said Dessie, benignly, "although equality of well-being has not much to do with equality of income, which, after a rather low point in wealthy countries, makes no contribution to happiness and bears little relevance to 'dignity'—if you think of self-esteem as dignity.[4] If the elimination of poverty is left, than humanism is a leftist doctrine because poverty detracts from happiness, self-esteem, and human development." He paused for reconnaissance. "But you are for the elimination of poverty—in your infelicitous way, making us both leftists; thus our fundamental disagreement is ignored. I confess that I would like to be a leftist but have had to rethink this preference when I found so many of the positions on the left occupied by rampant materialists. The old left-right axis does not correspond to the ideological needs of our time."

"So what makes you think the materialist-humanist axis is the dominant one in this age. Why not individualism-collectivism? Not the collectivism of the old Left, but the anthropologists' collectivism that now so dominates the cross-cultural literature that even I have come across it. I mean that division between (1) cultures that give priority to the achievement of personal goals and (2) those that give priority to group or collective goals."[5] Adam always liked to show off on Dessie's turf.

"Very good," said Dessie, with a degree of condescension that he hoped did not show too much. "As a cultural difference with geographical thermal lines, it is important. Cross-culturally, it affects the relations between life satisfaction and satisfaction with friends and family, on the one hand, and, on the other, it influences the relation between life satisfaction and such social factors as average wealth and heterogeneity.[6] But measures of individualism by states in the United States find that while your beloved individualism is correlated with gender and racial equality and does not seem to imply stress (as measured by heart attacks) or even residential instability, it is, however, modestly related to suicide and binge drinking. In a minute, when we get to the problems of a material-ist culture, you might recall that the individualism that has grown up with materialism seems to have nothing to do with artistic creativity."[7] Dessie was an individualist and had mixed feelings on these mixed findings.

"We are only scratching the surface," said Adam, with alarm in his voice. "If you list the economic and cultural conflict of the times, you will find so many possible axes that you will exhaust us before you finish your second spinach pie."

Dessie had jotted down a few notes on deep ideological axes and pushed them across the table to Adam. "Take a look," he said.

1. Individualism versus communitarianism (Henry Maine, T. H. Greene, Steven Lukes,[8] versus Ferdinand Tönnies, Robert Bel-lah, Amitai Etzioni, Philip Selznick)[9]
2. Environmentalism versus Bushism (Rachel Carson, E. F. Schu-macher versus George W. Bush)[10]
3. Materialism versus postmaterialism;[11] modernizing value sys-tem versus postmodernizing value system[12]
4. Protechnology versus antitechnology (David Landes versus Lewis Mumford, Jacques Ellul)[13]
5. Secularism versus fundamentalism (northern Europe and Pacific rim Buddhism versus Islam and parts of the American and Italian Souths)
6. Rational authority versus traditional authority (Weberian conflict: advanced countries versus most LDCs)[14]
7. Nationalism and ethnocentrism versus cosmopolitanism[15]

"I think you have buried the primacy of economics versus the pri-macy of culture that we touched on two weeks ago," said Adam, alert to the primacy of economics *über alles*.

"Good point," said Dessie, figuratively patting Adam on the back. "In some ways this historical attribution (causal explanation) is as important as the comparable individual attribution that has been called the most important set of attitudes a person can hold.[16] So we add:

8. Culture and mind (attitudes and values) as prime movers versus economic forces as prime movers (Max Weber and recently Havel[17] versus Marx and Tawney)[18]

Dessie looked back at his list. "You're right about there being too many," he said, "but what I find interesting is how few can be subsumed under either the humanist-materialist axis or the familiar left-right axis. One reason the "end of ideology"[19] arguments failed is that the left-right axis that these antagonists identified with 'ideology' comprehended so few of the important issues of the time. I don't want to make the same mistake with the humanism-materialism axis; it doesn't comprehend a lot of issues partly because it is an axis that applies mostly to countries that have gone through the modernization process."

"You are saying that what you call axes must themselves change with changes in the world's circumstances," said Adam, trying to be helpful in this strange territory. "What a pity that the world is not unidimensional!"

The heavy sarcasm went unnoticed, and Dessie went on. "Another way to think of the humanism-materialism axis is to think of materialism as an agent of change in a predominantly religious world: first in medieval Europe, then in the Buddhist world, and now in the Muslim world. In my humble view, materialism, having won in advanced countries, is now their agent of stasis, whereas humanism is the agent of change."

"You are backing into—what was it, your number 8?—the prime movers of history," said Adam, trying to keep issues and axes and ideologies straight. "And on examination, you are claiming a more humble role for your preferred axis. Humility is becoming even in a sage. Where are you leading us?" Adam was again feeling that his economic training had been somewhat short on the kind of values that were not priced.

"Only modestly humble," said Dessie, turning the compliment into an ironic jest. Reviewing his list, he said, "humanism is silent on technology (we are not Luddites), but, being against dogma and being for reason implies opposing fundamentalism of all kinds; humanism favors rational authority (which seems to embrace democracy), it is militantly (did he mean dogmatically?) procosmopolitanism, and, in its own interest, supports the power of ideas to change history."

"You manipulate these abstractions as though you were manipulating events," said Adam, uncomfortable in this domain.

"Like President Bush père, you question this 'vision thing,'" said Dessie with a smile. "But without some vision beyond the data of Ricardo, Walras, Edgeworth, Böhm-Bawerk, and your namesake Smith—well, I take that back about Smith—modern economists would be drawing curves and crunching data to no known purpose. Purposes are not given by data. Someplace Schumpeter says that although ideology is a great impediment to the search for truth, without ideology people would not even bother to search. But that is a different matter."

"I suspect it is interests and not logic or ideological coherence that determines what humanists are for and against," said Adam, coming back to the attack. "Take coherence, for example: the communitarians are not always on the humanistic side: their defining principles urge—perhaps even require—that their groups be graced by similarity and familiarity, qualities uncongenial to cosmopolitanism.[20] But you are sympathetic to many of their goals, so you make them humanists." He snorted again and continued. "Incidentally, the growth of cosmopolitanism, a tolerance for deviance, tracks the rise of market materialism rather well."

"So does the rise of education, public health, and the welfare state," said Dessie. "The rise of humanism itself is a product of the rise of wealth. That is the conundrum of the dialectic, if you can stand that language: only in wealthy countries, made wealthy by their materialism, can humanism challenge the dominance of the materialism that nursed it through its nonage." Dessie sighed. The extrapolation of trends, the dominance of persistence forecasting, made the job of a dialectician most difficult.

Adam looked skeptical. "There is something fishy here," he said. "Are you saying that historical dialectical arguments do not accept the lessons of history about what has gone with what in the past, that the relationships among past events are not predictive of future events because of some—what do you call it?—some 'antithesis' emerging from history itself?" Adam was not ready for such immanent reversals.

"I am merely applying an equilibrium model to the humanist-materialist domains," said Dessie. "In your narrow field, when supply increases to a given point, its effect on prices is to force a reversal of that rise in supply. Isn't that an immanent reversal?"

"Touché." Adam turned to a less familiar inductive argument. "So why haven't your busy little behaviorist friends studied this materialist-humanist cleavage the way they've studied individualism-collectivism and, to my sorrow, materialism itself?" Adam was not usually so dyspeptic, and Dessie forgave him.

"Well, that cleavage has not been forgotten either by my 'busy little behaviorist friends' or by more philosophically minded people. More than a decade ago, Jon Huer wrote a book, *The Wages of Sin: America's Dilemma of Profit against Humanity*.[21] In a more systematic (multivariate) study of more than two thousand adults of all generations, Vern Bengsten found two main dimensions: humanism-materialism and individualism-collectivism.[22] I have mentioned Inglehart's 'postmaterialism' as a humanist construct, and without too much tugging and hauling, one can find a humanist-materialist dimension in Shalom Schwartz's study of more than seven thousand teachers in forty-two nations where the values fall along two dimensions, one of which has at one pole the combined values Schwartz calls 'openness to change' and 'self-transcendence' as opposed to the other pole, 'self-enhancement' and 'conservation' (by which he means conservatism, not environmentalism)."[23] Dessie paused for a moment. "Well, this is pretty wonky stuff," he conceded, "but don't forget that the data fall into this pattern, and it is only Schwartz and I who are giving them wonky names. The underlying values are fairly clear. For example, two of the values closest to the pole labeled 'openness to change' and 'self-transcendence' are[24]

Humanist Pole on Schwartz Value Scale

Type	Definition	Value
Self-Direction	Independent thought and action (choosing, creating, exploring)	Creativity, freedom, independence (curious, choosing own goals)
Universalism	Understanding, appreciation, tolerance, and protection for the the welfare of all people and nature	Broad-mindedness, wisdom, social justice, equality, a world at peace, a world of beauty, unity with nature, protecting the environment

Adam was interested in spite of his skepticism of such value studies. "Well, it's only a working hypothesis," he said, sensing a slippage of his standards. "I would have thought an axis would have a clustering of values and beliefs along some statistical dimension. But, of course, left-right never did, its economic dimension being orthogonal to its civil rights dimension.[25] Yet it served a heuristic purpose for several generations. Perhaps a humanism-materialism axis can do the same thing in spite of its vagueness. At least it's provocative, and it might even be fruitful." He paused for a moment and added with a smile, "And it gives me something to shoot at."

"Your mention of the left-right axis's two dimensions—an economic dimension and a social liberal dimension (the latter being, dare I say it, a humanist dimension)—opens up just the kind of exploration of ideas that I would love to follow up. Your economic theory of diminishing marginal returns suggests that as societies become richer, they will deemphasize the economic dimension and stress the humanist-materialist dimension. That way, material sustenance is included as an important but diminished part of the picture. Progress comes from winning the battles along one dimension so one can focus on another." Dessie was in a transport of joy.

"You have a long way to go to map that one out," said Adam, not unkindly. "And one of the things you have to do is to show that your ideas of a humanist cluster are at least compatible with nature's ideas of our natural endowments. On that score, I think you will find that we hardheaded materialists are more in tune with nature than you are."

Nature's Priorities

We are a long way from the time when the chief agent of 'progress' was natural selection," said Dessie with the deep breath that Adam had cause to fear. "But we carry in our genes the instructions that guided us on that journey.[26] Do these instructions help or hinder the movement to the New Humanism?" he asked rhetorically.

"Have you discovered a humanism gene?"[27] asked Adam sardonically.

Fighting and Mating

Dessie ignored him. "There are two meanings to Spencer's term, 'survival of the fittest,'" he said. "The one that survived Darwin for a hundred years is the selection of those whose foraging and fighting skills gave sufficient advantage to their physical survival to enable them to outbreed rivals. The more recent modification of this interpretation, made famous by Dawkins's *The Selfish Gene,* focuses on qualities that are sufficiently more attractive to the other sex to give a breeding advantage to any variant of the species who has these qualities,[28] even if the variant individuals are somewhat inept at food gathering—hence the peacock. In capsule form, the first emphasizes fighting and the second making love, perhaps (species differ) after fighting for the right to make love."

"Isn't there a synthesis called 'inclusive fitness' or something like that?" asked Adam. "I am not happy with your opposition of love (your domain?) to foraging (which is mine). Nature must surely give genetic endowments to both."

"Of course," said Dessie. but making love (copulation) does more than make offspring. It releases hormones—vasopressin in males and oxytocin in females—that have the general effect of making all members of their species seem more congenial and lovable and of encouraging parenting behavior."[29]

"The hormones are nature's discreet social bonus to a process that is, after all, a conscious source of great happiness for humans and probably all other dimorphic organisms," said Adam in his lugubrious tones. "You quasi-philosophers want to talk about the pursuit of happiness but rarely mention intercourse. Although the pleasure of sex is treated gingerly in much of the feminist literature, here is an area where the relations between the sexes must be equalized to maximize happiness, as Mill reported."[30]

Dessie looked at his napkin and went on. "Also, through kin selection, altruism involving self-sacrifice may be advantageous for the group in the processes of natural selection. It is not the case that our genes carry only those instructions appropriate for Tennyson's 'nature red in tooth and claw.'"

"Who ever said that economic man was 'red in tooth and claw?'" asked Adam, adding, "Anyway, it would mean blood on the gray flannel suit."

"My metaphor was a little lurid," apologized Dessie, "but I wanted to make the point that if our inherited foraging motives and skills in market or other societies are not always the most important, something else is. Certain clues suggest that the first and primary drive among primates and perhaps all mammals (and social insects?) is within-species relationships:

> Infants are born with or acquire early a number of abilities and dispositions that will help them learn about people. They find human faces, voices, and movements particularly interesting stimuli to attend and respond to. They also possess and further develop impressive abilities to perceptually analyze and discriminate human stimuli. . . . There is also evidence that infants respond differently to people than they do to objects and seem to expect people to behave differently than objects do.[31]

Adam was silent as the lecture on physiology and evolutionary psychology proceeded from the mouth of his friend the humanist.

"For example," continued Dessie, "they imitate people but not movements of objects. Furthermore, those people who process faces and objects in the same areas of the brain turn out to be autistic.[32] At least one

kind of materialism is organically different from this perceptual humanism."

Adam saw an opening. "If you're right that responsiveness to people,
as contrasted to things, is 'normal,' then women are more normal than
men."[33] He smiled with glee, not sorry that this was off the point.

"Good," said Dessie, "then it is more normal to be, like women, less
materialistic."[34] He continued along his train of thought. "Something
about people gives whatever is human a salience and preference in the
perceptual system.[35] Compared to the perception of objects, person perception is influenced by the knowledge that relations with others are
interactive; people respond, they agree and disagree. As one author
reported, 'Reciprocity is its own reward,' including reciprocal understanding of each other's feelings—something that develops with matura-
tion up to about age nineteen—because of the complicated cognitive
processes involved (formal operations, in Piaget's term).[36] On the basis of
the findings of eleven studies, David Sears reports 'that attitude objects
are evaluated more favorably the more they resemble individual human
beings. Because perceived similarity . . . increase[s] liking, individual persons . . . attract more favorable evaluations than . . . less personal attitude
objects, such as inanimate objects or even aggregated or grouped versions
of the same persons.' And, in a Greeklike way, the whole person, rather
than the person's separate attributes, found such favor."[37]

"I always knew that," said Adam, continuing his fun. "When I draw
a supply curve in the shape of a woman, I get a lot more attention." But
as soon as he said this, he knew it was illicit.

"Psychology has rediscovered the emotions," continued Dessie, smiling in spite of himself. "In a cross-cultural exploration of the emotions of
joy, sadness, anger, and fear, Klaus Scherer reports that all the major
emotions are stimulated primarily by social relationships. 'It is rather
well established by now that such relationship needs are central compo-
nents of the motivational make-up of most social animals.'[38] Finally, people will endure a higher level of pain for the approval of others than they
will for money.[39] And with social support, people are more healthy, more
likely to live longer, and less likely to succumb to stress."

Adam went back to his sophomore epistemology. "You cannot prove
that people *ought* to be given priority in our value systems by showing
that our perceptive powers are people oriented," he said with the smile of
a sage. But he saw that making fun was not really very helpful and
decided to take these doses of sociobiology more seriously. "I hear you,"
he said. "What are we to make of it?"

Dessie continued. "Finally, if people trump things, things may trump abstractions, for the more an object can be visualized, the more readily is it retrieved from memory: *boat* is remembered more easily than *justice*.[40] None of this says that we should speak only about persons or make persons rather than groups or such abstract concepts as freedom and community the ultimate good, but there is a sense in which the focus on human objects is congenial and even 'natural' in a way that abstractions and nonhuman objects are not. Thus, because human stimuli heighten perception, elicit approval, arouse emotional salience, and enhance health more than do material things, we have some reason to say that, for the human world, nature gives priority to people and that, for us, nature puts people at the center of things."

Adam felt that nature was a Rorschach to be interpreted in any way congenial to an interpreter's thesis. Although he did not cling to the idea that economic man was nature's gift to economics, he wasn't happy about yielding this territory to some softhearted humanistic man, either. "Very well," he said, "but somehow nature must have given humans, like other animals, an acquisitive instinct to take care of their material needs."

Evolutionary Roots of Acquisitiveness and Love of Possessions

The literature that I've read is rather vague on materialist instincts, but what I have seen is not supportive," said Dessie, still in his serious mode. "If some 40 percent of our traits are influenced by our genetic inheritance,[41] one might well search the record for the influence of that inheritance on, if not materialism, at least acquisitiveness or possessiveness, as you suggest. One approach to evolutionary theory is through the behavior of very young children. Lita Furby reviewed the evidence in the Human Relations Files and concluded, 'The large majority of references stated or implied that children are naturally possessive and acquisitive and that society must inculcate something different if so desired.' But she was skeptical: 'Most of the material was too general and fragmented for solid conclusions.'[42] Conversely, certain repeated and possibly universal experiences might make the appreciation of 'what is mine' and what is not mine (yours, theirs) a universal *culturally* learned disposition.[43] In fact, children who are exceptionally acquisitive for material objects are distinguished by their poor linguistic and social development, a condition that tends to be fixed for the remainder of the child's life if not corrected by age six.[44] Healthy social development is marked by relatively low acquisitiveness."

"How old are your children?" asked Adam with his most innocent expression. And changing tactics, he said, "What about the verb *to squirrel away* and the standard reference to the behavior of the pack rat?"

Like a tour guide, Dessie said, "I'm glad you asked that question. Ernest Beaglehole searched for animal behavior that might suggest acquisitiveness and found that except for hoarding for nest building and food, there was no evidence of cross-species acquisitiveness that matched the human pattern.[45] Similarly, laboratory experiments with animals show that they will do their work for 'pay' but they increase their work as pay is decreased—more of a pay-maintenance than pay-maximizing behavior.[46] In another approach, Lawrence Becker, a property lawyer, searched for the origins of individual possessiveness in territoriality and was equally dismissive of any evolutionary foundations for human acquisitiveness and possessiveness. Among other points, Becker found that territoriality was a group rather than individual claim—territoriality worked through bonding."[47]

"Did you ever watch the way a woman on a train piles her handbag and books between her and the man who has just chosen to sit next to her?" asked Adam. "Have you ever watched your colleagues 'defend their turf,' even though it is only intellectual property (and student enrollments) they are defending? Whatever is 'mine' is part of the self and defended and sometimes expanded accordingly.[48] I am skeptical."

"Fellow members of our species—other people," continued Dessie without noticing Adam's disturbing comments, "are endowed by nature with powers of mutual attraction and emotional stimulation, and the brain is organized for such responsiveness. Possessions are not similarly naturally endowed; we allow desire for possessions to block our attraction to people at our peril. Although we may be required to break market 'laws' to reach the New Humanism, apparently we will do so with the support of our natural instincts." Perhaps the evangelist had triumphed over the naturalist, but he could not help himself.

"I see," said Adam, "If nonhuman primates reject equality for females (and this is not altogether clear),[49] then human primates should also reject the idea."

"Wrong," said Dessie. "The pain of violating the biogram should be registered, but ethical considerations can trump hedonic considerations. Bentham's two masters, pain and pleasure, are only semisovereign."

"Biogram! Humph!" snorted Adam. "What passes for 'nature' and 'natural' is very often simply the current practice defended by those who benefit from it." As he saw Dessie's startled expression, he hurried to say, "No, I don't mean private property, but rather something almost as sacred, the family. As Susan Okin says, we are a long way from nature in the practices of the modern family, but her main point is that technology has so altered practices of reproduction and nurturance that to reject their implications for the family is pure sexism.[50] Anyway," continued Adam, "your effort to ground your priorities in evolutionary or biological bases seems odd in a humanist. I would have thought that you would find cultural explanations more congenial."

The Culture of Humanism

*O*h, I know, I know," said Dessie in a kind of wail of anguish. "You tempt me onto this loose terrain of cultural interpretation expecting to see me sink below the surface of clear English and plain textual meanings. You probably want me to go French at this point: de Saussure, Derrida, Foucault, even Lévi-Strauss. What a morass!"

"You forgot Mary Douglas, who claims that meanings derive from the various parts of the body,"[51] said Adam, joining in the fun. "Actually," he added more seriously, "neither of us is qualified to talk about the golden age of science that we are passing through in this—ahem— sensate period of materialism.[52] I cannot stand this talk about the decline of culture by literary people who, as Snow remarked in his work on the two cultures,[53] totally ignore the magnificent advances in science in our time." Adam paused to reconnoiter. "I know that anthropologists use the term *culture* to mean everything learned, so we can't oppose *science* to *culture*. But by use of modifiers, like 'scientific' culture, we can subdivide that loose term without losing track of what we want to talk about."

"I think you are right about the golden age of science, but historically, 'the most eminent thinkers in the sciences have tended to be contemporaries of the greatest creators in philosophy, literature, and music'— although, curiously, not of the visual arts,"[54] said Dessie, quoting from Dean Simonton's work on genius and creativity. "One can cite exceptions to the Western humanistic wasteland, of course: Wittgenstein and the British analytical school and the Vienna Circle in philosophy, Marcel Proust and maybe Thomas Mann in literature; but music? Well, I can't think of any. You are right to be proud of the scientific culture of this materialist age, but why does this age not follow the pattern of historical clustering with great science going along with great philosophy and literature?"

"You were about to say the commercialization of the arts," said Adam, anticipating Dessie. "But if you think of the great corporate patrons of the arts as something like the great Florentine princes and Roman popes, I am not sure what differences you would think important."

"It isn't the sponsorship: it's the nature of the product. Let's face it," said Dessie, flushing with exasperation a long time brewing, "What America offers the world is a trashy, synthetic, ephemeral culture. Perhaps our materialism is not the cause; perhaps the cause is the technology that permits an instant mass distribution of music, literature, and the visual arts—the massification of culture. Some research (I forget where I saw it) shows that the closer the production of art is to its consumption, the more rapid the cycles of style, and the more rapid the cycles, the more ephemeral the product. That would accelerate A. L. Kroeber's long-term cycles: great civilizations discover a culture pattern, exploit its variations for centuries until exhausted, and then die out making room for other great civilizations."[55]

"You will think me a clod," said Adam with unwonted humility, "but shouldn't we acknowledge that there is no great culture without prosperity—as in the Periclean age and Elizabethan England?"

"Right," said Dessie. "Although basic science—really, the practical arts—rises with income from the beginning (as cause more than consequence), 'advanced scientific work occurred only when basic physical needs were fulfilled for almost all people in the society.'[56] This is at least superficially opposed to Tocqueville's proposition that more egalitarian societies are less culturally productive—but Tocqueville belonged to an age that was not yet divided into 'two cultures.' But to get back to your proposal that it takes great wealth to produce a great culture: perhaps. But the obverse is not true. Prosperity does not guarantee a great culture. Simonton cites the Byzantine empire to make that point—enormous wealth but little art, music, philosophy, science to show for it.[57] I come back to the question: Why is the United States like the Byzantine empire rather than classical Greece, Elizabethan England, or quattrocento Florence?" Dessie paused because he disliked what he was about to say. "Simonton gives a hint of which Tocqueville would approve (but that in science is not true): more egalitarian societies are less culturally productive. This would follow from the proposition stated earlier—namely, that there must be some distance between the producer and the consumer for art to flourish. Simonton has a political explanation as well: unlike T. S. Eliot[58] but like J. S. Mill, although with better evidence, Simonton finds that because diversity encourages creativity, 'about nine percent of the variation in creativity could be attributed to political fragmentation' as contrasted to political consolidation in empires. Taking twenty-year periods over the course of Western and Eastern history, he finds that twenty years after political fragmentation follows the breakup of an empire, many schools of philosophy flourish."[59]

"Fascinating," said Adam, with a new respect for Dessie's credentials as a humanist, "but I do not quite see how this contributes to our understanding of what you might call the culture of humanism—as contrasted to that of materialism."

After that compliment, Dessie wanted to be nice, but it was beyond his powers. "What exactly is the *culture* of materialism?" he asked. "In a sense, Fernand Braudel says that capitalism drives out culture. In the third of his phases of material life, he says, 'Finally the more sophisticated capitalist mechanism, . . . encroached on all forms of life, whether economic or material, however little they lend themselves to its manoeuvres.'[60] Or perhaps you mean the 'culture of consumption,' on which much has been written.[61] Some members of that wailing German diaspora have spoken disparagingly of the possibilities of any other kind of culture in a consumer society: as Hannah Arendt commented, 'A society obsessed with consumption cannot at the same time be cultured or produce a culture.'[62] And on the left, 'The appropriation of all culture in the service of commodity production is the distinguishing feature of late capitalism.'[63] If this is hyperbole, what, aside from science, would characterize a materialist culture?"

"You brush aside the whole world of verifiable knowledge, or what Alfred Weber called cumulative knowledge.[64] Doesn't a humanist care for life along with art, and if life, a longer life? Doesn't a humanist thrill with excitement as we explore the heavens—the heavens that figure so prominently in poetry and art? You may not understand the decoding of the human genome, but you should be excited by the discovery of the secrets of what makes humans what they are. These things must somehow stir your—well, your soul." Adam paused but could not stop himself. "You think I am a clod because I don't know nineteenth-century poetry as well as you do. Well, let me tell you that the world of clods is much broader than you think." Adam was breathing hard.

Taken aback, Dessie sputtered for a moment. Old Adam was absolutely right, and Dessie was ashamed of his precious, half-blind view of culture. "You're right," he said with what was for him a gracious bow. "As a humanist, I should also be at least a consumer of science and respond to the excitement of our age while resisting its duller, more vulgar experiences." Given what he had planned to say next, there was an irony in this colloquy that Adam might appreciate—or scorn.

"Back to the culture of humanism," Dessie began in a much more modest tone than he had used in a long time. "I wanted to use some of Simonton's findings to help define it. The main message of Simonton's analysis of the conditions under which great creativity flourishes is diversity. Does this sound like the cosmopolitanism I mentioned before? It should. Not all diversity has this cultural fruitfulness; Simonton found that diverse but subordinated peoples in empires were rarely creative.[65] Other research, however, suggests that marginal peoples who have had some experience of previous success (Scots, Jews, Ibos) are most inventive.[66] One is reminded of Arnold Toynbee's somewhat empty formula: challenge—but not too much—makes people creative.[67] A central premise of humanism is the welcoming of diversity. And from this flows the inventiveness and creativity that characterize great civilizations."

"Are you saying that the process of assimilation—that our cherished melting pot—melts the differences out of which a great culture grows?" asked Adam in surprise.

Dessie *was* saying that, but he was uncertain of its truth, so he slid over to another issue. "Something else," he said. "Simonton says that the great philosophers are not representative of their time but rather consolidate the thought of the previous age. More than that, they are, he says, 'extremists!' Aristotle, Aquinas, and Kant 'advocate extreme positions held by very few others' of their time.[68] The melting pot and the other-directedness that is inspired by a nation of immigrants may, in combination, help to explain why America is more like Byzantium than Elizabethan England."

Adam looked puzzled. "For a set of explanations that purport to account for a phenomenon as important as cultural desolation, this all seems pretty ad hoc to me," he said.

Dessie knew that was the case. But he also knew of a deeper issue that they had not yet faced. Adam, of course, was applying the standards of the philosophy of science to Dessie's discursive, exploratory discussion. But even Dessie knew that a proper econometric study of any one of the hypotheses he had mentioned would be a great contribution. Perhaps, he thought, any dialogue between economists and humanists must first confront an epistemological problem, wrapped in a cognitive problem, concealed in a semantic problem. "I am engaged in hypothesis formation with illustrative cases,"[69] he said, "not hypothesis testing."

Adam understood this, but any discursive exploration of possible causal factors seemed to him so undisciplined, so loose and easy, as to be uncongenial. "Let's get back to the central question," he said. "You keep talking about the centrality of the human person, but that entity keeps getting swallowed by politics, evolution, culture, and so forth. I don't see what you mean by *centrality,* or is that one of your figurative metaphors?"

The Choosing Person

/magine," said Dessie with one of his faraway looks, "that you are creating a society and seeking to shape those institutions that would best favor the development and well-being of people. You would be drafting a constitution, establishing a relationship between church and state, creating a judiciary part of whose function is to regulate behavior. Perhaps, like Thomas Paine, you would think of government as an institution whose main purpose is to 'restrain our vices'[70] or, like David Hume, believe that 'in contriving any system of government . . . every man ought to be supposed a knave, and to have no other end, in all of his actions, than private interest.'"[71]

Adam interrupted: "That's the trouble with government, no invisible hand to convert private interests to public interest or, as has been said before, to 'make a silke purse of a sowes eare.'"[72]

"What organ is most important?" asked Dessie. "Where would you invest the most resources, especially if you think of government's restraining power rather than its provisions for welfare?"

Adam saw that this was a rhetorical question and said nothing.

"By extending to the current democratic state the Aristotelian argument that by improving the virtues of the citizen, we thereby improve the qualities of the city-state," said Dessie. "I would suggest that the most important feature of nation building is the development of the powers of the individuals who must make whatever institutions are created actually work. The proposal is not philosophically new. About twenty-five years ago, Derek Parfit suggested that we should not try for the best outcomes but rather develop persons who 'should have the aims and disposition having which would make the outcomes best.'[73] That is, putting people and their development at the center of things has a constitutional value that is prior to but hardly a substitute for what the Framers debated. I am aware that structures are important,[74] but in accounting for the success and failure of the wide variety of governmental systems in the world, I suspect that more variance is explained by the culture and dispositions of people in each nation than by the institutional forms they work with.[75] Formally, the United States and the Latin American countries all have presidential systems—but they work very differently." He thought for a moment and added for Adam's sake, "I have seen evidence that the same priority holds for economic development as well."[76]

"I don't believe that government institutions do not influence policy and, therefore, subjective well-being,"[77] said Adam, recalling the course on political economy he had taken as a youth at Harvard.

"Of course they do," said Dessie. "My point is that hiding in the concept of political culture, which is often recognized as a shaping force, is a concept of human development. Otherwise you risk the great man theory of history—for example, the Framers would materialize out of nowhere. The New Humanism has a metatheory of history after all."

Perils of Anthropocentrism

For some time Adam had worn a worried look. "This focus on individuals instead of societies and their institutions worries me," he said. "It seems to atomize the society as well as to dissolve institutional roles and rules into individual attitudes."

"I thought," said Dessie, "you said before that markets depend on individual preferences; that is their glory. Now you worry about atomization. Computer simulations of a world of individual preferences predict that social fragmentation is inevitable.[78] What kind of a pot are you to call me black?"

"Never mind pots and kettles," said Adam. "Isn't it true that your demand that we put individuals, not institutions (like the market, or communities, or societies), at the center of things—a thesis we might call *anthropocentrism*—tends to atomize society?"

Dessie saw a huge ball of arguments rolling toward him and cringed. "You have an excellent point," he said with a more or less graceful bow. "What are the institutions of a humanistic society whose purpose is the development of individuals? I have some ideas on that, but, as in a court, could we adjourn that question until a later session—say, Spanakopita 7—when I plan to take it up in some detail?" He felt that he was wimping out (which he was), but he also wanted to do justice to Adam's question.

Adam smiled. "That's two spanakopitas from now. "I'm not sure I can wait. But before we adjourn I have one other question: doesn't this focus on development and self-development lead to an unpleasant self-focus, to narcissism?" he asked with a revulsion for examining his own rotten inner self.

Dessie thought of the number of times he had asked a friend about a play that friend had seen and been told about his friend's experience at the play. How to advance his vision of—well, yes—anthropocentrism without risking these perils? "I don't know the answer," he said modestly, "but I think it is possible to distinguish among 'self-knowledge,' 'self-consciousness,' 'self-awareness,' and 'self-focus.' I am not sure that Plato was right about knowing thyself; some of the best-adjusted people have little self-knowledge,[79] and the more complex a person's self-knowledge, the (slightly) less happy is that person likely to be.[80] But I do think it helps. Indeed, access to one's deepest feelings and values is an essential part of rationality—one that your little friends don't recognize but Amos Tversky and Daniel Kahneman did.[81] Among other things, it helps to keep choices transitive."

"If you ask me, there is a too much self-consciousness these days," said Adam, thinking of the popularity of self-help psychology and of his personal preference for people with harder noses who got things done.

"There's a chap in sociology, something of a medievalist," said Dessie, "who would agree with you about the trend but not with your evaluation of it. He said, 'The increased tendency of people to observe themselves and others is one sign of how the whole question of behavior is now taking on a different character. People mold themselves and others more deliberately than in the Middle Ages.' He thought this stemmed from greater rationality."[82] Dessie looked at Adam significantly, expecting a toast to this recently rediscovered prorationalist.

"But self-consciousness is an impediment to the easy relations with others that you think so important," said Adam, probing territory quite foreign to him.

"Maybe so," said Dessie without a trace of self-consciousness, "but its kin, self-awareness, artificially created by hearing one's own voice on a tape recorder and by seeing oneself in mirrors, although painful, makes people more honest.[83] Objective self-awareness also speeds recovery in illness[84] and buffers the effect of unhappy events.[85] But you're right in other respects: not only is self-awareness an unhappy experience,[86] it may also reduce altruistic acts[87] and decision-making competence.[88] On the whole, however, I think the commonsense position is correct: it is better to know one's own motives and values than not to.[89] You might think of it as the first of many trade-offs between happiness and human development," said Dessie, anticipating trouble.

Suddenly, Adam announced, "I've got to go. But first, tell me who is winning, MATERIALISM or HUMANISM?"

"My lunch, as always, is $8.75," Dessie said, handing the check to Adam. "Here is $9.00. Keep the change."

Spanakopita Six

Diminishing Returns to Happiness

"Are you happy?" asked Dessie in a cheerful tone as he settled himself in the front booth next to the window that always seemed reserved for him and Adam.

"Very happy," said Adam in his usual lugubrious tone of discontent. "Why?"

"Most people say they are, even in the less-developed countries,"[1] said Adam. "Those of your colleagues who dare mention the word *happiness* think this is most people's main goal in life,[2] and in this respect, for once, they agree with Aristotle as well as Bentham. Modern utilitarians and others, however, qualify their approval: happiness must be merited to end up on the positive side of the ledger.[3] Moral philosophers may do the same thing: as Kant says, 'Being adorned with no feature of a pure and good will, yet uninterrupted prosperity, can never give pleasure to a rational and impartial observer.'[4] How does utility theory handle this problem of who deserves more utility?" Dessie was really interested, although he also was expecting to score points on this issue.

Happiness and Ethics

Adam was glad they had moved from hedonics to ethics—not because he had better ethical answers but because he thought of ethics as a domain where, because data seemed irrelevant, people could defend almost any statement with enough casuistry.[5] "Utility theory is not a theory of morals," he said, "but, as I may explain later, economics has a theory of fairness that can be applied to utility theory: a firm pays its employees fairly when they receive the equivalent of their net marginal products. If they are unhappy with this, it is their unhappiness that is at fault, not the fairness of the wage. And if they are happy with less, well—" he paused for a moment and then brightened, "then they get a happiness rent." This pleased him because it gave an economic twist to a field where economics was a bit short of answers.

"I should have thought that it was the employer who received the 'happiness rent' when his employees were satisfied with wages worth less than their marginal products," said Dessie. "But that is a side issue, since Kant and others are talking about virtue rather than productivity. I gather that utility theory is as, well, as happy when a scoundrel makes a lot of money as when an honest person does."

But Adam had not finished. "And exchanges are fair when the both parties to an agreement are informed and willing to make the exchange— that is, when it is voluntary."

"Not only is there an economic literature on asymmetrical information that greatly qualifies the implications of what is 'voluntary,'" said Dessie, showing off a little, "but some modern utilitarian philosophers take account of 'a person's inability to predict outcomes by himself.'[6] In short, ideas of fairness depend more on complex theories of decision making—basically theories of interactive cognition—than you acknowledge."

"There are other elements, of course," said Adam, using Dessie's technique of ignoring counterpoints, "like honoring contracts and 'a fair day's work for a fair day's pay,' but the ethical standing of these statements must be self-evident. In any event, utility theory is not a theory of virtue or justice. Economists have to leave something to the philosophers and the lawyers."

"Of course," said Dessie tartly, "but that is no excuse for practicing social science without reading social science. No theory of contracts is a good ethical theory without some knowledge of the relative strengths and weaknesses of the contracting parties. That's why Robert Nozick's theory of entitlements[7] is not a sensible account. But to get back to the bearing of utility theory on ethics, economists believe, with Bentham, that 'money . . . is the most accurate measure of the quantity of pain or pleasure a man can be made to receive.'"[8] Dessie interrupted himself to make a collateral point: "I admire your defense of women, but it is incompatible with the idea that money measures happiness. The marriage contract is one contract where the daily rewards of affection and punishments of hostility will greatly outweigh the distribution of money."⁹

"We never said that 'the measuring rod of money' applied to utility in family affairs," said Adam defensively.

"Perhaps not, but on the main issue of ethical criteria for rewards," continued Dessie, "although you do say that economic utility must be earned, you are silent on whether this pain or pleasure, however measured, must be merited. This is quite unlike Bentham's other inheritors, the ethical utilitarians,¹⁰ who hold, with the rest of humankind, that in a decent world pain should follow evil and pleasure should follow good. It is excessively Emersonian of economists to believe that 'the only reward of virtue is virtue.' Or perhaps that is the economists' version of ethical equilibrium." Dessie found this amusing even though it really wasn't very clever.

"Well," said Adam, slightly annoyed, "if, as you said last time, it is a moral error to make hedonic rewards contingent on contribution, so be it. Economic exchanges cannot avoid that 'error.' But there is a better way of thinking about economics and morals. Boulding once defined 'Economics as a Moral Science' this way:

> Oddly enough, it is not welfare economics with its elegant casu-istry, subtle distinctions, and ultimately rather implausible recom-mendations, which has made the greatest impact on the develop-ment of common values and ethical propositions. The major impact of economics on ethics, it can be argued, has come because it has developed broad, aggregative concepts of general welfare which are subject to quantification.¹¹

In my view, he might have gone further to say that economists' contribu-tion to ethical life is their contribution to GNP itself, so that we could comfortably sit here passing ethical judgments on the pilots who brought us to that point—the economists."

"Thank you for the spinach pie," said Dessie, still amused, "but for the ethics, no thanks. Two weeks ago we discussed the perils of assessing people on the basis of their contributions to society and we decided—didn't we?—that since that left the weak, the sick, the badly educated, the discriminated against without any worth whatsoever, this version of ethics would not pass muster." He paused for a moment to see how to bring the topic back to happiness. But Adam preceded him.

"All right," he said, "I thought most philosophers followed Aristotle in identifying virtue with happiness. If that is wrong, then what is the relationship?" This was the better side of Adam, and Dessie, now in his pompous phase, did not deserve it.

"Do you want the philosophers, or do you want something a little closer to the way things are?" asked Dessie rhetorically. "Spinoza said that happiness and virtue must go together because a knowledge of God meant identifying with God's wisdom.[12] If that doesn't persuade you, try Kant, who said that it was a duty to be happy because that made it more likely that a person would not be tempted to transgress the moral code.[13] As it turns out, Kant was right: happy people are more likely to cooperate with others and to engage in prosocial activities.[14] Happy people are also more likely to be interested in moral issues than are unhappy people.[15] Moreover, the basic personality trait of 'conscientiousness' (attention to duty, responsible behavior toward others) is associated with happiness.[16] In my opinion, a utility or other hedonic theory that does not somehow relate happiness or utility to moral considerations is a defective theory." There! Dessie had actually said what had been on his mind for a long time.[17]

Maximizing Happiness

'There is virtual agreement about this [good] among the vast majority of mankind,'" said Dessie, quoting Aristotle. "'Both ordinary people and persons of trained mind define the good as happiness. But as to what constitutes happiness opinions differ.'[18] John Stuart Mill agreed about this universal desire, basing it in what he called 'human nature.'[19] Biologists and evolutionary psychologists are less certain. On the one hand (sampling the literature), the discovery of a 'pleasure center' in the brain such that, when rats are enabled to press a lever to stimulate that center, they will do so at the expense of all other desires,[20] the discovery of a certain kind of brain waves activated when people report themselves as happy,[21] and the further discovery of the role of the amygdala in processing emotions[22] all give insight into the physiology of moods."

"The fact that physiologists can locate the way 'utility' is processed in the brain doesn't tell us much about how it works when a person is confronted with a choice," said Adam. "What do you call that: 'a category error?'"

"Hold on," said Dessie. "If it turns out that the physiology of pleasure and pain has, so to speak, a mind of its own, then your vaunted *choice* is something else entirely. Anyway, as I was saying, these physiological mechanisms have properties endowed by evolution to make them respond in certain ways. In a piece called "The Evolution of Happiness," David Buss points out how this endowment both impedes and facilitates our searches for happiness. The impediments include the gross differences in what were the sources of happiness when our responses were formed and those that are now available.[23] For example, the stress response—the 'fight or flight' syndrome—was once a healthy response to external stimuli with survival value, but now it is often internally stimulated by modern environmental uncertainties and often greatly impairs the way we function and actually invites illnesses."[24]

Adam was not pleased with the direction of this discussion, for he saw Dessie sapping and mining utility theory. "If the world of the hunter-gatherers is necessary for our happiness, why are people in modern countries happier than those in the less-developed countries?" he asked.

Dessie went on. "To supplement what we said in Spanakopita 5 about nature's priorities, we should note that there are two views on whether nature intended us to be happy," he said. "One says that 'nature is not likely to have burdened us with characteristic unhappiness. . . . In the human brain more areas seem to produce positive experiences than negative ones (25 percent to 5 percent).'[25] The other says that 'natural selection . . . doesn't "want" us to be happy. It "wants" us to be genetically prolific. . . . We are built to be effective animals, not happy ones.'[26] Of course, the second view is correct, for evolution achieves its purpose through the drive to satisfy the pleasure centers and especially the drive to overcome pain. This is Buss's second point: the 'existence of evolved mechanisms [is] designed to *produce* selective distress.'[27] Similarly, Randolph Nesse says that 'over evolution, depression has helped to reorient people pursuing futile enterprises.' He goes further and paints the bright side of fear and even anxiety, which he says are small costs for their survival value.[28] To return to Buss: the mechanism of evolution, elimination of the unfit, 'has produced competitive mechanisms that function to benefit one person at the expense of others.'[29] This is not 'nature red in tooth and claw'—so messy for gray flannel suits, as we discussed last week—but it does put a different complexion on the likely success of our pursuits of happiness."

"And I thought economics was the 'dismal science,'" said Adam with a sigh.

"Wait a minute—all is not darkness, at least from my point of view," said Dessie. "I don't think Buss mentions anything about the proliferation of commodities to save these pursuits from failure, but he does say that 'on the positive side, . . . people also possess evolved mechanisms that produce deep sources of happiness: those for mating bonds, deep friendship, close kinship, and cooperative coalitions.' "[30]

"Are you telling me that food and sex are not rewards for effort in the jungle or even among the hunter-gatherers on Wall Street?" asked Adam incredulously.

"Of course they are," said Dessie; "but evolution is more comprehensive: a rhesus monkey will press a lever to the point of exhaustion just for the sight of another monkey.[31] The point is that the pursuit of happiness (or maximizing utility) cannot be satisfied in the market but rather takes us a long way from commodities and, indeed, from wealth itself. To the extent that utility theory is a market theory, it is often irrelevant to our pursuit of happiness." Moreover, he said to himself, a top-down theory of happiness where a general mood of happiness guides market choices wreaks havoc with utility theory.

"You already made that point," said Adam. "Let's agree: you pursue happiness, however hungry you may be, in fraternizing with your colleagues and I, with a full stomach, will pursue it by getting recognition, a promotion, and a larger salary."

"Don't be silly," said Dessie, "we'll both pursue it along a variety of paths. I only want to point out how inadequate a materialist culture and its sacred market are for the pursuit of happiness. But I think we are talking about different things: you are talking about preference satisfaction as though that meant the same thing as happiness, but, as we saw in Spanakopita 2, it often doesn't. People do make mistakes—unless you want to add perfect people to your perfect market."

Preferences and Happiness

Some people say that 'well-being is less based on preference than on some more objective set of achievements,' "[32] continued Dessie, quoting Amartya Sen. "But I think we should also point out that preferences often *follow* choices, not only because we rationalize our decisions after we have made them (the 'postdecision dissonance reduction' that relieves the pain of thinking one chose badly)[33] but, as William James once commented, also because we realize how we feel by observing how we acted (chose): I must have been frightened because I ran away; I must have been hungry—see what I ate.[34] Even if it were true that satisfaction flowed from achieving one's preference, one would have to sort out the various kinds of preferences and satisfactions: anticipatory, remembered, and experienced.[35] Then there is the possibility that preference satisfaction is a prescription for unhappiness. If, as Machiavelli, Hobbes, Rousseau, and Durkheim all believed, desires (preferences in that sense) are insatiable, then the hedonic treadmill stretches out before us in an infinite landscape. Furthermore, psychologists find that one cannot anticipate how one will feel about the later items in a consumption series because of *adaptation* processes (one adjusts to pain and pleasant feelings) and *contrast* (the hedonic value of what went before). Indeed, systematic conflicts between preference utility and the relevant beliefs about experience provide new arguments in the debate about the standard assumption of rationality and raise a new question about the status of choice as the sole measure of utility."[36] Dessie looked at Adam to see if he were still awake.

He was. "Would it be true that I would be happier if I did *not* get what I preferred?"

"Sometimes," answered Dessie. "It is presumptuous to believe that people can predict how their choices or courses of action will turn out, or, as research shows, what their preferences will be in the future,[37] or that addictive and habitual behavior applies only to drug addicts. Like rational choice, preference utility is amateur decision theory that will not stand inspection."

"Did you ever read that giant in your adopted discipline, Gordon Allport?" Adam asked with a wicked gleam in his eye. "Well, he said,

Social psychologists today might well ask themselves whether the issue of rationality versus irrationality did not achieve a more balanced solution in various historical American documents than it achieves in their own theories. After all, American democracy has proved viable for nearly two centuries. Its assumptions concerning the 'nature of man governed' cannot be wholly wrong."[38]

Adam leaned back as if to say, "The defense rests."

"As you once told me when I cited Aristotle," said Dessie, "'You can't wipe out decades of research by citing great names.' In any event, in their fear of the 'passions' that Albert Hirschman explores,[39] the Founders took great pains to check the impetuosity and irrationality of the people. Doesn't sound like an argument for rational choice to me. But rational choice is, for once, not the point: we are talking about happiness, and in this we are on or close to the familiar turf of utilitarianism, where maximizing happiness, in Bentham's sense, is taken for granted. Do you mind if we discuss that for a minute?" asked Dessie in his most ingratiating manner.

"I haven't finished my soup yet," said Adam.

Limits to Utilitarianism

*D*essie glanced at Adam's soup bowl and proceeded. "There are five principal counts against pure utilitarian arguments," he said, counting on his pudgy fingers.

"You are telling me in advance that you are stacking the deck against the utilitarians," said Adam. "Utilitarians are not fools; they have answers.[40] But go ahead."

"On the first count," continued Dessie, "the infirm ethics of a strict SWB standard, I will say only that the 'greatest happiness of the greatest number' leaves open the exploitation of a minority by a majority (Bentham said that the doctrine of rights was 'nonsense on stilts.') Thus, the utilities (including life itself) of individuals and minorities may be sacrificed to majorities because the slight preferences of the larger number outweigh the intense preferences of the minorities. In democracies, these minorities are protected by rights, and 'rights-based considerations . . . go against utilitarianism.'"[41]

"I see you are determined to talk about politics rather than markets, where this so-called first count does not apply," said Adam. "You could say that utilitarianism is a good market theory without being a good democratic theory." He was beginning to enjoy the discussion of utilitarianism after all.

"On the second count, the utilitarian image of humanity," continued Dessie, "'essentially, utilitarianism sees persons as locations of their respective utilities—as the sites at which such activities as desiring and having pleasure and pain take place. Once note has been taken of the person's utility, utilitarianism has no further direct interest in any information about them. [Utilitarianism especially shows] the neglect of a person's autonomy' and 'lack of interest in a person's integrity.'[42] The image is unattractive."

"That's unfair," said Adam. "Utilitarianism is a theory of pain and pleasure: to charge it with failing to be a theory of personality is, well, like charging economics with not having a theory of personality."

"It does: greed and rationality," said Dessie, continuing without a pause. "On the third count, the utilitarians' threat to freedom, the utilitarian case also is vulnerable. For example, most Americans consider atheism to be an amoral and repulsive doctrine. To silence this 'offensive' doctrine would, I think, marginally increase the happiness of the American people. In a subtle analysis, Sen shows the way utilitarian thinking can justify the torture by a sadist of an innocent person and the proscription by 'Prude' of 'Lewd's' choice in reading *Lady Chatterley's Lover.*"[43]

"In my opinion, the gamekeeper was no great lover," said Adam, smiling, "but I see your point about conflicts in preference ordering; who's to say that my preference would triumph over yours? We avoid that problem by simply forbidding interpersonal comparisons."

"You don't avoid them, you assume them; comparisons are latent in all judgments," said Dessie. "Also, recall the paradigmatic phrases of the dean of discriminative judgments on the superior merits of some pleasures compared to others. 'It is better to be a human being dissatisfied than a pig satisfied; better to be Socrates dissatisfied than a fool satisfied. And if the fool, or the pig, are of different opinion, it is because they only know their own side of the question. The other party to the comparison [Socrates or someone who has experienced both "higher" and "lower" pleasures] knows both sides.'[44] As we shall see, problems of contrast and adaptation make Mill's test inappropriate, but the point is that utilitarians (but not Mill) homogenize happiness and its sources in a quite unscientific way."

"So why can't I be a utilitarian in economic matters and an intuitionist or contractarian or whatever you like in other matters?" asked Adam.

Dessie thought of the principles of philosophy that require universalization instead of eclectic picking and choosing among philosophies as one finds them more or less satisfactory, but he had two more counts against utilitarianism that he wanted at least to mention. "Fourth," he said, "social comparison (that, like Canute, you command to stand still) is one of the offenders: if people's happiness depends on comparing their situations to others', and if others' situations advance at the same rate as their own, they will never be any happier. The fifth and final offender is our tendency to adapt to new situations: if a person is promoted and quickly adapts to the new level of pay and prestige, even without social comparison, that person can never be happier, no matter how much she achieves." Before Adam refuted this point, Dessie had something else he wanted to discuss. "A distinguished scholar of happiness phrased it this way: 'How harmful is happiness?'"[45]

But Adam slipped in ahead of him.

*O*f course happiness or preference utility (getting what you want) is a good," said Adam, who had learned from George Stigler[46] and lesser lights that the point of economics was not to maximize wealth but to maximize utility, however it was defined. "Indeed," he continued, "it is one of your ultimate goods—a good in itself in your sacred trinity. What more is there to say about it?" He paused and added, "Except that after almost two hundred years of utilitarianism, the happiness of the female half of the population is only now being seriously debated."

Dessie knew that although women were considerably more depressed than men, they reported themselves as happy in about the same degree.[47] But he wasn't going to get into that tangle. "If you have no measure of pain and pleasure, as Bentham said was the case, you are stuck with global statements of uncertain worth," he said. "But with a measure, we can actually study what goes with what, the benefits and costs of self-reported happiness," he continued, thinking of the contributions of both quality-of-life studies[48] and of the Zurich school of economists.[49]

"I thought you weren't supposed to count the consequences of intrinsic goods lest they lose their intrinsic goodness," said Adam, turning Dessie's shaky philosophy against him.

Dessie had to smile: this economist was learning the tricks of the philosopher's trade all too quickly. "Theoretically, happiness may not be called 'good' *because* it has beneficial consequences, but an understanding of this elusive intrinsic quality can be supplemented by a grasp of its consequences." He lowered his voice to a whisper so as not to be heard by the philosophers in the next booth. "Don't tell anybody, but in fact all good philosophers are also consequentialists." Then, resuming his normal and often all-too-audible voice, he went on. "As I mentioned a couple of weeks ago, happy people are more likely to be happily married,[50] have higher self-esteem, and have more self-confidence (sense of internal locus of control); they are more optimistic; and, partly because they are more outgoing (extroverted), they get better jobs and make more friends.[51] Happiness also helps a person recover from surgery.[52] In her extended studies of the effects of good and bad moods on behavior, Alice Isen finds that people in good moods differ from others in the following ways: 'Good feelings,' she says, 'seem capable of bringing out our better nature socially and our creativity in thinking and problem-solving. . . . They are potential sources of interpersonal cooperativeness and personal health and growth. . . . Positive emotions facilitate helpfulness and generosity.'[53] Also, since memories are often stored according to affective tone, a good mood stimulates happy memories. Happiness, so to speak, is a felicitous condition."

"Well, then," asked Adam, playing the Socratic stooge with a wry smile, "if you can count the benefits of intrinsic goods, why can't you count the cost of intrinsic bads?"

"I'm glad you asked that question," said Dessie, failing to notice Adam's smile. "To take the extreme negative case first, clinical depression is extremely costly. Not the least of these costs are those borne by the children of the depressed, who not only are more likely as children to suffer a disproportionate number of physical injuries[54] but also are more likely as adults to be mentally disturbed. At work, coworkers enjoy their work less if they associate with depressed persons, and at school depressed students upset their friends and often stimulate hostility toward themselves.[55] Depressed persons do less well in their studies than matched others. Also, the effect of depression on judgment is often but not always damaging."[56]

Adam brightened at the mention of costs. "So, as a measure of well-being, GNP suffers from its insensitivity to levels of unhappiness and depression in a society," he said with a cheerful air.

"That's not all that suffers," said Dessie, trying to deflate Adam. "There are also personality costs: for example, depressed people are less capable of autonomous behavior than normals,[57] and depressed children are more likely than normals to blame themselves for failure,[58] thus creating a malign cycle of pain and debilitation. Alcoholics who are also depressed engage in more fights and disturbances of the peace than alcoholics without depressive symptoms.[59] In fact, depression has been found to be a contributing causal factor in both alcoholism and drug addictions."[60]

"I would like to remind you," said Adam, showing off, "that there are also substantial economic costs in lost productivity: the mildly depressed have one and a half times the number of disability days that normals do and the severely depressed have five times as many lost days as the mildly depressed."[61]

Dessie, remembering the discussion of the economic value of life in Spanakopita 4, couldn't resist: "Is the life of a depressed person worth less than that of a happy person?" he asked in spite of his resolution not to needle Adam.

Adam was unneedled: "Well, the dependents of the deceased often do require financial subsidies from the state, and in Britain the direct cost of inpatient care for the depressed was about a seventh of the total inpatient cost of the health service." Adam was pleased to join Dessie in this sad account of loss.

"Do you think we could estimate the contribution of happiness to GNP net of the costs of depression and unhappiness?" asked Dessie, again forgetting his resolution.

"I think so," said Adam soberly, "although, to tell the truth, we economists have usually figured it the other way around: the contribution of national income to utility. We have always assumed that this was what economic growth was all about. Actually, it is your so-called happiness figures that show this most clearly: across twenty-three nations the correlation between happiness and GNP per capita is .69,[62] and a later summary of four surveys across fifty-five nations found a correlation of .58.[63] Of course it is not permissible to reverse these figures, but I would guess that the contribution of happiness to GNP is substantial." At last Adam seemed to be on home ground, even though he was using figures from alien turf.

Remembering how Gary Becker had estimated that increased longevity had added about 2 percentage points to GNP,[64] Dessie was about to ask if Adam thought that happiness's probable contribution to GNP made happiness worthwhile, but recalling his resolution to avoid facetiousness (and his comments two weeks earlier), he held back. Anyway, he also remembered that two authors he greatly respected had reported that in their calculations, 'a one standard deviation increase in SWB produced a 2 to 3 percentage points greater increase in income. Two standard deviations increase in SWB was an 8 to 12 percentage point increase in income.' "[65] Happiness did substantially increase GNP, and his sense of facetiousness was quite misplaced. He silently apologized to Adam.

"This question of causal ordering of prosperity and happiness is not as clear to me as it seems to be to you," said Adam. "Are people happier because they have better jobs and marriages, or do they get these better jobs and spouses because they are happier?"

"Both," said Dessie. "Some of what I was saying a few minutes ago comes from a longitudinal study lasting more than sixty years and giving opportunities to analyze what comes first and therefore could be a cause. In this sense, happiness studies are a little like the extrovert studies finding that extroverts are happier when they are with others, whom they seek and who give them pleasure, but they are also happier than others when they are alone.[66] Happy people seek out situations that make them happy, but their happiness facilitates the search. But you know all this;

what is interesting is what might be called the dark side of happiness, the side not mentioned by our Dutch friend who asks 'How harmful is happiness?' "

The Dark Side of Happiness

/s this like the childlike qualities of Lady Macbeth? Or should I ask about the malignance of Peter Pan?" asked Adam with his own childlike smile of innocence.

Smiling in spite of himself, Dessie soberly started his exposition of the dark side of happiness. "Well," said Dessie, "in spite of what Isen found,"[67] others have reported that depressed people are more accurate predictors of the future.[68] Some of the most attractive features of happy people contribute to this inaccuracy about the future: their self-esteem and sense of controlling their own fates leads them to exaggerate the probability of good outcomes and to minimize the probability that they will fail or that something bad will happen to them, even though it may be happening to others all around them.[69] You will be well advised to select a depressive for an attorney."

"If you are a happy person," agreed Adam. "But if you are unhappy, better to get advice from an optimist." Being a little on the dour side, Adam spoke from the heart, but actually he was thinking of something else: What happened to rationality?

"You might want to rethink your selection of an adviser," said Dessie, "because there is some evidence that happy people tend to be a bit rude. One experiment revealing this surprising finding is amusing. Subjects are placed in a happy or sad mood by a procedure tested many times: they are asked to think about happy or sad experiences in their own lives. They are then confronted with the fact that a friend owes them twenty dollars but may have forgotten this debt. They are asked to choose one of the following approaches to their debtor friend:

1. 'I wonder if I have enough money on me today?'
2. 'Do you have any money on you?'
3. 'I could do with twenty dollars now.'
4. 'I think you owe me twenty dollars.'
5. 'I want you to repay my twenty dollars.'

Happier subjects are more likely to choose the last two responses, while unhappier ones tend to choose the first two."

Adam, who knew little about experiments, was both amused and impressed by its ingenuity, but like everyone else, he sought a different interpretation. "Why couldn't it be that happy people are confident of their friends' goodwill and approach them directly while unhappy people are more fearful?" he asked.

"Perhaps," said Dessie. "But the same, shall we say lack of diplomacy, occurs among the happy when the groups with contrasting moods sit down to a meal cooked by a host who prides himself on his cooking. What approach do they use?

1. 'This meal might need something.'
2. 'Have you tried this with ketchup?'
3. 'Do you have ketchup?'
4. 'There is no ketchup on the table.'
5. 'I want some ketchup.'[70]

"I don't like ketchup," said Adam, laughing. "Okay, so the dark side of happiness includes this tendency to be a bit rude. I hope that's the worst of it."

"It's not," said Dessie as his face lit up in contemplation of the dark side. "Happy people are more likely to believe that they live in a just world, a world where people get what they deserve and deserve what they get."[71] It was on the tip of his tongue to say "a perfect market," but he remembered his resolution just in time. "It is a 'blame the victim' syndrome," he said, "where, for example, most rape victims are thought to have brought their misfortune on themselves and people who are mugged are said to have been careless or they wouldn't have been mugged. There is a cause for this, of course: happy people like to think that their happiness is both earned and merited, but beyond that, the belief in internal attribution usually associated with happiness leads naturally to the belief that people are responsible for their own fates."

Like Dessie, Adam, too, thought of the perfect market, where everyone gets what he or she 'deserves,' but he was sensible enough not to mention it. "Well, we went over something like this in Spanakopita 2, when you wanted to call the belief that people are responsible for their own fates a noble lie. Have you demoted it?"

Dessie was in a quandary. "The funny thing is," he said, "that internal attribution has enormous payoffs when applied to the self, where it both predicts life satisfaction[72] and helps to create those situations that justify that prediction. But happy people also apply it to others, where it is often cruel as well as unfair. The solution," he continued, "is to apply this notion of responsibility for one's own fate only to oneself and not to others, but I know of only one case where that has been done."[73]

Adam saw his chance. "To choose one's interpretation of causation according to whether or not one likes the results is pretty shady," he said. But seeing another implication, he went on. "By some similar line of reasoning, might one say that happy people, who are more likely to be successes, should apply this sense of responsibility for their own fates but that unhappy people should not because that self-responsibility would only make them unhappier?" He continued with his punch line: "But doesn't that leave the unhappy people without the inner resources to change their situations?" Adam particularly enjoyed turning all this psychology stuff back on Dessie, who used it so triumphantly.

Dessie sighed, said "Yes," and went on with his exposition of the dark side of happiness. "Has your utility theory contemplated the notion that the satisfaction of preferences—and the consequent increase in happiness—would make people less interesting and complex? That does seem to be the case: at least one metanalysis found that 'self-complexity' was negatively (although weakly) related to measures of happiness.[74] In a sense, this follows from other findings that show that introspection[75] and rumination about unhappy events make people unhappy.[76] Self-knowledge is not a route to happiness, nor does happiness contribute to self-knowledge."

"If happiness impedes self-knowledge, I see trouble ahead for the compatibility of happiness and human development in your sacred trinity," said Adam, not in the least troubled by the impending trouble for Dessie.

"Complexity of self-knowledge is not the only complexity that happiness seems to oversimplify," said Dessie, both relishing this attack on the simplicity of the economists' wholehearted utilitarianism and sorry to make trouble for his preferred version of humanism. "It seems that happy people are more given to stereotyping (for example, with regard to race and sex) than unhappy people. The authors of the study that reported this say, 'Results support theories that characterize happy mood as a mental state that predisposes reliance on heuristics [stereotypes, in this case] and sad mood as dampening such reliance. . . . Happy moods signal a safe environment leading to a lowering of one's psychological guard and resulting in greater reliance on heuristics.'[77] Beyond that," added Dessie, "a cross-national study found that happiness was not related to 'richness of mental life.' "[78]

"I am beginning to wonder," said Adam, "whether Mill should not have rephrased his famous preference for Socrates over a 'fool satisfied' to say something about how a satisfied person is likely to be a fool. Do you suppose our colleagues know that?" he asked, thinking more of Dessie's colleagues than his own. Then, true to form, he wondered how happy was too happy? "At what point does joy interfere with realism?" he asked, partly because he wanted to know and partly because he doubted that there were data of this precise nature.

"About fifteen years ago, some research showed that the ratio of positive to negative moods was optimal (in terms of general effectiveness) at 0.62,"[79] said Dessie, a bit amused at this spurious precision, "but then in 1997 this optimal ratio was upgraded to 0.90.[80] Don't worry: this, too has been upset, so that the current belief is that 'there is nothing wrong with the high levels of happiness in present day society. As yet, it is still not established how much more happiness will be too much.' "[81]

"What a relief," sighed Adam. "I am delighted to hear it—but not too delighted, of course."

Dessie was on the verge of reminding Adam how other studies had found that happy people were more creative, had better judgment, were more future oriented, and were better at problem solving,[82] but he wanted to get on with his indictment even though he knew he was storing up trouble for himself later. "Not only do happy people more easily accept stereotyped versions of reality, but for the same reason they are more conformist than unhappy people. 'Individuals who tend to respond in socially desirable ways are truly happier individuals,' say the researchers who looked into it.[83] If you want independent thinking, find a modestly unhappy person (modestly because if he is extremely unhappy, he will tend to think mostly about himself)."

Adam was busy wondering how this would fit into the utility-maximization theory he had grown up with. From an economist's point of view, conformist thinking was a bad thing, not because conformists were dull (which was irrelevant) but because they did not support the innovation on which the market thrived. "Does that mean that happy people are less likely to upset the going order?" he asked in search of a political silver lining to the economic cloud Dessie had just produced.

"Right on," said Dessie with enthusiasm. "Unhappy people are understandably readier for social change than happy people.[84] Happy people are also more politically conservative than unhappy people, even though generous welfare provisions tend to increase general happiness.[85] Conversely, happy people are more likely than unhappy people to act on their feelings and perceptions; when they are activists it is because they believe in their power to control their fate.[86] So," Dessie concluded, "our Dutch friend who asked 'How harmful is happiness?' was right to ask, but his own answer[87] does not take account of 'Socrates dissatisfied' and applies only to conservatives."

Adam, like his late friend Jim Tobin, was a Keynesian and hence no conservative, but he was also a rationalist and by chance had heard that in one study happy students had emphasized the social virtues "while their unhappy colleagues stressed 'rationality,' 'independence,' and 'self-control,'"[88] all virtues he admired and thought necessary for a well-functioning market. Also, he knew that the appreciation of future uncertainty associated with unhappiness led to prudence and saving, qualities desperately needed in the American economy. "So what's the answer?" he asked in perplexity, disturbed by what appeared now to be the overly simple theory of utility with which he had been working. "If people should not maximize their utility, what goals should they have?"

Dessie knew the answer to that one, but he planned to elaborate on it the following week in Spanakopita 7. In any event, he had another item for today's agenda.

Diminishing Returns to Happiness

/t is plausible," said Dessie, broaching his new topic, "to think of situations where a person says, 'I am happy, but I want more out of life than that.' Perhaps the person goes on to say, 'I want to know myself better,' even though self-knowledge and self-awareness are not good routes to happiness.[89] Or, 'I would like to help others become better persons.' Implied in this latter statement are ideas of altruism and justice. In these situations, one of the elements of global positive affect, 'life satisfaction,' conflicts with another, 'happiness.' Happiness is not enough, and one cannot get along with only the one maximand, utility."

"The obvious answer," said Adam, "is that she is using *happiness* in two different ways: one is to describe her present mood, the other is to describe her anticipated mood in some other activity."

"Very good," said Dessie, as though he were commending a dull student for a bright answer. "As I said a few minutes ago, research shows that anticipatory, experienced, and remembered happiness are different and give different concurrent readings.[90] That is part of her problem, but there is more to it than that, for she is not thinking of the happiness that will come from her development. The plurality of goods implies that we must ask how much happiness we should give up now to increase a quite different good—human development—later. Or, to take another example, shall we shade justice here to get more human development there—

an odd situation where one may be trading two moral goods, justice and virtue. The latter trade-off sounds fanciful until one thinks of the budgetary trade-off between police and courts, on the one hand, and schools, on the other."

Adam sighed. Dessie was making life so complicated. How much simpler to have, like Aristotle (or the studies of subjective well-being), one maximand to which all else could be related. "Go on," he said.

"The first 'solution' I wish to propose is to follow consciously the procedures we unconsciously follow anyway: employ our models of the human person and our models of the good society as tests for assessing institutions and their practices, people and their behavior. It is silly to think that choices need a single metric: we choose to take care of our children at one time and to clean the yard at another. Where's the metric?"

"You sound like those philosophers who ground their opinions in 'our moral intuitions' when they mean the prevailing opinion in the particular circles in which they travel," said Adam. Then, thinking of a stronger counterargument, he said, "Aren't you forgetting the first principle of market behavior: it is a learning situation. If commodities don't offer the highest utility, then people will learn to adjust their choices and choose whatever does offer more utility, like friendship."

"There are three reasons why people don't choose the good with the highest utility yield," said Dessie, counting on his spinach-soiled fingers. "First, increased money and commodities offer short-term but not long-term satisfactions, a classic 'trap.' Second, people don't have direct access to their limbic system or the 'wisdom' of their amygdalas but rather tend to think that they are made happy by what they think makes others happy. As we agreed in Spanakopita 3, in a market-driven, materialist society, that leads to the middle-class 'economistic fallacy': money is the prime source of happiness. And third, they believe—how could they not?—that they will like later whatever they want now, the error, mentioned earlier, that Kahneman's research has exposed."

Adam saw the economists' cherished faith in choice and preference ordering undermined and could not accept it. "By the same arguments that undermine the market, you are undermining democracy," he said, knowing that he was not joining issue with Dessie's points; bereft of economic research (as contrasted to psychological research) on actual choice procedures, however, he took the easy route.

"Democracy has a special relation to well-being[91] that we will have to skip for the moment," said Dessie with the momentum of a heavy vehicle. "The second solution," he continued, "is to examine how any one of the goods contributes to the others. Among Bentham's criteria for maximizing pleasure and minimizing pain was 'fecundity'—that is, the degree to which a given pleasure bred other pleasures, or how much pleasure might be bought by a certain level of pain.[92] Enlarging this concept beyond pleasure and pain, one might justify happiness by its contribution to the other two goods in our trinity, human development and justice. Where happiness contributes to one or both of these goods, it gains new justifications. And, indeed, there were some hints in our earlier discussion today of ways that happiness contributes to human development."

Adam tried to think of ways that pursuit of utility in the market could both reduce greed and increase rationality. He couldn't think of any. "Go on," he said.

But Dessie would have gone on anyway. "There is third way in which happiness can be justified in a world of plural goods—namely, by distinguishing between *being* happy and *pursuing* happiness. John Stuart Mill observed, 'Aiming thus at something else, [people] find happiness by the way. The enjoyments of life . . . are sufficient to make it a pleasant thing, when they are taken *en passant,* without being made a principal object.'[93] If, then, happiness is the by-product of some activity with moral status, at least two of the three goods are satisfied by a single act. But the main point is the curious reinforcement of the value of plural goods: with a single good, even happiness, one risks losing it by too great a concentration on it. As the consequentialist arguments for happiness exemplified, seek justice and you will be happier than if you pursue happiness."

"I suspect that there is some sleight of hand here," said Adam. "Are you sure you're not saying rather simply that people will be happier when they do good or develop themselves than when they pursue some good you have not yet credited?"

"No, I'm not sure of that," said Dessie with a burst of magnanimity. "But my main argument would still hold: there are diminishing returns (in happiness, if you will) to pursuit of happiness devoid of increments of human development or justice. This is more than saying that living for pleasure is a bore, which it is, for it is also saying that any pursuit of happiness that does not incur incremental value from something else will fail."

"I smell do-goodism," said Adam in one of his vulgar moments.

"Not, I hope, the odor of sanctity," said Dessie, not offended by the smell of doing good. "With plural goods without a common denominator, no one good is a measurement of the worth of another but rather each is measured by the sacrifice in opportunity costs of the goods not chosen. Diminishing returns to each good are measured in terms of the other goods forgone, and this principle is as much of a logical 'axiom' (to

120 use Schumpeter's term)[94] as is the original idea of declining marginal *utility*, where utility is the standard measurement. Under these circumstances, we would seek some balance among happiness and human development and justice where diminishing returns are measured by relative loss of one as the other two are pursued.[95] And, as I mentioned, the criteria for any combination of goods are our concepts of developed persons enjoying their lives in a good society, defined as one that facilitates these three ends." He put his fork down and wiped his lips without disturbing his self-satisfied smile.

"I have to meet an unhappy student," said Adam, "whom I can now advise to develop his better parts or do justice to relieve his unhappiness."

Spanakopita Seven

Better People

*A*dam arrived at Clark's before Dessie and fell to wondering what Dessie had in store today. He feared the worst: more on the wonky side of the problems of humanism that left him uneasy and uncertain about how to respond. Last time, in Spanakopita 6, when they had talked about what Dessie called happiness and Adam called utility, they shared a common goal, although it was expressed in quite different languages using very different kinds of data (or, in his case, inference): happiness/utility was a good thing. True, Dessie had found some faults in happiness as a goal, but he did not oppose it. Today, Dessie threatened to talk about that vague and unsatisfactory concept "human development," with who knows what kinds of consequences for the well-ordered society (he used Rawls's term unconsciously) that we enjoyed—well, a partially well-ordered society, partially enjoyed.

"So. Brooding on rational man's 'irrational exuberance,' or is it 'infectious greed' today?" asked Dessie in his most cheerful tone.

"Don't sneer at rationality," complained Adam. "What with 'deconstruction,' 'postmodernism,' and 'posthistoricism,' your friends make a trope of reason and violate its simplest principles."

Dessie had read *Liberties of Wit*[1] with appreciation and, being lodged safely in what was once called the "new criticism" (plain reading of the text), he was no friend of deconstruction. "Touché," he said, meaning "You touched me," not "you wounded me." "But while on the subject, may I ask you whether your concept of rationality covers the rational choice of what we should be doing next?"

"You know as well as I do that rationality is, in this context, an application of the best means to the chosen ends. It has no bearing on the selection of ends,"[2] said Adam, proud of his use of sophomore-year philosophy.

"Wow!" said Dessie. "Very good!" This infuriated Adam. "But if one accepted the arguments in Spanakopitas 2 and 5," continued Dessie, "one would have to agree that human beings were at the top of the value chain and that their welfare, which you have always recognized, includes their development as well as their happiness. To put it colloquially, developing better human beings is what we should be doing." He thought of a Kennedy-type aphorism: "Ask not 'What did you earn?' Rather, ask, 'What did you learn?'"

Better People

*W*ho can be against 'better people?'" asked Adam.

"Right!" said Dessie enthusiastically, but then hesitated as he thought of Weber's comment on human perfectibility, "It has been detrimental to take the liberty of trying to make [a person's] 'life' into a work of art."[3] But he decided to let it go as he proceeded like a Jesuit among the brighter infidels. "Doesn't it follow, then, that instead of GNP, we should be maximizing our GNPP?" He smiled his owlish smile, which he fancied as enigmatic.

"Gross national people product," said Adam after a very brief pause. "Here is where we part company. The effect of what you are saying—perhaps its purpose—is to displace economics as the major policy discipline to which we all pay attention and to substitute a branch of psychology—say, developmental psychology—in its place."

"That is not my purpose, but if it follows from substituting human development for economic development, then the ancien regime must give way," said Dessie. "You guys took control over several centuries when you displaced religious advisers. And, because you have done it so well, value priorities have changed and, well, 'a long farewell to all your greatness'[4] would be most becoming at this stage."

Adam was annoyed but controlled it. "I see a 'Council of Human Development Advisers' modeled after the Council of Economic Advisers," he said, "and the equivalent of the Fed's adjustment of interest rates by some agency concerned with the rise—yes, and fall—of IQ, congressional committees on emotional balance and self-esteem,[5] and along the lines of the American Civil Liberties Union, a not-for-profit American Autonomy Union." He thought for a moment. "Come to think of it, I would join the AAU to keep the council and the IQ Fed out of my hair."

"Hang on," said Dessie, "true to form, you think what isn't done by the market must be done by the state. There are other institutions, like the family and the schools, that are already deep in the business of trying to create better people without raising an alarm. So, for that matter, are all governments—but we'll come to that later. And, because you don't see it, you don't believe in it, but, like the wind, there is a culture that exerts an unseen but ubiquitous force on all our acts. We have seen its force in the nineteenth century in the changed attitudes toward slavery and in the twentieth in changing attitudes toward women. The Fed was not a participant in these activities, although one might say that market forces were important in both cases, as they will be in changing our attitudes toward human development, though possibly mostly in opposition."

Adam had cooled down and was now the more reasonable of the two men. "As I said, I favor better people," he said calmly, "but the fact is that it seems strange in the midst of relative prosperity and general contentment with democratic governments to take such a radical step. It's not an elegant phrase, but 'if it ain't broke, don't fix it.'"

"You are conditioned to look at institutions instead of people," said Dessie with some asperity. "When the American public is asked about current problems, the character of people 'these days' is often the first problem mentioned. Is the American character 'broken'? Of course not. Does it need 'fixing'? In the sense of better ways of understanding modern life, more controlled emotions, and better understanding of moral questions, of course it does."

"I suspect that this is one area where self-help is the best way to go," said Adam, fearful of Dessie's latent paternalism.

"Think back to your New Year's resolutions, to your resolve to spend more time with your children, or think of the dieters, gamblers, and smokers who have resolved at one time or another to change their behavior. Studies of these ever-recurring resolutions and their breakdowns call them the false hope syndrome and report how the deferred gratifications of reform are so often swamped by the immediate gratifications of the precise behaviors a person seeks to change.[6] It isn't easy, but the ability to defer gratification can be learned.[7] Laissez-faire in this field, as in many others, is a way of avoiding problems." Dessie paused for a moment and came back on a higher level. "In any event," he said, "this proposal is not a 'radical step' or a departure from one of the West's most revered traditions. Aristotle was one of the first: 'Lawmakers make the citizens good by training them in good habits—at least that is every legislator's intention; and those who fail as legislators are those who do not establish a good system of education.'"[8]

"If legislators in Aristotle's time failed to establish a good system of education, what makes you think they'll do a better job of it today?" asked Adam.

"If the classical writers, including Plato in quite another vein, were ardent supporters of human development," said Dessie, ignoring Adam's question, "it is the Enlightenment that gives the idea its greatest expression. Remember Humboldt's goal, the 'highest and most harmonious development of [humanity's] powers to a complete and consistent whole?'[9] But the greatest of these Enlightenment figures was Condorcet. In his famous *Sketch,* he said,

> Will men approach a condition in which everyone will have the knowledge necessary to conduct himself in the ordinary affairs of life according to the light of his own reason, to preserve his mind free from prejudice, to understand his rights and to exercise them in accordance with his conscience and his creed; in which everyone will become able, through the development of his faculties, to find the means of providing for his needs, and in which at last misery and folly will be the exception, and no longer the habitual lot of a section of society?[10]

Writing from prison, Condorcet answered his own question by finding in the advancement of science the 'strongest reasons for believing that nature has set no limit to the realization of our hopes.' And he believed that the impetus was so strong that neither priests nor rulers could stop it.[11] He formulated a theory of immanent development that contributes to the kinds of reasoning that supports the value of human development. Human development may be thought to be part of nature's design."

"Until you said that about immanent development, I was rather moved," said Adam, for whom Condorcet was mostly a mathematician still cited by specialists in voting. "But I am not a partisan of 'immanent' anything," he paused for a moment and added, "except in systems with fairly well established equilibrium tendencies."

Dessie smiled. Of course market economics was, like evolution, one of the greatest employers of immanent tendencies, but he went on. "Speaking of immanent tendencies, we don't have to go back to the eighteenth century but can turn directly to someone who, aside from his desire to nationalize the land, was one of the best supporters of the premises of market economics. I mean Herbert Spencer. Remember, he said that when the current process of evolution had come to fruition,

> none will be hindered from duly unfolding their natures; for whilst every one maintains his own claims, he will respect the claims of others. [No longer will there be legislative restrictions to burden people.] Then, for the first time in the history of the world, will there exist beings whose individualities can be expanded to the full in all directions. And thus . . . in the ultimate man perfect morality, perfect individualism, and perfect life will be simultaneously realized."[12]

"He was stealing from his enemies, Marx and Engels," said Adam. "'In place of the old bourgeois society, with its classes and class antagonism, we shall have an association, in which the free development of each is the condition for the free development of all.'"[13] He smiled benignly at Dessie.

"As you might expect," said Dessie, ignoring Marx, "some more or less contemporary theorists are passionate about human development, sometimes seeing it as the natural process of civilizing trends. Erich Fromm is among the most optimistic: he says humans have an inherent 'tendency to grow, to develop and realize potentialities which man has developed in the course of history.' He thinks of them as 'an active factor in the social process,' whatever that may be."[14]

"You know that kind of thing won't convince anyone who isn't already predisposed to your New Humanism," said Adam.

Dessie secretly agreed and thought of a real, worldwide program supporting his cause. "The United Nations Development Programme is actually doing something about human development. Almost fifteen years ago, its leaders said, 'A global compact for human development should be based on the recognition of the need for a new human order. Each issue should be analyzed for its impact on people.'[15] Bravo!"

"Okay, so the UNDP encourages hygiene, better schools, and more education for women, but that hardly provides us with the criteria for what constitutes better people," said Adam, insisting on sticking to the point.

"Well, then, Abraham Maslow says there is a hierarchy of needs that has the properties of a Gutman scale—that is, you can't get to level 3 without passing through level 2. His levels are composed of needs of which the most basic are physiological and safety needs. After having satisfied them, one can attend to level 3, the 'belongingness and love needs,' which, when satisfied in turn, permit one to move, sequentially to the 'esteem needs' and, finally 'the need for self-actualization,'[16] by which he means a combination of self-expression and self development."

"Ugh," said Adam. "I know you know that this so-called need hierarchy is not a multilevel scale at all but at most only a two-level scale, with the first four levels satisfied in any order, higgledy-piggledy; only the last represents a different level."[17]

"I know, I know, I know," wailed Dessie, but without sufficient contrition. "All I want to do is to introduce another concept of human development, one that has had enormous influence on others, including Ronald Inglehart."[18] Dessie paused for a moment, rather sadly reviewing the unsatisfactory follow-up on the glorious beginning of perfectibility themes in the Enlightenment. "As a member of ISQOLS,"[19] he said, "I know how much progress has been made in one of the Enlightenment's main other themes, licensing the pursuit of happiness, but whereas Bentham and the utilitarians carried forward the idea of happiness as a prime goal, the human development project became diffuse and almost lost in the discussion of how to bring up children and how to school them properly. From Benjamin Franklin to the Chatauqua movement prior to World War I to the idea of self-actualization after World War II,[20] the human development project received American support, but these treatments lose their persuasiveness when they cut their ties to the scientific literature on cognitive, emotional, and personality development. 'The unspeakable ignorance of mankind in respect to the influences which form human character'[21] that Mill found in his time when he argued for the equality of women has been somewhat relieved, and there is no excuse for continuing the discussion without reference to what we know." He paused again. "You want some nuts and bolts, and I think you would find them in Loevinger's measures of ego development.[22] So far I have given you clay without straw," said Dessie, enjoying his mixed metaphor.

"Only those crazy Egyptians would want to put straw in bricks, anyway," said Adam. He thought for a minute and decided to offer his view of human development. "Perhaps," he said tentatively, "you would find the economists' version of human development mentioned in Spanakopita 5 more congenial: we call the product of such development human capital and value it highly."

"Nonsense," said Dessie abruptly. "According to the Saint of Human Capital, Theodore Schultz, the term means only those qualities that increase a person's marginal product.[23] We cannot treat this narrow range of talents as equivalent to the development of human faculties we usually mean by 'better people': sensitivity to others, appreciation of form and language, readiness to perceive and then respond to duty—all the cognitive, emotional, and behavioral qualities that make for a rounded and complete personality. Saint Theodore is a truly great man— he and I were at the center together in 1956–57—but after all, he can express only a view of humankind congenial to an economist."

Cognitive Development

Because Adam tended to get restless when the discussion wandered from what was immediately germane to their argument, Dessie decided against an explication of schema and balance theory and to focus instead on one seminal theory that was a counterweight to rational choice. "Come to think of it," he began, "cognitive development is a kind of human development that lends itself to Pareto-like treatment: higher levels can do everything lower levels can do and something more. Jean Piaget is a giant in this field, and he has developed a scale from a sensorimotor stage through various more advanced stages, tracking children from early childhood through young adulthood. He has done this with a set of highly ingenious experiments where, for example, he tests the concept of 'conservation of matter' by pouring water from a wide vessel where it registers only, say, an inch high, to a narrow vessel where it registers, say, six inches high. Which vessel has more water in it? As children mature from 'concrete' to 'formal' operations, they learn that the two vessels have the same amount of water in them."[24]

"Delightful," said Adam, genuinely pleased with the trick played on children, "but I am not sure how that advances our discussion of human development."

"Because these cognitive changes imply so much for the way people cope with the world," said Dessie. "For example, at the 'preoperatory' stage, the individual cannot yet take another's point of view since he knows and understands only what is in his own mind—that is, he is cognitively egocentric. He has not yet learned reciprocity. He makes assertions without conceiving of the need for evidence, since his thought is self-confirming. In interaction with others, he gradually learns that they do not share this point of view and that support for an assertion is necessary. He becomes a social being."

"Okay," said Adam, "so he learns all these things and masters formal operations and becomes an insurance salesman or a schoolteacher. How are we better off?"

"People who can understand each other make a better society," said Dessie with a little impatience. "And they can criticize society more intelligently because they can see that the world presented to them is only one of several possible worlds—that is, they can think hypothetically and abstractly. But going up the Piagetian scale is not enough: adolescents at this stage believe that by conceiving of a better world, they change it. One needs further experience and learning to see that understanding is only the basis of possible change, not a sufficient condition for such change. Nevertheless, the discovery of invariants (for example, the conservation of matter) and of concepts of reciprocity (based on an understanding of reversibility in the physical world) and the consequent change from egocentrism to sociocentrism make formal operations the basis for moral thought."[25]

"Moral thought," repeated Adam. "Some of my colleagues are very good at moral thought, but at least one of them comes very close to plagiarism, covering his tracks with a welter of footnotes. If I had to choose between benevolence and plain, old-fashioned honesty, in spite of your friend Kant, I would choose the latter."

"Two things would enhance honesty, but I don't think you would like either of them: living in a room full of mirrors[26] and consciousness of death,"[27] said Dessie, hardly able to contain himself. "But to get back to your point about the fruitfulness of moral thought, Piaget shows that when one has achieved the stage of formal operations, one can take a perspective on oneself. Because one's own inner world is not the sole basis of one's thought, one can adapt one's schemas to objective reality (accommodation) as well as classify one's observations in preexisting schemas (assimilation). Piaget's theory gives cognition a maturational sequence, which has been tested and confirmed cross-culturally,[28] and a social base: the necessary condition for sociocentrism and moral maturity is peer-group interaction, cooperation with equals."

Adam was skeptical. "Are you saying that the inner-city teenager who is part of a peer group (that is, a gang) is better off than one learning from a two-parent family? Don't you think Piaget is rather hopelessly culture bound with his sample of tidy, well-behaved Swiss children?"

"On Piaget's cultural blinders, I do agree," said Dessie, "but P. R. Dasen did find that in all cultures, the sequence of learning is from sensorimotor to preoperational to concrete operations to formal operations.[29] That's the point, and it bodes well for a genuine theory of cognitive development: irreversible (well, up to a point), scalar, measurable, and cross-cultural."

"How can this be, if, as I have heard, genetic endowment of intelligence accounts for about 40 percent of the explanation?" asked Adam.

"The figures are in dispute—as are the meanings of the measure you are thinking of, intelligence quotient (IQ)," said Dessie, recalling what he had read about the genetic contribution to IQ. "But don't forget that one reason Piaget developed his tests was because he thought IQ (Benet's version) told us so little about thinking ability. Nevertheless, since IQ is the measure most often used in schools and cross-cultural tests, we must use it. I won't bore you with details, but if you want to explain occupational success (and in your field you must), IQ accounts for less than 10 percent of the variance and family background only a little more, with educational achievement explaining the most, giving us some promise of real improvement.[30] But don't forget that at least a third of the differences in occupational attainment have nothing to do with either education or cognitive skills. After certain family and credentialing factors are taken into account, such personality characteristics as industriousness and emotional control, along with luck, seem to be more important."[31] Dessie felt that he was lecturing and becoming a bore, which was true.

"Your antipathy to economic explanations is showing," said Adam. "Why not acknowledge that poverty is a major source of both low intellectual ability and poor schooling?"

"Right," said Dessie, continuing right on with his own train of thought. "IQ is not a proxy for family background,[32] as you might guess from the fact that IQ differences among children from the same family are as great as between children from different families.[33] Nevertheless, family background is important; taking it together with education and cognitive skills, we can account for about half of the variation in occupational status.[34] Moreover, 'equalizing the way children are treated at home would do more for outcome equality than would school equalization.'"[35]

"And poverty?" asked Adam again.

"Right," said Dessie again. "Poverty in childhood is indeed a major determinant of low cognitive skills. For example, class differences in IQ do not show up until after age eighteen months, when the IQs of the poor begin the downward drift that lasts to age five or six.[36] A famous British study of poor canal boat children found the correlation of IQ with age was .75."[37]

"There you have it," said Adam. "A conscientious materialist can claim that his methods offer as good a handle on cognitive development as do more fancy psychological methods."

"The 'fancy psychological methods' have a place in reversing the effects of the indifferent materialist market," said Dessie. "A Milwaukee experiment placed children from single-parent African-American homes in care facilities with high caregiver/children ratios and raised the children's average IQ from 75 to 124. When they returned home, their IQs regressed to 109, but this gain persisted through the early school years.[38] Furthermore, at least until the late 1960s, there was a forty-year decline in the relationship between poverty and IQ."[39]

"What I infer from this," said Adam, ignoring what Dessie had just said, "is that cognitive development is a function of economic growth. This would be true partly because richer countries can provide better schooling and better child care and because their prosperity reduces the poverty in the home that seems so cognitively debilitating. So one can be a materialist and expect that the values and culture of materialist societies will respond to the need for cognitive development of all our children, as apparently they have." He beamed with pleasure at the selective support for his position that Dessie had provided.

Dessie smiled at Adam's pleasure, partly because he agreed with Adam—up to a point. "There has been a massive gain in IQ over the past fifty years that can't be accounted for by increased schooling,"[40] he said in apparent confirmation of Adam's point. "And, to stimulate your pleasure center, Lane suggests that the gain in IQ may derive in some part from market demands for choosing and thinking, as Schumpeter said it would,[41] although the point of overload is sooner reached[42] than you materialists believe. But the correlation between IQ and per capita GNP is pretty slack, partly because it is possible to have high poverty levels and high per capita GNP at the same time.[43] In fact, the United States has the highest child poverty rate (21 percent) in a sample of twelve advanced countries.[44] Furthermore, James Grant, the executive director of UNICEF, said in 1994, 'We have seen a vast deterioration in the condition of the American child in the 1980s and the cost of pulling them back into the mainstream now will be mammoth. . . . The U.S. shows a significant under-performance in the records for children reaching the fifth year of schooling.'"[45]

Adam couldn't take much comfort from this but noted with modest satisfaction that it was not a matter of culture but of finances.

Dessie continued, "Grant also pointed out that when economic capacities are taken into account, the United States ranked dead last.

Why? One clue is that the United States shared this low ranking with other anglophone nations that share a common culture with a unique reliance for child care and child health care on the market."

"Do you know that rats who live in environmentally enriched environments have heavier brain mass than those who live in simpler environments?" asked Adam, apparently out of the blue. "And that increase in the brain mass occurs mostly in the cortex?"[46]

"Are you all right?" asked Dessie solicitously.

"And that markets represent the most complex environment that most people will ever experience?" continued Adam, warming to his thesis. "Indeed, the brain develops along the lines of our occupations and challenges: 'Large differences in trunk and finger neurons were found in the brains of people who were typists, machine operators, and appliance mechanics' but not in sales staff."[47]

Dessie couldn't resist. "Do you suppose," he said with a sober face, "that the part of the brain dealing with matter is enlarged in materialists and that this inhibits the development of humanist portions of the brain?" But he had no sooner said that when he thought of a way to turn to his advantage the evidence on becoming what one does, which he recognized as a strictly Aristotelian notion. He prevented Adam from answering by asking, "Do you know that in studies of various occupations and levels of wealth among less advanced people, it is what people do and not how rich they are that is related to higher intelligence? It is not the herders, with their superior store of wealth, who are smarter, but the hunters and fishermen, who live daily by their wits. That is why hunter-gatherers adapt to a labor market more easily than do peasants."[48]

"Are you suggesting that a failed market system that stimulated and challenged its participants without making them any richer would contribute just as much to cognitive development as would a successful market economy?" asked Adam incredulously.

"Of course not," said Dessie sharply, "but not because there is a close relationship between individual wealth and IQ. There isn't.[49] Rather, it is because such quasi-public goods as schools and health facilities would be inferior in a poorer society."

This was unfamiliar turf to a person brought up on rational choice, and Adam felt uncomfortable. He looked for a way out and thought he saw one in the emotions, which he conceived to be the opposite of cognition and, he believed, less loaded with all these uncomfortable behavioral studies. "When you came in, you asked me about 'irrational exuberance' and 'infectious greed,'" said Adam. "Just who is the Piaget of the emotions?"

*T*he honors are split," said Dessie evasively. "Most political philosophers have feared the emotions and, like you, favored rationality, which they called reason, although Rousseau and Edmund Burke (who hated Rousseau) were partisans of the emotions. In general, though, people favor the qualities they think they have. Hence Aristotle's support for philosophy."

"You mean that the reason for favoring rationality is the belief that one is rational rather than a fear of the irrational?" Adam asked, wondering about his economics colleagues working on the emotions of greed.

"Over the brief course of what we call civilization, two principal themes emerge: fear of 'the passions' (take a look sometime at the population of Dante's *Inferno*) and veneration of what is often called love, which on examination often turns out to be control over hostile and aggressive feelings—what we would now call emotional control." Dessie was going out on a limb in this interpretation but was quite sure that Adam would not object. "On the first of these," Dessie continued, "I think the interests of elites led them to believe that mass publics were ruled by 'the passions'—excitable, irrational, hostile[50]—until the competing mercantile elites found that this belief impeded their interests. At that point they gracefully accepted the idea that people could also be ruled by 'interests' that were calculable and rational and that made the unregulated market possible. At least that is my reading of Hirschman's *The Passions and the Interests*,[51] although it is not necessarily Hirschman's.

"Why not say, along with Schumpeter,[52] that the world was taught rationality by economic need, money, and the market?" asked Adam with a semblance of innocence.

Dessie knew that if people became what they did, there was some plausibility to this allegation, but that same line of thinking pointed to the technology of work, where some research supported the 'become-what-you-do' hypothesis[53] rather than Schumpeter's 'rationality-from-choosing' hypothesis. Research on consumer markets tends to emphasize the irrationality of consumer decisions.[54] In any event, it would be hard to show that businesspeople were more "rational" than the military or, for heaven's sake, academics. "Cognitive development is primarily a problem for childhood socialization, although, of course, people do learn throughout their lives," said Dessie, eager to turn to the emotions.

"So what is there to be said for the emotions?" asked Adam. "We economists get along quite well without reference to them." He paused and added, "Except for greed, of course."

"For a while, psychologists thought of emotions as 'interruptions' of cognitive processes, valuable chiefly if they drew attention to danger," said Dessie. "Like economists, they focused on cognitive processes, neglecting emotions for reasons David Sears outlined in a talk in the early 1990s.[55] But even then, some psychologists pointed out that any society that repressed or did not value emotions was not a good society. Imagine a society without pity and love, anger, shame and guilt, joy and grief and sorrow! You wouldn't want to live in it. Nor would it be safe, for the emotions and moods (like the happiness discussed in Spanakopita 6) are sources of information both about the environment and about ourselves.[56] They are evolutionarily programmed for that purpose and have survival value."[57]

"And economic value?" asked Adam, as though survival value were a noneconomic value.

"It's all laid out in Lane's treatment of *The Market Experience*,"[58] said Dessie, primed for the question. "He says, 'The market stimulates arousal and is saturated with emotions, such as happiness, worry, guilt, confidence, disappointment, thankfulness, frustration, and satisfaction.'[59] Maynard Keynes, anticipating Greenspan's 'irrational exuberance,' referred to investment decisions as the product of 'animal spirits.'[60] Frank Knight said that human activity, including economic activity, 'was largely impulsive.'[61] To understand economic behavior, one must understand the emotions."

"I get the point," said Adam, without much conviction, "but since there are dozens—perhaps hundreds—of emotions, and since I doubt if we know much about educating the emotions, and, further, if they have the physiological bases you say they do, I doubt that this recent interest in, well, the passions will get us anywhere."

"Intelligence has a physiological basis, but that doesn't mean we can't improve it," said Dessie, taking up the last point first. "As for the multiplicity of emotions, you're right, and much work is going on sorting them out and finding their respective etiologies.[62] It is bewildering, but, if you will excuse me, I would like to take a moment to look at the cross-cultural work on emotionality."

"I suspect that each society has its own preferred and forbidden emotions," said Adam, thinking of his experience with a Greek student who reported that when he went back to his home country, people thought he was homosexual because he had learned a version of the American expressive style.

"Yes and no," said Dessie enigmatically. "Some cross-cultural studies find, for example, that the Latin American norm is positivity, the Confucian norm is passivity,[63] and the norm among the Dobu (South Pacific) and to some extent in Tezpotlan (Mexico) is suspicion and hostility.[64] Curiously, these norms did not greatly affect self-reported happiness, with two exceptions: in collectivist countries, where the reliability of questions on moods was lower because people had not thought about their moods; and in Japan, where *very* was a dirty, four-letter word."[65]

"That means that there are as many ideas of emotional development, if there is such a thing, as there are cultures," said Adam, again hoping to derail the focus on subjectivity.

"No, for three reasons," said Dessie. "First, when emotions among advanced Western countries are studied, there is much similarity and consistency. Klaus Scherer and associates studied the self-reported emotional experiences of joy, sadness, fear, and anger in eight European countries, analyzing the antecedents, intensity, situational stimuli, and personality correlates of these emotions. They found very few significant differences by national culture, although, to the authors' surprise, the British were more sensitive than others to physical pleasure and the Swiss were more emotionally expressive."[66]

"I'm suspicious already," said Adam. "Do you know any Swiss people?"

"But even across the East-West dimension (and emotional conflict is a much less serious problem in the East),[67] there are reports of surprising similarities. Thus another study found that Chinese people and Americans reacted with similar emotions—because of similar attributions—when presented with information on a person's success or failure.[68] This is surprising when you consider that East and West usually have fundamental differences in attribution.[69]

"I have no doubt that you can find similarities among nations if you try hard enough," said Adam. "And I could find differences, if I were so disposed."

"And second," continued Dessie ignoring the allegation that he was cooking his data selection, "there is enough evidence on the regulation of emotions to see that across the negative emotions (anger, hatred, fear), the virtues of self-regulation are well recognized.[70] It is also apparent in studies of sympathy and empathy that regulating these benign emotions contributes to favorable outcomes. Self-regulated emotions also contribute to mental health in adulthood,[71] and if infants under a year old show this capacity to regulate their anger, their later capacity for 'effortful or focused attention' is better."[72]

Adam interrupted. "When emotions are under cognitive control, as you would say, don't they lose their intrinsic (!) value as emotions?" He thought he was sounding like a psychologist, but his main purpose was to stop being a pliant Socratic stooge.

"Because a desire to control their environment is one of the most passionate desires people have, uncontrolled emotionality is not experienced as more felicitous than is controlled emotionality," said Dessie. "Indeed, a large part of the effect of control springs from self-observation and consciousness of what is happening, often prompting the self-punishing feelings of guilt and shame.[73] There are large rewards in controlling anger among friends, and people in many cultures report trying very hard to do so.[74] But your skepticism may come from your relative youth"—Dessie was six months older than Adam—"since the younger are more emotionally volatile and feel less in control of themselves than do we older people."[75] For a long time he had been trying to pull age rank on Adam and finally had worked it in.

"Okay," said Adam, smiling, "so the passions can be measured and are not, you say, hopelessly culture bound, and there is a more or less common focus on what to do about them." He paused for a moment: "But can this regulation be taught and learned?"

"In your own backyard," said Dessie. "James Comer in New Haven has developed a program folded into the regular school curriculum to teach children how to handle their grief and anger, how to negotiate rather than fight, and how to cooperate in the classroom."

"I've always favored reading and writing in lower schools and math and the classics in upper schools," said Adam. "Are you sure these, excuse me, 'frills' are worth the time?"

"The programs are a little like Valium and Ritalin in mental hospitals," said Dessie, improvising. "They help children stay in school, calm down, and attend to their lessons. For example, the results included 'a 34 percent drop in suspensions in the New Haven Schools, a more congenial classroom atmosphere, fewer fights and disruptiveness, and an increase in children's ability to think before they act and to pay attention and learn.'[76] Actually, training in emotional control was more effective in reducing drug abuse than programs specifically focused on that problem. Perhaps it is a frill in schools for well-brought-up bourgeois children, but for inner-city schools it is well worth the time." He thought for a moment, recalling the Columbine High School massacre, and said, "On second thought, the bourgeoisie also need self-regulation of their emotions."

Adam was not fully persuaded, but for the moment he was pacified on the question of how to control the passions. But he was troubled by what this information implied. "I still don't see how you can handle the variety of emotions in any kind of parsimonious way," he said. "In that respect they're not like rationality or intelligence."

"I'm glad you mentioned that problem," said Dessie, wondering, if the roles were reversed, how he would feel asking Adam leading questions about the kinky oligopoly curve. "Third," he continued as though there had been no interruption, "there is a summary measure of what is called emotional intelligence (EI). It is defined this way: EI 'refers to *the capacity for recognizing our own feelings and those of others, for motivating ourselves, and for managing emotions within ourselves and in our relationships.*'[77] Physiologically, the emotions are lodged in the subcortex or limbic system, as contrasted to the neocortex, where the functions measured by IQ are located. EI links the two. Component parts include self-awareness, self-regulation, motivation, empathy, and social skills.[78] And at least by one measure, EI is independent of IQ but is closely related to such personality traits as empathy and happiness.[79]

"What good is it?" asked Adam, sensing another wonky measure like Maslow's need hierarchy.

"Well, it is a much better predictor of occupational success than is IQ," said Dessie, thinking this would be the coup de grâce for an economist. He continued, "'Many people who are book smart but lack emotional intelligence end up working for people who have lower IQs but who excel in emotional intelligence skills.'[80] In my opinion, this is a fascinating development of a long-neglected focus on the forgotten side of the brain."[81]

Adam was impressed in spite of himself. "How, then, are we doing with our emotional intelligence?" he asked.

"Badly," said Dessie. "Massive surveys of teachers and parents in the 1970s and the late 1980s 'show the present generation of children to be more emotionally troubled than the last. On average, children are growing more lonely and depressed, more angry and unruly, more nervous and prone to worry, more impulsive and aggressive.'"[82]

"What happened to all these programs for teaching children emotional self-regulation?" asked Adam, discouraged by these findings.

"Underfunded by a society whose faith lies in market solutions," said Dessie, scoring a somewhat tired point that he felt he had to make to this neoclassical economist. "They do it better in continental countries, like France, not driven by market fetishism."[83]

Adam watched Dessie appropriate the rest of the crackers with growing distress. Saltines don't go with spinach pie; they go with soup. What would be the diplomatic thing to do? "Doesn't this human development stuff have a moral dimension?" he asked suddenly. "Everyone thinks that's the heart of the matter."

The Development of Virtue

I'm glad you asked that question," repeated Dessie, taking the remaining cracker. "You are absolutely right, as usual. For most people, 'I would like to become a better person' means less grouchy with their children, more dutiful toward their spouses, a more responsible member of the community. For example, at least recently, middle-class people worried about the perceived discrepancy between their performance in the family and their concept of how they ought to perform, especially fathers worrying about spending enough time with their children.[84] Work morality also has recently been important; although most people reported enjoying the work they did,[85] they worried about their performance. Only a little over a decade ago, more Americans (51 percent) said 'I have a strong inner need to do the very best I can regardless of pay' than did workers in any other country.[86] Even more have worried about saving, which they often regard as an ethical (impulse-control) question."[87]

Adam, forgetting about the crackers, was pleased to see that this moral development business applied to work and saving. "I told you so," he said. "Materialism has its ethical side, after all."

"The moral side of materialism is an ethical conflict over when to override material gratifications," said Dessie abruptly. "Family time versus work time; dedication to work conflicting with dedication to pay, gratification now versus security later. Funny kind of ethics." Dessie had in mind the familiar observation that the Protestant ethic, which some say launched the great capitalist enterprise, was a moral principle quite outside the principles of greed and rationality that dominated neoclassical economics now presiding over market enterprise. 'A system that depends for its success on a heritage that it undermines cannot be sustained on the record of its bountiful fruits,'"[88] quoted Dessie.

Adam was about to sneer at these Cassandras but remembered how the heritage of familism undermined Asian capitalism in the late 1990s and that the massive corporate failures of 2001–2 had been attributed to "infectious greed." But why not let utility theory do some of the work? He recalled how George Stigler had allowed for a kind of moral utility emanating from the "warm glow of public rectitude"[89] and decided to try to recapture moral credit for materialism via that route. "I don't see why you can't have moral utility side by side with materialist utility," he said almost plaintively.

"You can, of course," said Dessie. "But don't forget that Stigler, as an economist, is perfectly happy with a tautological theory of utility: one knows that utility is a property of something if people choose it, and one knows that if they choose something, it has, for the choosing person, the quality of producing utility.[90] Conversely, if you make satisfaction of conscience a 'moral utility,' you really lose analytical ability." He paused for a moment and added, "But, of course, it is true that satisfying one's conscience does contribute to well-being."

Adam had enough of the lecture on method and wanted to get back to the main subject. "You were showing me the delights of moral development, which surely can't be only about the moral problems of capitalism."

"Could there be anything that fits the use of the term *human development* without moral development?" Dessie asked rhetorically. "I doubt it, not only because the public thinks first of moral development but because philosophers do, too. I won't bore you with the record, but just to sample, consider how a recent theorist brings the moral dimension into her account of the essence of humanity—what it takes to make people fully human. She says, 'I argue that without essentialism of a kind, we are deprived of two moral sentiments that are absolutely necessary if we are to live together decently in the world: compassion and respect.'"[91]

"Speaking of tautology," said Adam in disgust. "How do you know that to be 'fully human' you have to have certain moral qualities? You know it because you defined it that way."

Dessie knew that Adam was right and that all moral preferences were only reasoned assertions. But the question of moral development did not hinge on the epistemological standing of the concept of morality. "However that may be," he said in the famous evasive phrase known to all professors caught in a bind, "a broad conception of human development must include moral development, or else it degenerates"—Dessie chose the word with care—"into human capital. Emotional self-regulation is part of moral development, since the function of morality is often to constrain aggressive or hedonistic impulses. So we are partway there. We might start by defining the 'moral point of view.' First, it means controlling self-interest." Dessie paused and added with a malicious grin, "If I am treading on anyone's toes, please let me know. Second, it means doing things on principle. Although we can almost always find a principle to justify what we want to do, the search for principles is morally therapeutic. Third, universalizing the principle—a kind of categorical imperative injunction. And fourth, consider the effects on everyone alike, not just your friends."[92]

"Well, that's very nice and rather more inclusive than honoring contracts," said Adam. "So that's what moral development is all about!"

"Not quite," said Dessie, moving like an irresistible force against a movable object in a vacuum, "but the universalism does proscribe moral relativism, so much admired by our anthropological friends who have gone native." Dessie knew this was unfair, but he had been bitten by attacks on his Westerncentrism before. Moving on, he said, "Moral development, like cognitive and emotional development, needs some further constraint. Remember Piaget?" he asked, linking moral development to cognitive development.

"Oh, yes," said Adam, holding his head, "I remember him."

"Well, an American scholar—actually a Harvard scholar—by the name of Lawrence Kohlberg developed a set of six moral stages based on Piaget's concepts. Kohlberg grouped these stages into three levels: preconventional, conventional, and postconventional. The preconventional levels are based on the principle that 'right is acting to meet one's own interests and needs and letting others do the same. Right is also what is fair; that is, what is an equal exchange, a deal, an agreement.' "[93]

"What's wrong with that?" asked Adam, at the same time fearing that he would be assigned to some inferior moral level.

"Hold on," said Dessie, "you will want to get off on the second floor—although I warn you that each floor or level has a mezzanine: two stages to a level. At the conventional level," he continued, " 'a person . . . takes the viewpoint of the system, which defines roles and rules. He or she considers individual relations in terms of place in the system.' "[94]

"So now we have the point of view of society represented offering scope for regulation," said Adam. "What could be more moral than that? But I think I prefer the first floor."

"Wrong," said Dessie. "Market principles and practices are at the stages located at the conventional level—that is, they are sensitive to public opinion (Kohlberg's stage 3 in level 2) and because of their reliance on law and order (stage 4 or mezzanine of level 2). But market theory, at least, has no room for the independent consciences prescribed at stage 5 on the postconventional level 3. On this level 3, a person takes the point of view of a 'rational individual aware of values and rights prior to social attachments and contracts. . . . He or she considers the moral point of view and the legal point of view, recognizes they conflict, and finds it difficult to integrate them.'[95] At stage 6 (on level 3), they are more easily integrated, but, if you will excuse me, I won't give the details on stage 6 or the hypothetical ultimate stage because nobody achieves these stages."

"So much for Kant," said Adam gleefully. "I will excuse you."

"Lawrence Kohlberg believed that the moral injunctions of these levels, each of which was divided into two stages, as mentioned, 'are prescriptive codes embodying logic, reciprocity, reversibility, equality, and universalizability.' Also, he finds that in his stage theory, one can distinguish form from content so that the content may vary from culture to culture but the forms of moral reasoning remain constant.[96] Although Kohlberg has run into trouble on the irreversibility, the invariant sequence criterion, and the coding of the accounts, the measures have held up pretty well to empirical scrutiny."

"And compassion?" asked Adam, not really understanding the Pandora's box he was opening.

" 'Consider this, / That in the course of justice none of us / Should see Salvation: we do pray for mercy,' said Dessie, pretending he was Portia but thinking how appropriate it was that both Portia and Pandora were women—and Athena, the goddess of wisdom, too! "As it happens," he continued, "you have stumbled onto one of the great—well, at least most troublesome—quarrels in moral development: Should moral reasoning include compassion? Kohlberg's measure relied on logic, but Carol Gilligan's measures embrace empathy, compassion, tolerance, and understanding of others. With several of her colleagues, she writes that at least with respect to moral reasoning, 'Piaget's emphasis on formal logic almost guarantees adaptive failure.'[97] The reason for this, they say, is that 'life choices are made in a world of relationships; [hence,] reason must be reunited with relationships, thereby making feelings an inseparable part of human thought.' "[98]

"It sounds more like two ships passing in the night than like a collision," said Adam. "One party wants to talk about moral reasoning with the properties that all other reasoning has, including logic; the other wants to talk about kindly feelings, or, as you said, the double blessings of mercy. Fine. Where's the conflict?"

"The conflict lies first in the meaning of the term *moral reasoning* and second in a much more important matter: what do people actually do when they make moral judgments? By some accounts, they first feel their way to an answer and second think their way.[99] I find definitional problems a bore, but on the second point, I suspect that Gilligan is nearer right, at least for half the population."

"And the other half?" asked Adam, intrigued by Dessie's cryptic remark.

"The male half," said Dessie, feeling ashamed at having had to expose what might appear to be sexism. "Men do better on Kohlberg's tests, and women do better on Carol Gilligan's in both China and the United States.[100] For our purpose of exploring the New Humanism, it doesn't really matter, but given the evidence on the hedonic benefits of companionship,[101] I think we would all do better with the Gilligan relational agenda for moral development. As we shall see, this won't be the only case of feminization of concepts and programs in our humanist agenda."

Adam had a problem. He favored Kohlberg's emphasis on logic, but his sensitivity to women's interests led to respect for Gilligan's interactional theory. "Whoever wins," said Adam, skirting the issue, "your idea of human development as moral development faces big problems. As you may know, there is a huge demand for the teaching of character in public schools, with 84 percent of public school parents wanting 'moral values' taught and about two-thirds wanting schools to develop standards of right and wrong. But the record of teaching morals in schools (including an effort based on Kohlberg's ideas) is pretty dismal."[102]

"Don't forget Comer's success in reducing bullying and fighting in the New Haven schools," said Dessie. "In both childhood and adulthood, capacity to regulate emotions has a strong effect on immoral or antisocial behavior. Thus, one study finds that 'in infancy and early childhood, the ability to inhibit and control one's behavior has repeatedly been associated with a range of measures of conscience and committed (internalized) compliance (e.g., following commands wholeheartedly, making reparation, not cheating, and resistance to temptation), concurrently and over time.'[103] We know something about emotional self-regulation and can do something about it," added Dessie, again linking morality to emotions but never accepting the theories (for example, those of Alfred Ayres and Charles Stevenson) that moral statements were nothing but emotional expressions. Dessie recalled that Baier's "moral point of view," mentioned only a few minutes earlier, involved such cognitive processes as doing things on principle and universalizing that principle.

"Well, one way of teaching morals without mentioning morality is to talk about controlling emotions," said Adam in an unusually subdued mood, "and I suppose that is an advantage that the critics I mentioned haven't understood. But what would happen, if, as William Morris recommends, you just let children grow up naturally without trying to teach them 'morality?'"

"We don't know much about feral children, like Mowgli, but we know a little bit about what happens to moral behavior as children grow older. For example, some studies of the way rewards (candy bars) are distributed in common work tasks show that, as Kohlberg and Piaget said, concepts of fairness develop only as logical reasoning progresses. But these same studies show, as Gilligan predicted, that older and more developed children (of both sexes) sought ways of reconciling conflicting interests quite independent of perceived desserts. All children—indeed, all people—are self-interested and favor themselves, but older children combine this with merit so that their self-favoring allocations are greater when, through effort and contribution, they deserve more. With increased age (and experience), children saw equality as the best way to resolve conflicts.[104] Although your model of untutored and unconstrained moral development may be *The Lord of the Flies,* actually, among nonferal (civilized?) children, hedonistic reasoning decreases with age. And the development of empathy is part of that process."[105]

"I'm going to have to go in a few moments," said Adam, "but am I to understand that in the United States at least and probably in all advanced countries, we see over time the progress of many cognitive skills (at least from World War II to about 1970), the retardation of emotional development, and—but what has happened to moral development since World War II? Can anyone claim there has been moral progress over this period?"

"Good question," said Dessie, chasing the last bit of spinach pie on his plate. "National crime statistics bear about the same relation to general morality (honesty, prosocial behavior) as do suicide rates to national happiness averages: they aren't predictive.[106] Taking the long view, it seems that the Piagetian sequence from egocentric to sociocentric tracks cognitive development from economically 'primitive' societies to economically more advanced societies.[107] There is also evidence that compared to traditional villagers, urbanized 'modern man' is more compassionate to the weak—that is to women and children.[108] But as we take a shorter view of more recent trends of value orientation, the picture changes. For example, the authors of one American study report, 'The changes we found between 1968 and 1981 can perhaps be best described as a shift away from a collective [community] orientation to a personal competence . . . orientation.'[109] And, as the Fordham people who keep track of these things show, some moral indicators go up and some go down.[110] I can't answer that question, but I do know that we are at a point when it is possible to work for human development with much better knowledge than our Enlightenment forebears."

Adam chimed in, "One thing more: to keep up our reputation and comply with moral norms, you should leave a bigger tip for Marian. Even though the currency of this act is only material, she will interpret it as an act of appreciation. See you next week."

Spanakopita Eight

Getting Rich the Right Way

The red booths were the same, and the service was, as usual, brisk, but Adam seemed both older and more tired. His weariness probably had nothing to do with his bouts with Dessie, but he thought it did. Nothing is more troubling than an assault on one's belief system, and he felt that, like a seventeenth-century priest exposed to the Reformation, the relentless undercurrent of attack was both unfair and wrong. When Dessie came in, Adam said, "Look, I'm not a hedonist, and I do believe in human development and a better quality of life for all. It's just that I think the way to achieve these things is the proven way: the market democracies we know have taken us a long way along this road, and as we grow richer, people can choose individually how to spend the increased discretionary income to better themselves and their lives—as they please."

Dessie was in a good mood. "I understand your position," he said. "It is the position of most of my colleagues and most of the public, too, for that matter. I started there myself," he said, as though he had passed from there to a higher sphere where Adam could not travel. "But for two reasons, markets as they now function are inadequate instruments for our well-being. As I said a couple of weeks ago, one is that for people in advanced countries above the poverty line, material gain brings no increase in happiness even though it might provide a means of satisfying their preferences. The main cause for this failure is that the things that do make people happy—a felicitous family life, companionship, and intrinsic work satisfaction—are not priced and do not go through the market. My second reason, as I said last week, is that human development ranks higher in every reflective value scale that I know about than does material gain; human development should take precedence over economic development. The market seems to be one of several instruments for economic development but has ambiguous effects on human development."

Dessie paused to see how this excessively reasonable statement was being received. Weary Adam presented a blank face, so Dessie went on. "Any defender of a status quo has an advantage; he can sit tight and simply ask 'Why change?' The challenger has to explain not only 'Why?' but often 'How?' and 'With what expectations of success?'"

"Other prophets of economic and social change, like Malthus, Spencer, and Lange,[1] have not fared very well," said Adam with his usual sobriety. Of the two statements about the end of history mentioned in our first Spanakopita, Marx's on the future was rather less fortunate than Fukuyama's[2] on the persistence of present trends."

"It is a silly statement, whatever spin you put on it," said Dessie. "But if, like Fukuyama, one simply projects the persistence of current institutions—with a little explanation to go with it, one will be disappointed. Things change. If you can stand it, I am going to ask for help understanding how the less-developed countries (LDCs) will achieve the New Humanism. How is your digestion?"

"The stomach-mind relation is a bit unstable," said Adam.

Two Economic Systems?

*D*essie cleared his throat. "Problems facing the LDCs are quite different from the problems facing the advanced countries," he said, knowing that Adam preferred universals to such distinctions. "The LDC problem is how to get rich without letting the process of enrichment spoil their later chances for becoming humanist societies. In this respect, I would follow Keynes's rather-too-lightly ignored suggestion that when we are rich enough we can have a very different economic system, one in which 'avarice is a vice' and where 'all kinds of social customs and economic practices, affecting the distribution of wealth and economic rewards and penalties, which we now maintain at all costs, because they are tremendously useful in promoting the accumulation of capital, we shall then be free, at last, to discard.'[3] That is, we need one economic system for the accumulation of capital and another for the New Humanism, where, as Keynes said, we are free to 'pursue the arts of life.'"

"Two systems of economic analysis?" queried Adam. "Given your attitude toward economics, I should have thought that one would be more than enough." He hoped this little joke would divert Dessie from what sounded like pure heresy. It did not.

"Yes," said Dessie. "I believe with Keynes that when people become, on average, rich enough so that the value of economic goods declines in relation to noneconomic goods, it is time to rethink our economics."

"Up to what you coyly called 'rich enough,' you agree that the greater the income, the greater the utility," said Adam. "After that point, no longer does more money imply greater utility—oops, 'greater happiness.' Do you know anyone who has reached that point and says, 'Enough, I don't want any more money'? Candidly, what would you do if someone offered you high royalties for a book reporting on our dialogue?"

"Candidly, I would rather talk to you than spend, let alone make, a lot of money," said Dessie, adding in a friendly fashion, "You must feel that way, too, or you would be having a brown bag lunch at your desk while finishing a text that would rival Samuelson's. But if we can get away from these somewhat intimate observations, I would like to repeat one point: more money makes people in the LDCs happier but does not make most people in advanced economies happier, whatever their opinions are. Specifically, considerable evidence shows that the 'consumption culture' is not a happy one.[4] Most people don't know this, but do you not agree that people may have erroneous opinions?"

"All right, you said that before, and I suppose it is a reason for looking at things differently at the two levels of development. What else?" asked Adam, eager to hear the worst.

"Second," said Dessie, "between the two levels of development, there is the difference in the impact of government spending on economic growth: For the LDCs, the higher the ratio of government spending to GDP, the lower the rate of growth. In fact 'each increase of 10 percent in [this] ratio led to an expected decrease of 4 percent in the average annual rate of growth.' But the ratio of the public sector to the GDP in advanced countries has no effect on the growth of these countries.[5] If the role of government in the two levels is so different, the whole nature of their political economies must be different."

"Well, I hate to be technical," said Adam, "but it could be that there is so little variation in ratio of public to private sector economic activity among advanced countries that the distinction between the two levels is artifactual." He knew that this was Charles Wolf's excuse for the difference,[6] but he couldn't believe that the difference between Scandinavian and American public sector ratios was so trivial.

Not being very good at them, Dessie did not like these statistical caveats and proceeded accordingly. "And third," he said, "there are some very interesting differences in the effects of freedom on happiness across societies. Here it goes the other way: increased economic freedoms (for example, unrestricted rights of transaction) and political freedoms (for example, free speech and assembly) have a close correlation with happiness in advanced economies but not among LDCs.[7] Call this the rising marginal utility of freedom, if you want, but whatever you call it, it suggests yet another break in the universality of our social science generalizations."

"Does every break in a generally smooth curve suggest to you the need for a totally different mode of analysis?" asked Adam, beginning to feel uncomfortable.

"At the point when the effects on society of greater income, greater government, and greater freedom are different, doesn't it make sense to rethink the causal models applied to the different sets of cases?" asked Dessie. "Furthermore, to some extent, the tasks of the two levels of development are different and therefore their social values are different. It is the difference between modernization and postmodernization, to use Inglehart's terms.[8] On the one hand, LDCs are busy modernizing—that is, moving from agriculture to industry, fighting endemic poverty, establishing the rule of law, sometimes redefining boundaries, and (even for Islam, with a century's lag) switching from religious to secular authority. On the other hand, the best of the advanced societies are moving beyond this to postmodern goals, deindustrializing in favor of the tertiary sector, treating poverty as a disease to be eradicated, attending more to the aesthetics of their cities, seeking some balance between universal care and individual autonomy, and in other ways searching for a better quality of life."

"There is something dangerous about defining 'them' as different from 'us,'" said Adam. "You break the bonds of empathy that tend to favor the similar and familiar and you risk derogating the very people you would like to help."[9]

This was very distressing to Dessie, who thought of himself as left of center and who had always supported more aid to Third World countries. His next point seemed to promise relief. "Good idea," he said. "Let me bring this comparison of rich and poor closer to home. In the United States, the effects of education on values, attitudes, and behavior suggest strong reasons for thinking of, in this case, less educated and more educated nations as different. Let me summarize what Lane found in his review of literature on the effects of education. In the United States at least, compared to the better educated, less educated publics are less interested in politics, less supportive of open discussion and more willing to forbid it, less tolerant of disliked groups, less likely to support due process for the accused, more rigid and moralistic on issues defined as 'right' and 'wrong,' more nationalistic, less able to weigh the costs of the policies they support, and less consistent in the face of counterarguments.[10] I don't know how it is among economists, but I find that political scientists' recognition of these differences (and they devote their lives to the kind of education that encourages these cognitive and attitudinal effects) is inhibited by their laudable desire to give power to the powerless. That is irrelevant here, but what is relevant is that these educational differences reported of the United States also characterize the differences between LDCs and advanced societies."

"That's elitist," said Adam with something less than a smile. "If these differences are so important, do you want to return to an educational qualification for the franchise?"

"You know," Dessie said in a plaintive tone, "it is a lonely business trying both to be liberal and to face the facts." Then, changing his tone, he added, "Almost as lonely and isolating as being an economist listening to me—if anyone is listening."

Getting Rich in the Right Way

*O*h, I'm listening, all right," said Adam, "I'm just not believing, at least not yet. But we started talking about materialism, which you wanted to trash. Do I understand you now to be saying that materialism is okay for poorer countries but that advanced economies are beyond that gross level of living and can devote themselves to higher things? Okay," continued Adam, "The first duty of the developing nations is to get rich."

Human Development while Getting Rich

"Not just that," said Dessie, "they should get rich in a certain way. You guys talk a lot about strategies of import substitution and export-driven growth. Without denying any of that, let me point to the difference between Nicaragua and Senegal. In the late 1990s, Senegal and Nicaragua had about the same per capita income, but Nicaragua's human development index (life expectancy at birth, adult literacy rate, and school enrollment) was almost twice that of Senegal.[11] Put the other way, South Korea had a per capita income about double that of Costa Rica, but the two countries rank about the same on a human development index. There is a strategy of getting rich that focuses on human development, and many other strategies that do not. Follow Sen[12] and the United Nations Development Programme rather than the IMF[13] and the World Bank—although the latter, it is true, has recently reformed.[14]

Adam partially agreed with Dessie but had to remind him of one thing: "National income and the human development index are fairly closely correlated; without economic growth, the index is likely to be static."

Cognitive Development while Getting Rich

What more should a developing country do? Dessie remembered how Venezuela's minister of intelligence justified his job and quoted him to Adam: "We think that our [true] riches are not in oil but in our brains."[15] And Dessie added, "For those concerned with economic growth, the merit of the argument rests not only on the rapid depletion of oil but on the wealth-producing potential of human capital."[16]

"You're getting awfully close to identifying productivity, which is the meaning of human capital, with the worth of the individual," said Adam with a wicked smile.

"To repeat," said Dessie patiently, "during the period of accumulation, as Keynes remarked, there are 'all kinds of social customs and economic practices, . . . we shall then be free, at last, to discard.'[17] That is why we need two different economic analytical systems."

Adam's ideas about thinking had been grossly distorted by the model of rational calculation popular in his discipline, but he was willing to entertain a little heterodoxy in this field. As long as "the interests" dominated "the passions," he could accommodate some heterodoxy. "Okay," he said again, "back to the thinking you wanted your 'better people' to do last time."

"Getting rich in a fruitful manner depends on *how* people think," said Dessie, rejecting most of what he wanted to say about cognitive development. "Landes put it one way: 'Two things . . . characterize any modern industrial system: rationality, which is the spirit of the institution, and change, which is rationality's logical corollary.'[18] And Tetlock and associates spelled it out further:

> In many contexts, people are striving to achieve neither epistemic nor utilitarian goals, but rather . . . are struggling to protect sacred values from secular encroachments by increasingly powerful societal trends toward market capitalism (and the attendant pressure

to render everything fungible) and scientific naturalism (and the attendant pressure to pursue inquiry wherever it logically leads).[19]

For this purpose," continued Dessie, "some secularization is probably necessary, not because religion is inimical to human development or always to materialism, where the studies are conflicting, but because some religions are hostile to the epistemology of science and growth." He thought for a moment and added, "But if you are thinking that a Reformation, à la Weber, is necessary, remember how Japan and the Asian tigers used Buddhism, Shinto, and their secular companion, Confucianism, to bolster their development without a Reformation. Furthermore, consider what Malinowski said about *Magic, Science, and Religion:* when the Trobrianders knew how to do something, like building a canoe, they used science; when they didn't, they used magic and the supernatural.[20] Under these circumstances, science must develop to explain the explicable, and religion can survive on the many inexplicable questions that remain, such as 'Why do humans exist?'"

"Didn't we cover that in asking 'What should we be doing?' in Spanakopita 2?" asked Adam, surprised that there were any questions that Dessie did not think were explainable by behavioral or physiological methods.

"The point I am making," said Dessie patiently, "is that developing countries must adopt the epistemology of a scientific world while not destroying the resources of religion for later use when the New Humanism comes."

"In the meantime, religion may destroy people's economies," said Adam, thinking of the cargo cults of the people of the South Pacific.[21] Switching themes, he asked, "Aren't you going to talk about that other 'Great Transformation' that runs parallel with Polanyi's, 'From Status to Contract'?"

From Status to Contract

"That's an earlier transformation, from agricultural communities to industrial cities," said Dessie in his most didactic manner. "The point here is not the one about going from family to contract that Sir Henry Maine made[22] or the one about bonds of affection giving way to bonds of interest that Tönnies was so concerned about.[23] But you are right to raise the issue, for my agenda does include some reversal of the transformation that Maine and Tönnies described." Dessie thought for a moment and then asked, apparently irrelevantly, "Do you remember the Hawthorne experiments that found that increases in productivity that seemed to flow from changes in lighting and rules in a factory actually were produced by the apparent concern of management for the well-being of the workers?"

Adam snorted. "Actually, a later review of their data showed that it didn't work that way,"[24] he said, taking pleasure in showing Dessie that behaviorists made mistakes.

"Well," said Dessie, ignoring the interruption, "a leading researcher in that seminal program compared the Trobriands with the Americans and pointed out the salient difference in their priorities: 'Social motives, far more than expectations of economic gain [guide the islanders' economic activities]. Today, we make the contrary assumption. We believe that if we get the factors of production [properly put together], 'the human problems of effective and meaningful association at work will take care of themselves.' "[25] I want to emphasize that this is just the kind of reversal of priorities that is possible when we realize that each domain has a materialist-humanist mix and that we can sometimes change the mix without greatly altering the product."

"I doubt if any of your humanist friends would rather live in the Trobriand Islands, where life expectancy was about forty," said Adam, guessing at life expectancy among natives. "You are skirting something in that status to contract business," he added. "You are forgetting the transformation from collectivism to individualism."

Individualism on the Road to Humanism: Self versus Others

"The problem of individualism is this," said Dessie. "We have to unleash individual initiative for both economic growth and for self-development—and then take steps to tame it. I know you will pounce on this modified endorsement of the individualism that you love so much, and I have no very good way of avoiding your embrace," he said, looking fondly at Adam.

"Ten-foot pole," said Adam, cryptically.

"Shall we start with Tocqueville's concept of individualism?" asked Dessie ominously. "He means something quite different from selfishness or 'love of self.' Rather, he means 'a mature and calm feeling, which disposes each member of the community to sever himself from the mass of his fellows and to draw apart with his family and friends, so that after he has thus formed a little circle of his own, he willingly leaves society at large to itself.'[26] The concept has traveled a long way in the past 170 years," Dessie continued. "One branch makes of it a 'moral axiom,' as we saw in Spanakopita 5, while another branch makes it a cognitive orientation. For the moment, I want to follow the cognitive orientation: individualism as the priority of one's own goals over group goals.[27] In general, individualism is regarded as a precursor of and a condition for the rise of capitalism,[28] but we are talking about what the LDCs must do to arrive at the point where they can afford to undo it—well, some of it. Again, after the experience of Japan and the Asian tigers, we know that familistic orientations can be very productive, but it seems that there are built-in limits to how far familism and *giri* and cronyism can go in market systems without bringing about the system's downfall.[29] In a conflict between familism (or collectivism) and materialism, materialism seems to win, leaving individualism dominant among the richer nations. In a different line of thought, observe that there are many anthropological reports about the retarding effect on effort of cultural obligations requiring that earned goods must be shared with other members of an extended family.[30] Since individualism is part of the culture of advanced economies and collectivism is more prevalent among LDCs, the transition to individualism is part of the cost, if that is the right term, of economic development." He thought for a minute and continued, "By cost I mean something that will have to be partially unlearned when the Great Day comes."

"You sound like Penelope, unraveling at night what you stitched together during the day," said Adam.

Functional versus Evaluative Individualism

Ignoring Penelope, Dessie went on. "Just as there is a preferred way of getting rich and a preferred way of moving toward the epistemology of science, so there is a preferred way of selecting among various kinds of individualism. If one calls the kind of individualism that distinguishes the individual from the group *functional* individualism—and thus permitting the vesting of responsibility for a person's own fate in that person—there remains the question of evaluation: is the individual or the group the primary object of welfare? Functional individualism is silent on this question, so we need a second kind, *evaluational* individualism,[31] to fulfill our mission to put people at the center of our value system. The market's functional individualism has the benefit of releasing individual energies for important tasks, but it does not value individuals per se. As in Darwinian evolution, individuals are dispensable in the market's functional individualism, for it is aggregate demand and supply that are important. The costs to individuals are irrelevant."

"There is no reason to give Darwinian evolution a bad name; after all, here we are," said Adam, as though the fact that he and Dessie were "here" was a sufficient proof.

Self-Attribution: The Effective Core of Individualism

"In both kinds of individualism, the driving force is self-confidence," said Dessie as though confirming the fact that he was "here." "You will recognize this, of course, when I refer to self-confidence by its proper name, the 'internal locus of control' that we talked about in Spanakopita 5. It is a necessary feature of both economic development and human development. Individualism without internality, if that were possible, would get you nowhere because no one would believe that she was an effective agent."

"I had always thought that 'internality' had something to do with hunger," said Adam, smiling and forgetting the previous discussion of the topic. "And how is this sense of personal control learned?" he asked with a sly smile.

"I was coming to that. You'll love it," said Dessie, almost glad to give comfort to his friend. "The market teaches internality. People daily experience contingent reinforcement as they work for pay and plunk down cash for some good. There is a lot of evidence that what people like about the market is not so much the wealth it produces as the sense of choice and freedom that it engenders. In a remarkable set of answers to open-ended questions asking people to explain the workings of the American free-enterprise system, three times as many mentioned its qualities of freedom, especially freedom of opportunity, as mentioned the high standard of living it generated. Almost none referred to limitations placed by market rules or business practices on their choices.[32] In a more usual survey format by Harris, 79 percent said that the value of the market was "freedom for the individual to choose where he works, lives, what he says," almost as many as said that the value of the market was the obvious one, a high standard of living.[33] The point I wish to make is not the priority of freedom over material welfare (which other value studies actually affirm) but that even more than democracy, markets provide contingent reinforcement for the belief that one controls one's own life."

"Home at last," said Adam with a broad smile.

The Benign Cycle of Internality—and the Malignancy of Its Loss

"It gets better, I think," said Dessie, stuffing a little more spinach pie in his mouth. "Man's primary motivational propensity is to be effective in producing changes in his environment,"[34] he continued, quoting a distinguished experimental psychologist. "Thus, doing something and seeing what you hoped would happen actually happen is intensely rewarding. Learning in this way that one is effective, one becomes more effective. There is a 'benign cycle' to internality, so when the market contributes to the sense of personal control, it also makes more generally effective people."

"I told you the market is a great teacher," said Adam, who had changed his earlier belief that the market was only a field of choices.

"And, for the unemployed and the poor, the market teaches that one is a cipher and quite ineffective," said Dessie, spoiling the picture by including those not served by the market. "That learning is called 'learned helplessness.'[35] In that state of helplessness, the person says to himself, 'What's the point of trying? Fate or the system, or the big guys on top control my life.' Losing 'the illusion of control'[36] (or the illusion of free will) is not just disillusionment; it is demoralization."

"That is a silly argument for two reasons," said Adam. "First, if people succeeded in their efforts all the time, they would become habituated to success, and nothing would be learned. For the lessons of contingent reinforcement to be meaningful, failures as well as successes must occur. And second, you are suggesting that the overwhelming majority who find the market responsive will then want to change to something else—that is, having learned how satisfying market choices can be, they decide to abandon these rewarding choices for something they have never experienced."

"Internality is portable," said Dessie, as though he were speaking of pensions. "If the lesson that one is usually a cause is well learned, it is a source of the belief that one can alter one's fate in a variety of situations, including those outside the market." Dessie paused. "Internality is a market grave digger," he added with a smile.

"You are excessively morbid today," said Adam. "I do not want to eat lunch in the company of grave diggers."

"Yorick was a jester, not a professor or an entrepreneur," said Dessie in a muffled voice. "But this is not a funereal scene—or quite a triumphal march," he added. "This second 'Great Transformation,'[37] like the first one, involves a lot of learning. One kind of learning is to understand the value of what you call human capital, what Sen calls 'capabilities,'[38] and what I call human development. This includes but is not limited to cognitive development, whose core is the neglected concept of a scientific epistemology.[39] Another element is the development of a certain kind of individualism that first includes the notion that one's individual goals are important but, as Tocqueville suggested, avoids selfishness by comprehending the welfare of the group in one's own welfare. Learning that one's goals are important is part of a larger idea that all individuals are important—generalization, as in Kant. The market teaches some of these things but not others. It teaches people in a materialist setting whose goals must be partially unlearned as we take further steps along the path of this second 'Great Transformation.'" Dessie paused for a moment before continuing, "If these several learnings do not bring us to the promised land, well—

"Well, what?" asked Adam, fearful that Dessie would say that he would slit his throat.

"Well, we'll have to start over again," said Dessie with a benign smile.

What Will Move Us from Here to There?

Adam was relieved. He would not like to think that a breath of realism had given his idealistic friend a mortal chill. To encourage Dessie, Adam salvaged something from the other man's soliloquy that seemed novel and interesting: "I knew, of course, that the market had made us richer, but I had not thought—or at least doubted that you would think—that it had taught people to assume responsibilities for their own destinies. What do you call it? 'Internal locus of control'? Come to think of it, though, there is a much earlier precedent for something like that. John Bright, the radical Manchester liberal, opposed poor relief, arguing the superiority of encouraging self-reliance: 'Mine is that masculine species of charity, which would lead me to inculcate in the minds of the working classes the love of independence, the privilege of self-respect, the disdain of being patronized or petted, the desire to accumulate and the ambition to rise.'"[40]

Having said this, Adam partially regretted it because he did not think support of the market implied opposition to welfare. Rather, he wanted to know what Dessie thought would transform society in the direction he desired. "What do you think will move us from this materialist society to what you call a humanist society?" he asked with genuine interest.

"To return to the grave diggers you dislike, I am not counting on that early prophecy, 'What the bourgeoisie . . . produces above all are its own gravediggers,' or on the large numbers of twentieth-century echoes of that prophecy,"[41] said Dessie. "Nor do I rely on the immanent properties of human nature that both the Right and the Left have offered. For example, Herbert Spencer said in 1851,

And when the change at present going on is complete—and each possesses an active instinct of freedom, together with an active sympathy—then will all the still existing limitations to individuality . . . cease. . . . Then, for the first time in the history of the world, will there exist beings whose individualities can be expanded to the full in all directions."[42]

"Let's see," said Adam. "That was about 150 years ago; enough time has passed for you and even for me to have 'expanded our individualities to the full in all directions.' What happened?"

"Well, if Spencer is a little off, a later voice from the Left, one that we talked about last time, found in human nature 'an inherent tendency to grow and develop,'"[43] said Dessie, ignoring Adam. "Neither Left nor Right is persuasive. In Spanakopita 4, I think I proved that there are biological substrata supporting primary attention to people and especially to kin, but to expect these potentials to flower now into a different kind of civilization confounds potential with outcome. Why now, after all these years with more or less the same biological endowment?"

"That is where an economic interpretation might be better," said Adam, "though of course not Marx's or Beard's.[44] Economic systems change, and these changes make economic explanations for major social changes plausible. As we said in Spanakopita 3, 'No great intuition is required to grasp the fact that the way people earn a living influences the way they think.'"

The Intraculture and Intrapsyche Dialogue

"You're right, as usual," said Dessie, applying an emollient to his friend's sores, "and I think I can add some insight into the broader Aristotelian notion that people become what they do. But first, consider what is proposed by the transformation I am discussing. It is not as though the forces of materialism were all lined up on one side and the forces of humanism were lined up on the other, like football teams in their helmets and shoulder pads. Rather, all peoples and historical periods are materialist to some degree. Thus, in his reinterpretation of Sorokin's data on 'sensate' (materialist) and 'ideational' (religious) periods, Simonton finds that in the dominant sensate eighteenth-century period, some 45 percent of the leading thinkers were ideational, whereas in the dominant German romantic (ideational) period, 30 percent of the intellectual production was sensate."[45] By the way, Sorokin believed that the triumph in the West of the sensate ideology would inevitably lead to 'relativism, materialism, and ultimately to nihilism and chaos.'"[46] Looking at Adam's startled face, Dessie quickly added, "Well, forget the prediction, but remember the point that all societies must have some materialist and some humanist or ideational themes."

"Are you saying that the transition from materialism to humanism is simply a modest shift of emphasis among the leading intellectuals with the rest of humankind following meekly along their pioneer tracks?" asked Adam, wondering what happened to the promised battle among the giants in the next "Great Transformation."

"The leading intellectuals rarely reflect what the 'rest of humankind' is thinking,"[47] said Dessie. "But that's not the point." He paused and went on. "There are three points: One is that the change of values from a minority to a majority can be an evolutionary affair, more like the emancipation of women than the emancipation of slaves."

"If your cultural transformation from materialism to humanism is like what you called the 'emancipation of women,'" said Adam, again listening to his specially tuned ear, "you will find that people's overt acceptance of humanist values is only the preface to a whole volume of subliminal ideas that people hardly recognize are part of the story."[48]

Dessie was delighted to find Adam so sensitive to the subliminal or quietly assumed precepts of society. But he had work to do and resumed his march: "The second point is that within the breast of each person may be a conflict such that she is not so much 'converted' as self-persuaded. 'I have half a mind to enlist in the Peace Corps.'"

"A humanist homunculus in every materialist," said Adam, thinking of his namesake's 'man within.' But what will you do when the humanist conscience urges harder work to earn more to pay for the third child's college education?"

"I will cheer for the conscience, of course," said Dessie, "and, as you will see in a minute, I will hope that the third child gets into the college of her choice." Dessie then went on with his topography of humanism. "And the third is the erosion of materialist dominance by increments from one domain to another, say, first in religion (making churches allies of the humanists), then in the family as parents deemphasize material success and stress, say, independent thinking, and finally infiltrating the economy as bankers—and not just their wives—join the boards of nonprofit organizations, introducing more men to the doing of good while helping them learn the language of humanism."

"My wife is a banker," said Adam, meditating on this new view of the battlefield with fifth columns on each side. He returned to his original question. "I still don't see what will move us from here to there, no matter how mixed up the cultures will be."

"First," said Dessie, "I want to show the importance of one humanist idea in all economies and therefore in all transitions—I mean the importance of interpersonal trust. The failure of such trust greatly impeded the movement of the Philippines from their patron-client economy to a mercantile economy;[49] it kept the natives of Tepoztlan (Mexico) from cooperating in mutual-aid projects that would have increased their productivity,[50] and, in contrast, its presence in Chan Kom, a Mayan village in the Yucatan, permitted a major increase in their productivity and adaptation to modernity.[51] More systematically, Kenneth Boulding and Neva Goodwin argue that interpersonal trust is a condition for economic productivity,[52] Putnam shows that trust is a condition for democracy,[53] and Inkeles and Diamond point out that their cross-cultural data are 'highly suggestive of a strong positive association between economic development and a psychological disposition to trust other people.'[54] If interpersonal trust is at the same time an ingredient of economic modernization and the heart of the humanist agenda, then your materialist drive for increased productivity is an ally of my humanist drive for a society where people are at the center of things."

"I see what you're doing," remarked Adam, somewhat annoyed this time. "You are claiming to be an ally of the market for the purpose of destroying the market. Clever, but it is not clever verbal scoring that counts but rather actual events. Events are not so easily manipulated."

"Sorry. I use words to track, explain, and predict events, the same as you do," said Dessie. "There's more to come. You won't like it, but there are several dialectics to get through before we get to that final—well, penultimate—moment. Although *dialectics* means 'logical dispute,' I will use the term in the Hegelian sense: something creating an opposing force that transforms the original situation."

"Since, as you are well aware, economists employ deductive reasoning more than most, I would prefer the original meaning, 'logical dispute,' but go ahead," said Adam in a resigned manner.

The Benign Cycle of Internality as a Dialectic

"I want to refer back to what I said about the way the sense of personal control is learned by market experience," said Dessie. "I have said that people who learn that they can change their circumstances will do so as it dawns on them that the market offers dross in a world of golden opportunities. The problem is for people to learn from the market or anywhere else that they are effective and, to some extent, can control what happens to them and at the same time to unlearn what the market teaches them about the source of happiness and what is of enduring value. They must then begin to learn what have turned out to be more effective sources of happiness and what is and always has been of enduring worth."

"You are inviting me into your trap by praising the market only to show that it leads inexorably to its own demise," said Adam, more amused than angry. "The better the market does its job, the sooner it must give way to something else! You tried that with the declining marginal utility of wealth. What next?"

The Educational Dialectic

"Education is next," said Dessie. "Allow me to elaborate on a point that came up last time and to quote from Edward Denison on the effect of education on economic growth in the periods up to 1969: 'The fourth biggest source of long-term growth was the increase in the average amount of education held by workers employed in the business sector. The resulting increase in their skills and versatility was the source of 14 percent of the 1929–69 growth rate and 12 percent of the higher 1948–69 rate.'[55] This is Schultz's investment of human capital that you mentioned in Spanakopita 5."

"Great!" said Adam, who, in spite of his weariness, was almost transported to a state of joy—or at least what passed for joy for him—by Dessie's accommodating remarks.

"Wait," said Dessie. "It wouldn't be a dialectic if it were a straightforward one-way influence. Taking a dialectical approach, consider how the rising economic value of human beings undermines the materialistic system that nourished them. Here come the grave diggers again.[56] If people are economically more valuable, they will receive more education, and more education leads to less materialistic values.[57] And incidentally, as Schultz believed, there is a cross-generational effect. The more educated a person's mother, the less materialist will that person be.[58] Moreover, the educational dialectic works even better when we get to tertiary education. Secondary education tends to socialize youth to the norms of the society; it is conservative. But tertiary or college education leads to the questioning of these norms;[59] it is an acceleration, perhaps, of humanist learning. Let the dialectic do its work: the market system encourages education for human capital, and that 'human capital' repudiates its economic source of value. It is not the Marxian dialectic, but Marx would like it."

"Don't count on it," said Adam, who somehow knew what was coming. "Wait until you see the record of rising materialistic values among U.S. college students in the 1980s and 1990s[60] before you rely on education to push us toward your utopian New Humanism."

"One more thing on education," said Dessie, impatient to score a point for public goods. "You won't like this either, but in my opinion, the reason for growth is not to make private people rich but to increase public services such as health and education. Contrary to the dominant conservative position in the United States, I think funds are less productively spent by private individuals than by the government, at least by a peaceful democratic government in a country marked by 'private wealth and public dearth.'"[61]

"That is pure heresy," said Adam, smiling, "but I am inclined to agree with you up to the point where government tax rates reduce the growth that permits these productive public expenditures. Anything else?"

The Occupational Dialectic

"If, in this dialogue, you will excuse the term *dialectic* once again," said Dessie, "I would like to point out the way that occupational changes undermine the materialist societies that produce the changes. Thus, we have gone from agriculture to industry, from industry to services, from services dealing with people to services dealing with information—the information revolution. This means that we have gone from working with things to working with ideas and data, a change that according to one careful account increases a form of cognitive development. That study found that time spent 'working with things' was negatively related (−0.68) to a measure of intellectual flexibility as contrasted to the effect of time spent working with people (+0.65) and time with data (+0.80).[62] Remember the postmaterialist dream of 'a society where ideas count more than money?' Well, as the occupational dialectic does its work, we may approach that dream."

Adam, knowing that the Graduate Record Exam scores were higher for economic students than for students in literature, history, and some social sciences (with the exception of psychology), wondered if working with data, which some economists did, was different from working with words, which the humanists did. But out loud he said, "What you have just discovered is that people in white-collar occupations are smarter than people in blue-collar occupations. Are you surprised? I don't see any intrinsic reversing relationship such as is required by what you call a 'logical dispute'—sorry—a 'dialectic.'"

"What I had in mind," said Dessie meekly, "was the way occupations are created and destroyed by technology. By the way, the Bureau of Labor Statistics lists among the jobs projected to grow faster than others to the year 2005 a rather larger group of 'computer engineers and scientists' and especially 'systems analysts,'" said Dessie, who had been boning up on this issue. "Moreover, the job losses are projected to be larger among certain manual railroad job categories and among farmers. What seems to be happening is a fairly large increase in jobs working with people and a smaller increase in jobs working with data combined with a continuing decrease in jobs working with things.[63] These projections suggest a slight brightening of the workforce and a larger decrease in materialism."

Adam, who knew more about labor statistics than Dessie, demurred. "Your data, if that is what they are, are a little out of date," he said. "The BLS now says that the fastest-growing occupations will be the semiskilled jobs (health workers, child care workers, waiters, and so forth) for which little training is required and which are invulnerable to computerization and overseas replacement.[64] These are jobs for which pay is the main reward—that is, jobs teaching materialism."

This was bad news for Dessie, but he chose to emphasize the principle and the invisible long-term outcome over the short-term changes Adam was reporting. "In 1900 39 percent of jobs were in agriculture; by 1982 this proportion had dropped to 3 percent. In 1900 who would have predicted such a change? Each state of technology and its related set of consumer demands builds on and makes obsolete the previous stage. The conflict and resolution of the technology-occupation changes are as strong a force in human development and erosion of materialism as is the increase in education."[65]

"Well, I'm not surprised that technology makes cognitive demands on people. But I thought you lefties were all upset about what you call 'deskilling'—that is, the tendency of market economies to reduce labor costs by substituting machines for people to reduce the requirements for expensive skills."[66]

"The man whose life is spent performing a few simple operations . . . generally becomes as stupid and ignorant as it is possible for a human creature to become,"[67] said Dessie, quoting Adam's namesake. "But more careful and more recent studies show that, in fact, jobs have become increasingly complex and more intellectually demanding in most industries, including office work, but not in many other service jobs."[68] He paused, thinking first of Intel's plant in Costa Rica and then of the sweatshops in Haiti, and added, "I think this applies to some Third World industries, though not all of them."

"It's extraordinary what happened between the early-nineteenth-century 'dark Satanic mills' and the industrial revolution in Third World countries," said Adam, looking on the bright side.

"I'll join you temporarily on the bright side," said Dessie. "Listen to my friend Alex Inkeles:

> Living in a country that is more highly developed seems to be ego-enhancing—it gives individuals a greater sense of personal worth, satisfaction, and competence beyond what would be predicted from knowing only their education and occupation. [It also seems] to develop qualities that contribute to stable politics and effective economic behavior because such individuals are more trustful and tolerant of others yet are more confident of their own capacities.[69]

Up to a point, modernization is good for you. It is only after that point that I (and Inkeles, too, for that matter) worry about its effects."

"So how does that affect the decline of materialism?" asked Adam.

"People usually choose their first jobs in conformity to family values, and then the first job generally reinforces these values. Thus, among jobs focused respectively on people and services—or on money and gain or autonomy and challenge—those who chose any one of these pairs thereafter prefers that kind of job.[70] If materialist jobs breed materialists, so jobs focused on people and services and autonomy and challenge breed nonmaterialists. Furthermore, parents teach their children the values that the parents themselves have found useful on the job—in one study, obedience or initiative.[71] The shifting character of occupations is marked, at least in part, by the relative rise of nonmaterialist jobs." He paused to reconsider what he had said. "But don't forget that materialism is a cultural theme as well as a set of individual values, beliefs, and motives. Even academics, who are working more for reputation than for money, are likely to be infected by it."

"What do the teenagers working at routine jobs at McDonalds learn?" asked Adam with scorn.

"They probably learn something about the value of work," said Dessie, sure that he could back this up with research but aware of contrary research that made him hesitate. "And, indeed," he continued "it seems that one of the predictors of adult marital and occupational adjustment is a record of hard work (at school or in real life) during adolescence. But one suspects that this is not at all part of the occupational dialectic, for what they learn at their low-paid, low-skill service jobs is the value of money as well as the value of hard work.[72] As Aristotle prophesied, people who *earn* money value it more than others."[73]

"Your occupational dialectic is a mixed bag—if a dialectic can be called a bag," said Adam, still doubtful about either the desirability or the fact of a drift away from materialism.

"As always, things move in different directions," said Dessie, "but the information revolution is a powerful reality. One other point. Edward Denison complains that government is creaming off many of the brightest people for work that does not register in the pitiful economic growth statistics he has to work with.[74] The fact is that civil servants, like the military, work in an environment that does not depend on the profit motive and may foster a service orientation. At least it has been found that government workers are less materialist than workers in the for-profit sector.[75] And it is true in general that government employment has increased faster in the West than has private employment.[76] Whether you call it a dialectic is immaterial: the fact is that the changes in employment are unfavorable to the growth of materialism." Dessie wanted to say "Q.E.D." or "I rest my case," but, as a matter of fact, he had several more hypotheses in mind to show why the decline of materialism was inevitable.

"Funny!" said Adam, "as I look around and see all my friends chasing dollars and watch the stock market invite into its snake pit the homemakers and taxi drivers of the world, I don't think I see this emaciation of the materialist population that you describe. Nor does the general public: 'It is widely believed that our unceasing quest for material goods is part of the basic makeup of human beings. According to the folklore, we may not like it, but there's little we can do about it,'"[77] said Adam, quoting Juliet Schor, one of Dessie's friends.

"Economists are not supposed to rely on what is 'widely believed' or on casual observation, especially from a booth in a hash house," said Dessie. Then, exhausted but modestly hopeful, he added, "The forces of MATERIALISM and HUMANISM are in a delicate balance; the outcome is unclear, but we humanists have reason to hope. See you next Wednesday."

Spanakopita Nine

After the End of History

"There's a chill in the air," said Dessie, referring either to the weather or to his sense of impending defeat in this session.

"I hadn't noticed," said Adam, feeling rather cheerful for someone of his lugubrious temperament.

"Into my heart an air that kills," continued Dessie in his melancholy strain.

"I thought you were looking for the promised land, not looking back on the 'land of lost content,'"[1] said Adam with a twisted smile.

"There is no turning back," said Dessie, switching from Houseman to Alex Inkeles in a disconcerting way. "We must choose 'either a modernism linked to a passion for power and to bottomless greed . . . or a modernism restrained by humility and tempered by humanism.'"[2]

"Okay. I said I was willing to grant you a certain tension between what you call humanism and your version of materialism, but you cannot establish a new ideological axis by fiat," said Adam.

"Do you hear voices prophesying humanism?" asked Dessie, as though listening to ethereal music coming out of the jukebox. "Hark! There goes Engels: 'The struggle for individual existence comes to an end and at this point, . . . [man] leaves the conditions of animal existence behind him and enters conditions which are really human. . . . It is humanity's leap from the realm of necessity into the realm of freedom.'[3] And there goes that old charlatan Herbert Spencer: 'When the change at present going on is complete, . . . none will be hindered from duly unfolding their natures; for whilst every one maintains his own claims, he will respect the claims of others.'[4] And hear the mellifluous voice of Maynard Keynes, the second-best economist of our time: 'In the long run . . . mankind is solving its economic problem. . . . Meanwhile make mild preparations by encouraging, and experimenting in, the arts of life. . . . The permanent problem of mankind [is] learning to live well.' "[5]

"The permanent problem of mankind is to look reality in the face, however ugly," said Adam, ashamed that Keynes had wandered into the business of prophesy.

"Well, some others tried to look at reality's ugly materialist face and didn't like what they saw. I won't bore you with details, but that White Russian Menshevik, Pitirim Sorokin, prophesied that our materialism would lead to 'relativism' and 'chaos';[6] the prophet of postindustrialism, Daniel Bell, called our 'materialist hedonism . . . the cultural contradiction of capitalism;[7] and nineteenth-century philosopher Frederick Lange thought the materialist market 'leads to censure of charitableness . . . and depreciates religion.'[8] Looking reality in the face doesn't seem to reconcile a lot of observers to the reality that you endorse."

Adam was unimpressed by these prophets of doom and even suggested another: "You forgot that the 'care for external goods should lie on the shoulders of the "saint like a light cloak." . . . But fate decreed that the cloak should become an iron cage,' "[9] he quoted triumphantly. But he preferred home turf. "Keynes had his economic predictions right," he said. "Economically, we live about four times as well as our grandfathers and about eight times as well as did people in Engels's time. And here we are in Clark's eating spinach pie and living well. So why should materialism decline? Indeed, aside from the prophets you mentioned and your so-called dialectics, what reason is there to think it has declined?"

"So far, I have been arguing that ethically and hedonically, materialism *should* decline and that there are immanent forces in the market society that suggest that it *will* decline. As to whether these forces have matured and materialism *is,* in fact, declining, that is a different matter. Are we ready for this second Great Transformation? Well, there are data," said Dessie, without enthusiasm.

"Let's see," said Adam, with an appetite for evidence that a humanist might call avaricious.

The Tenacity of Materialism

*W*ell," said Dessie, with unaccustomed hesitance, "I should explain that there is research by Ronald Inglehart that deals with the relative decline of materialism. That research comes in two stages, the stage where post-materialism was the goal and the stage where postmodernization is the goal or at least the outcome."

"Goals are easy," said Adam. "Does anybody get there?"

"Yes. The Scandinavians and the Dutch," responded Dessie enigmatically.

The Promise of Postmaterialism

Dessie took a deep breath. "Beginning in 1970 and continuing every few years thereafter, European (and later U.S. and world) survey research on values provided the data Inglehart analyzed in the light of Abraham Maslow's theory of a 'need hierarchy.'[10] As I said in Spanakopita 2, that theory asserts that human needs are hierarchically ordered so that only if the basic physiological and safety needs are satisfied can other social and psychological needs emerge in their ordered sequence. Inglehart claims that postmaterialism (which I will explain in a minute) appeals only to people socialized in peace and security—that is, only after their physiological and safety needs are met. This postmaterialism is contrasted to materialism by differences in responses to the following eleven (out of twelve) values." He pushed a piece of paper across the table.

Materialist and Postmaterialist Values

Cluster of Five Postmaterialist Values	Cluster of Six Materialist Values
Have say on job	Fight rising prices
Less impersonal society	Strong defense forces
Society where ideas count	Economic growth
More say in government	Stable economy
Freedom of speech	Fight against crime
	Maintain order[11]

"In my opinion," continued Dessie, now pushing his own agenda, "those postmaterialists are humanists in disguise (well, not disguise, since they do not even know that they are postmaterialists): they are charter members of the New Humanism."[12] He paused to gather his forces.

"It's a funny scale that makes a person choose between freedom of speech and economic growth," Adam broke in. "Actually, in many parts of the world, what free speech they have has come as one of the fruits of economic growth. Recognizing that fact, you might end up as (oh horrors!) a materialist yourself."

"The questions are ones of priorities," said Dessie, "and Inglehart doesn't force the pattern—the responses just fall out that way. But you're not alone in questioning the measure; others have done so, too."[13] Dessie didn't want to get bogged down in methodological questions and hurried on. "Inglehart's second stage is breathtaking in its scope and in the light it sheds on the transition to humanism we are about to—well, we will someday enter. Inglehart used three waves of the World Values Survey (1981–82, 1990–91, 1995–98) to study value changes in sixty-five countries representing about three-quarters of the world's population. He plotted a figure with type of authority on the vertical axis (traditional authority as inherited chiefs and religious leaders at one pole and modern authority as elected representatives and appointed bureaucrats at the other). The horizontal axis represents the polar values of survival at one end and quality of life at the other. Placing forty-three countries on this grid, he found that the lower left-hand corner was occupied by Nigeria and India, whereas the upper right-hand corner included—at the very tip—Sweden and the Netherlands. The United States was over on the quality-of-life side of the security/quality of life axis but oddly only in the middle on the vertical axis measuring traditional-modern authority—that is, compared to the most advanced countries, the United States reveals relatively more support for religious than elected authority.[14] You can see this in figure 1," he said, pushing another piece of paper across the table.

"I think I see a grid where GNP per capita is the main distinguishing dimension," said Adam, treating the figure as a Rorschach.

"It's one feature, of course," said Dessie, aware that Inglehart's theory relied on socialization in periods of affluence and security,[15] "but there are others, like religion, that seem almost equally effective in promoting or retarding the humanist values embraced by postmodernization. The distinguishing features of the nations characterized by postmodernization (where economic growth is no longer a primary value) were the following relative emphases:

Hard work is a less important value

Tolerance and imagination are more highly valued

Women are regarded as not only more equal but also as occupational mates

Moral absolutes are qualified by consideration of the circumstances of each act

Homosexuality is much more acceptable

The family is less central and less revered

Measures of 'trust in people' are higher[16]

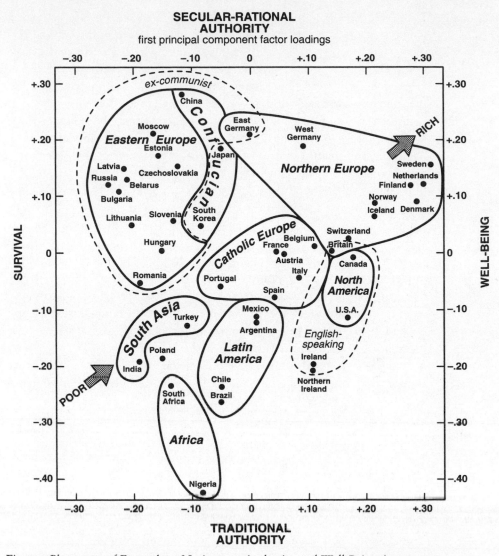

Fig. 1.   Placement of Forty-three Nations on Authority and Well-Being Axes, 1990–93.

Figure locates where given societies fall on two key cultural dimensions: Authority Values (Secular-Rational versus Traditional) and Life Values (Survival versus Well-Being). Positions are based on the mean scores of the publics of the given nation on each of the two dimensions.

(Reproduced from Ronald Inglehart, *Modernization and Postmodernization: Cultural, Economic, and Political Change in Forty-three Societies* [Princeton: Princeton University Press, 1997], 93. Permission from Princeton University Press to reprint this figure is gratefully acknowledged.)

Except for that curious item about the family, these, too, are humanist values that promise well for the New Humanism in Scandinavia and the Netherlands." He paused, as though weighing whether to make the next point. Drawing a deep breath, he went on. "In sharp contrast with modernizing nations, postmodernizing nations show a declining support for the state and increased support for 'do it yourself.'"[17]

Adam looked pleased but forbore saying anything about laissez-faire lest he upset Dessie. Yet he noticed that this so-called postmodernization embraced two features of the feminist agenda (or one of the feminist agendas): the mateyness of work colleagues without regard to sex and the deemphasis of the family.[18] It crossed his mind, as it had Dessie's, that humanism was congenial to the feminist movement. For Adam this was conflictful, but for Dessie it offered a new source of support for his agenda.

Dimly aware of Adam's ruminations, Dessie referred again to postmodernization. "May I point out that these data from Inglehart are findings, not prophecies or predictions; they show the drift of history not just the 'necessary' outcomes of immanent forces." Again, Dessie thought he had proved that one version of the promised land was, to mix metaphors, at least on the launching pad.

"Impressive," said Adam in a glum mood. "And you must be able to support this with data showing the decline of materialism in both Europe and the United States."

The Fragility of Postmaterialism

Dessie's face suddenly fell, and his euphoria disappeared. "Well," he said hesitantly, "there are data but they are somewhat disappointing. Inglehart can show that his measure of postmaterialism (which I mentioned earlier) has increased for several decades around the world, faster in the United States than has materialism, as you can tell from this figure, which I happen to have brought along today." He handed Adam a sheet marked "Figure 2. Policy Materialism–Postmaterialism as 'Goals for the Nation,' 1972–92." "But the truth is that because there is a large middle group with mixed answers in Inglehart's samples and because the measure of materialism is rising almost as fast as the measure for postmaterialism, it is hard to say what is going on." Dessie dropped his voice almost to a whisper and said hesitantly, "There are other troubles with his measures, too, that have raised questions about what their changes actually mean."[19]

"I didn't hear," said Adam, although he had heard perfectly well.

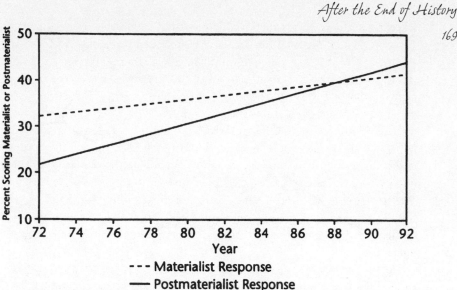

Fig. 2. Policy Materialism–Postmaterialism as "Goals for the Nation," 1972–92.

Question: "For a nation, it is not always possible to obtain everything one might wish [hands card with various goals]. If you had to choose among them, which one would seem most desirable to you? Which one would be your second choice?" 1. "Maintaining order in the nation [scored materialist]; 2. "Giving people more say in important political decisions" [scored postmaterialist]; 3. "Fighting rising prices" [scored materialist]; 4. "Protecting freedom of speech" [scored postmaterialist].

(Data from National Election Studies. Figure courtesy of Yale Social Science Statistical Laboratory. Permission to reprint from Robert Lane, *The Loss of Happiness in Market Democracies* [New Haven: Yale University Press, 2000] is gratefully acknowledged.)

The Materialism of the Young

"So I tend to rely on another, ad hoc measure of materialism among high school seniors that has a kind of face validity and has a record going back more than twenty years. In this account"—Dessie handed Adam a diagram labeled "Figure 3. Importance of 'Having Lots of Money' or 'Making a Contribution to Society' "—"you'll see that materialism rises pretty consistently up to 1990, when it declines fairly steadily for about five years. The forces of humanism ('importance of contribution to society') are stronger than the forces of materialism for a few years in the late 1970s, but then, although gathering strength, they are weaker than the forces of materialism for most of the 1980s. In 1987, the forces of humanism begin a fairly steady rise for the next eight years until, please notice,

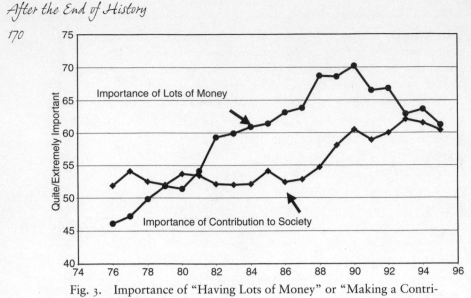

Fig. 3. Importance of "Having Lots of Money" or "Making a Contribution to Society," 1976–95.

(Reproduced from W. Lance Bennett, "The Uncivic Culture: Communication, Identity, and the Rise of Lifestyle Politics," *PS: Political Science and Politics* 31 (1998): 741–61. Bennett got the data from Wendy M. Rahn, "The Decline of American National Identity among Young Americans: Diffuse Emotion, Commitment, and Social Trust" (working paper for the study of political psychology, University of Minnesota, 1997). Permission by the American Political Science Association to reprint the figure is gratefully acknowledged.)

twice in the mid-1990s the two forces touch and struggle for supremacy. It's a pretty dramatic struggle, and although our guys are the underdogs for most of the two decades, at the close of the measured period we humanists begin to hope again."

Adam examined the figure but was not impressed. "In only four of the twenty years are your guys actually ahead," he said. "I don't know what moves these attitudes, but there is some suggestion of randomness here. Haven't you got better data?"

"Well, from the same kinds of data but using slightly different measures, we must look through this glass even more darkly," Dessie said. "In addition to the question about the importance of money, Rahn and Transue analyze responses to questions asking, 'When you are older, do you expect to own more possessions than your parents do now, or about the same, or less?' and 'Compared with your parents, what is the smallest amount that you could be content or satisfied to own?' All three questions show a pretty steady increase in American high school materialism from 1976 to 1990, with only the slightest hint of a decrease in the following five years.[20] It's pretty bleak."

Adam was sympathetic and a little surprised, given the steady drum-beat of anticonsumerism he had run across in the press. "Haven't you some other body of data that looks better?" he asked, almost hoping his friend had something up his sleeve.

Dessie was afraid of that but gamely produced another figure. "Well," he said reluctantly, "here are the results of a survey that has been conducted annually among college freshmen giving answers to questions over the thirty years from 1966 to 1996 about students' purposes in going to college. Again, two answers are contrasted, 'be very well-off financially' and 'develop a meaningful philosophy of life.' As predicted, the forces of materialism weakened regularly in the 1966–78 period until they were about equal to the rising humanist 'philosophy of life' group. Whereupon"—there was a catch in Dessie's throat—"the humanists lost their claims to supremacy. The materialists rose sharply to a plateau around 1990, staying there for the remainder of the period measured. They were about 30 percentage points higher than the anemic humanist group. Here," Dessie said, handing Adam another sheet, this one marked, "Figure 4. Goal Materialism among U.S. College Freshmen: Percentage Saying It Is 'Very Important or Essential' to 'Be Very Well-Off Financially' or to 'Develop a Meaningful Philosophy of Life,' 1966–96."

Adam looked at the figure and smiled. "What happened to the prophesied victory of the forces of 'good' over the forces of 'evil'?" he asked with compassion as well as irony.

"They were overpowered," said Dessie. "Further studies of post-materialism in the United States and Europe have been very discouraging. Juliet Schor says that 'by the mid-1980s, the American people were far more oriented toward economic growth and materialism than before. Most significant, young people were leading the charge back to material values.'[21] Elinor Scarborough tracked postmaterialist changes and, after pointing out that the rise of postmaterialism in Europe took place only during the 1980s[22] (when our guys were losing over here), with no general rise over the 1973–91 period (and an actual decline between 1990 and 1991), she says that the pattern across all countries measured suggests that a *ceiling effect* occurs whenever a country gets to about 20–25 percent postmaterialists.[23] She also finds that the increase in education alone could account for most of the rise in European postmaterialism,[24] which, although damaging to Inglehart's explanation referring to the effects of growing up in peace and prosperity, supports the educational dialectic I proposed last time. (Notice)," said Dessie in oral parentheses, "(how this fits in with the evidence that the education of women makes them less materialistic.)[25] Finally, two other scholars looking at the European data

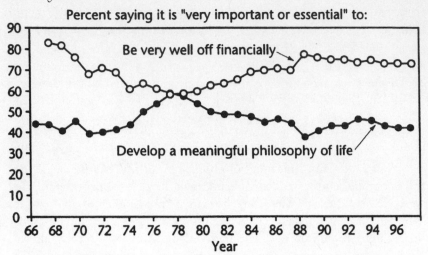

Fig. 4.   Goal Materialism among U.S. College Freshmen: Percentage
Saying It Is "Very Important or Essential" to "Be Very Well-Off Financially" or to "Develop a Meaningful Philosophy of Life," 1966–96.

(Data from Annual Surveys of more than two hundred thousand students entering American
colleges annually as published in the *American Freshman* [Los Angeles Higher Education
Research Institute, UCLA] and subsequent series. Figure created by David Myers and reproduced with his kind permission. Further permission to reprint figure from Robert Lane, *The
Loss of Happiness in Market Democracies* [New Haven: Yale University Press, 2000] is gratefully acknowledged.)

find that 'since the late 1980s, the proportion of postmaterialists relative
to materialists has either ceased to increase or has even declined in several
West European countries. . . . We surmise, then, that the postmaterialist
age has, for the moment at least, come to a halt.'[26] And we all thought we
had a convincing theoretical analysis," said Dessie with a sigh.

Adam wanted to make his friend feel better. "I remember Alvin
Hansen talking to Sumner Schlicter at Harvard after World War II," he
said, apparently irrelevantly. "On the basis of mostly Keynesian models,
Hansen had predicted massive unemployment after the war. On the basis
of talking to businessmen about their investment plans, Schlicter had predicted very little. Schlicter was right, but, as Hansen said, 'I had the very
best models.' It happens to the best of us. Should you talk to some—" But
he just couldn't pronounce the word *economists* to his distressed friend.
Instead he asked, "How do you account for this relative humanist failure?"

Dessie knew that the failure to fulfill these prophecies did not result
from the failure of the market economy—quite the opposite: it resulted

from the failure of humanism. Why? Why were materialist values so tenacious and the appeal of humanist values so weak? Higher ground: true to his profession, he sought higher ground.

The Transition from Materialism to Humanism

*A*ll transitions are difficult and painful," said Dessie, with a little more pomposity than usual. "The transition from agriculture to industry (and capitalism) that Polanyi called the 'Great Transformation'[27] probably disrupted more lives than any other, but the terms of struggle were understood: it was about economic advantage."

Leaving the Economic Axis

"Ill fares the land to hast'ning ills a prey / Where wealth accumulates, and men decay,"[28] quoted Adam, drawing again on what Miss Sachs had taught him in tenth-grade English.

"That struggle," continued Dessie, "was simply part of the longer struggle that John Hicks describes in his economic history,[29] comprehensible in that sense. But the one I am proposing—or rather, the one I discern as nascent in our culture—is quite different. It depreciates the economic axis in favor of another. I fear I will prejudice my case, but about thirty years ago a group of critics thought they saw in the ephemeral youth rebellion of the 1960s a first step toward that shift in axes. American youth, said French critic Jean Revel, 'do not want merely to cut the cake into more equal pieces; they want a whole new cake based on the rejection of an unsatisfactory lifestyle.'"[30]

"And what happened to that so-called Great Transformation?" asked Adam with scorn. He paused for a moment and then added, "Are you saying that your proposed transformation is more like the Reformation than the industrial (and market) revolution?"

"The point I want to make is that the transition from materialism to humanism involves an odd struggle between an entrenched ideology of *means* and an emergent philosophy—oh, all right, ideology—of *ends*. Economists themselves justify wealth only as the source of something else, something that has value—namely, utility or happiness. Now that we know that for most people in rich societies, it is not true that more money buys more happiness, the dominant materialist philosophy of means stands naked and exposed. In a dim way, Revel and Habermas and the others understood that the materialist lifestyle is unsatisfying to many people, but they did not know why." Dessie paused. "Nor, indeed, do these many people pursuing their materialist lifestyles. That implies that rotating axes is very difficult."

"As I have said before," said Adam, "there is something fundamentally wrong and even dangerous about an assumption that you know more about what makes people happy than they do."

Does the Transition Justify Paternalism?

"There are four answers to that," said Dessie, counting on his pudgy fingers. "First, consider the problems identified by Frank Knight: 'In a social order where all values are reduced to the money measure, . . . a considerable fraction of the most noble and sensitive characters will lead unhappy and futile lives.'[31] As that fraction increases, shouldn't we do something about it?"

"Okay," said Adam, much more impressed by Knight than by Revel, "economics and indeed, the market itself have answers only for those problems yielding to that 'money measure.' But the market is not society. Utility theory is not a general theory of happiness but only a theory of preference satisfaction in market situations."

Dessie had gained his main point. Happiness, subjective well-being, positive moods were all partially independent of the market. It followed that people *could* be happier in nonmarket societies than in market societies and that materialist pursuits *could* frustrate as well as satisfy the pursuit of happiness. He pursued this point with a set of special cases that came under the same heading. "Consider the nature and names sometimes given to the popular pains: *malaise, alienation, anomie,* and on the continent of Europe, *ressentiment,*" he said. "Far worse, consider the medical reports of rising clinical depression in modern market countries throughout the world,[32] depression whose causes are unknown to those who suffer from it. Moreover, in the United States, 'about 5% of the people have GAD [generalized anxiety disorder] at some time in their lives, and about two-thirds of them are women,'" said Dessie. "This disorder is defined as a 'condition characterized chiefly by debilitating worry and agitation about nothing in particular or anything at all.'[33] That's about 14 million people who need help in identifying their problems and getting help." Dessie paused before continuing. "The point I am making is that for one set of unhappy people—the alienated, depressed, and anxious— the most difficult step is to identify their problems. The next step is likely to be to find relief in social support quite outside the market and politics, and only then is the therapy offered by the market and government agencies at all useful."

"As is the case for most medical problems, people can buy medical counsel and Prozac and Zoloft (with a prescription) in the market," said Adam. Without being callous, he nevertheless smiled at the witticism he was about to make. "Are you saying that the passions should be given equal consideration with the interests that Hirschman said had triumphed to pave the way for capitalism?"[34]

"We have agreed," said Dessie, also smiling, "that even when the pain is from a known and identifiable source, if it is not priced, the market will not serve to relieve it. The market is not sensitive to the pain of loneliness, of sense of unfulfillment, or indeed, of wasted lives. If, now that we know a little more about pain and pleasure,[35] you would stop thinking of utility as preference satisfaction and go back to thinking of it as happiness—that is, as a passion—you would be on the road to making economics relevant again."

"I say I am 'very happy' because my stupid dog has come back; you say you are 'very happy' because your beloved wife has finally returned to you. The measurement addicts you cite say we measure the same level of happiness. What nonsense!" said Adam, breathing hard at the violation of an economist's ban on interpersonal comparisons of utility.

"Third," continued Dessie, "If a substantial part of the malaise includes a sense of powerlessness, as it does,[36] any remedies that involve resolute action are ruled out by the pathology that needs help. Laissez-faire, when to *faire* is exactly what one cannot do, is a cruel prescription."

"And fourth," said Adam, seizing control of the agenda, "as the axis rotates away from material issues, economists are also rotated away from influence in favor of people like you. What is proposed is not so much a revolution of ends over means as a coup by a group of social scientists eager to rule society according to *their* prescriptions." That was nasty, and Adam regretted it but couldn't help wondering if ad hominem had anything to do with putting people at the center of things.

"Fourth," continued Dessie, putting a different twist on Adam's unfair attack, "as C. Wright Mills put it, what the professor 'ought to do for the individual is to turn his personal troubles and concerns into social issues and problems open to reason, [encouraging] skills aiding rational insight into the self—self-educating, self-cultivating man.' That, said Mills, is 'the sociological imagination.'"[37]

"So we have the authority of this lefty sociologist to pry into people's affairs to make them public affairs," said Adam, still in his offensive mood. Turning more reasonable, he said, "Okay, quite apart from the ethics of your deciding for others what they ought to be doing, there is the problem of whether these others want the goods you are offering and will help you get them."

"Are you questioning the demand for happiness?" asked Dessie incredulously. "It won't (and shouldn't) persuade you, but you do recall that on this point Aristotle said, 'Both ordinary people and persons of trained mind define the good as happiness.'"[38]

"We could do worse than follow Kant on this," said Adam. "'No one can force us . . . to be happy in his way, but each must seek his own way to happiness in the way that suits him.'[39] You, dear Dessie, have helped point out the limits of the market as a source of happiness, but within the domain of goods and services, it has served us well. Happiness in other domains and the absence of happiness in the various kinds of mental anguish you portray are private matters."

Dessie now realized that for those focused on institutions instead of people, the word *private* was an available escape. Blocking this escape by putting people at the center of things was a larger task than he had thought. Still, there was Adam's valid point about the demand for the two goods he was promoting—for the kind of happiness that satisfied but was not popularly recognized and for human development—a point that might help to explain the tenacity of materialism.

The Demand for Nonmaterial Satisfaction

"Look," said Adam, reading Dessie's thoughts, "the normal—or even abnormal—person who gets a raise is pleased and is likely to decide she is doing the right thing and will do it again to get the same pleasure. She is, in your terms, a materialist, but that materialism is a set of values learned from experience. All right, it is a contingent reward, but that changes nothing: if an outcome is pleasing, it will be sought again. You cannot change that sequence of reinforcement and repetition, nor would you want to, for it is, almost by definition, rational."

"In the short term, the drug addict, alcoholic, and compulsive gambler are rational," said Dessie with an air of dismissal. "Of course you are right about the short term. But the many, many studies I have been citing over spinach pies these last eight weeks show that for most people in rich societies, higher *levels* of income fail to yield higher levels of happiness or life satisfaction. The new point here is that materialism is reinforced because of people's failure to distinguish between the short and long term. Pursuit of short-term pleasure at the cost of longer-term happiness is a classic trap. The trap is built into our investment institutions[40] and, indeed, may be an American cultural symptom.[41] I think it helps to explain why people do not learn that materialism is a dead-end route to long-term happiness. And it comes close to answering Schumpeter's argument about the superiority of markets over politics."[42] Dessie sighed.

"As I said in Spanakopita 6, people do learn from experience; we do not expect revelation but rather a slow accommodation to reality. Well, I take your point that short-term gains impede learning and working toward longer-term advantages, but"—here Adam hesitated—"usually there are aids to learning about the longer term available from other sources." He first blanched and then blushed as he realized how many nonmarket influences he was inviting into the arena.

Dessie crowed. "Fine," he said, "So you and I have a mission: We must supplement the market's short-term teaching on utility with our vision of nonmarket and longer-term gains in happiness." He hoped to enlist, or at least embarrass, Adam by including him among the missionaries.

"I'm an economist," said Adam in the belief that that would excuse him from any missionary service.

"Further," continued Dessie in his explanation of why materialism persisted in the face of its disappointing yield in life satisfaction. "The problem for the nonmaterialist is not just his difference from the multitude in the matter of taste, for he also differs in the matter of institutions to serve that taste: he must go outside the market for his satisfactions. Foster homes have never been very satisfactory, but the 'most noble and sensitive characters' of which Knight speaks must, in this culture, find some 'foster home' (such as a church or reading group) for their satisfaction. This required shift in institutions will filter out as many people as does the shift in taste and will accordingly reduce the 'demand' for nonmaterial satisfaction."

"Anyone who prefers a church or concert to a shopping mall is free to go there," said Adam. "What's the problem?"

"Sorry, I just wanted to point out the sources for a lack of demand for nonmaterial satisfaction," said Dessie. "But if I may, I would like to point out again a problem economics has imposed on itself in its analysis of this shift in values. Because of your change from the conception of utility as happiness to the conception of utility as preference satisfaction, you do not know what to do when the things that once made people happy change but preferences do not. Unless 'rational choice' implies perfect knowledge of one's own soul—or should I say tastes?—it is an obstacle to clear thinking."

"Okay, you made that point earlier," said Adam in a surly tone. "So I can repeat my question: if *you* know that human development is a good thing, but the poor humans whom you want to develop do not know this or even don't want it, how can we make this trip to utopia on which you have set your heart?"

The Demand for Human Development

"Demand," said Dessie thoughtfully, "is an ambiguous concept: for you guys, effective demand means money-backed action in the market; for politicians it may mean a petition from organized groups. But with reference to human development, it might mean a very private priority of values, will, and action. You might test it first by what people say they want and then by whether their beliefs about their development are related to an overall index of life satisfaction. By those tests, people do want to develop themselves, and their satisfaction with their progress in that respect does affect their happiness. At least Andrews and Withey found that positive responses to such questions as those dealing with the 'extent to which you can adjust to changes in your life' did influence their happiness and were second in weight only to a sense of achievement. More significantly, these authors' measure of how well people thought they were doing to 'develop and broaden' themselves also ranked fairly high in its contribution to happiness—fifth among thirteen relevant concerns.[43] Other quality-of-life studies support these findings.[44] Does the fact that people are sufficiently concerned about their growth and development to affect their happiness imply an articulate public demand for help? No. Of course not. Concern for personal development is one of the fairly large number of important things that cannot easily be either marketized or politicized."

"There is the prior question of whether satisfaction with one's development is a cause or an effect of happiness," said Adam sharply. "In Spanakopita 5, you told me that happiness contributes to self-esteem and hence it might well contribute to satisfaction with one's development." Adam paused for a moment and his face lit up. " 'Top down,' that's what you called it when overall mood influences the interpretation of experience rather than vice versa."[45]

"I was only exploring your question of whether there was any reason to believe that people actually *wanted* to develop themselves," said

Dessie quietly. "They do, but not the way Kant and Mill would have them develop: they don't usually want to be unique or individualized in any way; rather, they want mostly to be like other people.[46] These wants are largely unconscious as well as private, partly because the individualistic culture stifles such heterodox views." He thought for a moment of monasteries, self-help movements, Yale senior societies, and Alcoholics Anonymous and added, "But if a culture licensed such conscious efforts at self-improvement, they could be both public and socially reinforced. Those aspects of culture that could do this, however, are subordinated by interests profiting from materialism, interests so powerful and so prevalent that their appeals (and those of economists) seem to be 'natural.'"

To get back to the point, Adam asked, "Is there any evidence that people actually *act* on their desire to improve themselves—or their dependents, for that matter?"

Dessie looked sad. "Materialism's agent, the market, inhibits the desire for human development in a special way," he said with some passion. "Self-development implies the creative use of leisure, but a student of changes in use of leisure time reports first that the use of any increment of leisure time tends to be devoted to watching television, whether or not people liked the programs; second, he says, 'Rather than marked increase in self-growth and personally expressive leisure activities (such as participation in the creative arts, culture, education, or physical fitness), we find instead increased time being spent in sleep, in resting, in personal care, and in automobile travel.'[47] In that sense, I am sorry to say, there is very little effective demand."

"Thank God for the 'Overworked American,'"[48] said Adam, only half in jest.

"Do people care about the development of others?" asked Dessie rhetorically. "Of course they do. The faults of others is the stuff of gossip, which is universal, but we have no measure of changes in the nature or frequency of gossip. Nevertheless, our fellow compatriots' concern about the 'American character' seems unusually high. Asking 'What are the ways the country is getting worse or better?' an early, major study of the quality of life in the United States found that almost five times as many people thought that the 'behavior and attitudes of individuals' were getting worse than thought they were getting better (52 percent to 11 percent). People were more concerned about other Americans' character than about inflation, unemployment, corruption, crime, and all other possible sources of concern."[49]

"And do people do anything about that concern aside from complaining to their neighbors and the pollsters?" asked Adam skeptically.

"Not much, but something," said Dessie. "For one thing, people expect the schools to undertake character education, and over the thirty-four-year period from 1960 to 1994, the United States quadrupled its expenditure (in constant dollars) on education, reducing the teacher-pupil ratio by about a third."

"How about their concern for the development of others in their care?" asked Adam, adding, "That's probably a better test."

"If the value of human development were salient," said Dessie mournfully, "we would not see the 'tremendous erosion of the role of parents in the lives of children.'"[50] And adding a comment barbed for Adam, he continued, "In market societies, family integration has declined, partly, at least, because of the claims of market work on both parents."[51]

"Like the perpetual rising middle class, the family has been perpetually declining," said Adam with a show of erudition. "In 1897 Durkheim observed that 'family integration and solidarity were decreasing, thus weakening the family's power to maintain personalities and prevent anomie.'[52] But I will not challenge the obvious acceleration of that decline since World War II. Can you be surprised that materialism is tenacious when the alternative that you're advocating—family life and companionship—has only inarticulate support, if that?" Adam thought for a minute and suddenly realized the oddity of the discussion about the causes for the apparent triumph of materialism: except for Dessie's last barbed sentence, it had dealt mainly with individual attitudes and values. "I think you've taken your agenda of putting people at the center of things a bit too far," he said. "For better or worse, haven't the family, religion, communities, and the market itself played a large part in materialism's failure to decline?"

The Failure of Institutional Support

Dessie forbore the usual, "I'm glad you asked that question" and plunged into his text.

The Failure of the Market to Prepare for Humanism

"It seems churlish to say so," he said, "but the market delivered only half of what Inglehart and others thought was a sufficient basis for post-materialism: it provided affluence but not security. In a period of rising prosperity (1994), Robert Reich reported on the 'anxious class,' 'consisting of those Americans who no longer can count on having their jobs next year, or next month, and whose wages have stagnated or lost ground to inflation.' At the same time, Harris polls reported, 'Over and over people tell us they are concerned about their jobs, that they don't feel secure, that the economy is doing badly.'"[53] Affluence, the part of welfare that the market measures, may in fact be less important than security, which is unmeasured and almost a market externality. In one study (1993), people reported that security was the most important aspect of the money they sought, more important than either the freedom or pleasure that money yields."[54]

"I think I hear you saying that when utopia—that is, an economy that is at the same time dynamic and offers security to all—has come, then utopia will indeed be here," said Adam, amused at his own wit.

"Humanism or postmaterialism has many noneconomic sources," continued Dessie. "It's a question of weight. Although Inglehart acknowledges the problem of insecurity,[55] he slights it in favor of affluence. As I mentioned, Scarborough found that education could account for most of the variance in postmaterialism; although a declining force outside the United States, religious preferences still account better than do economic variables for some of the British salient postmodern attitudes.[56] Finally, some U.S. research finds that such family features as market work by mothers and high father absence are important causes of materialism.[57] Materialism's tenacity in the face of its failure to yield happiness must be traced not only to the market's failure to provide economic security but also to the failure of religion, the family, and communities to provide alternative satisfactions. After all, compared to the market, they are older and more reliable sources of value and meaning and, yes, life satisfaction."

"I think you're on the right track at last," said Adam with relief. "It was silly of you to think that because material striving would succeed, it would fail in its mission of social progress! That defies both common sense and, as I understand it, learning theory, which says that if behavior is reinforced, it will be repeated. But the failure of families and religion to provide satisfaction—utility, in that sense—might well drive people into a more intensive search for material satisfaction, though I would resist any theory of materialism as primarily compensatory for failed love or faith or anything like that."[58]

The Religious Contribution

"Materialism competes with other loyalties and values," said Dessie. "If these competing values or the institutions that foster them decline, then, in a kind of hydraulic fashion, materialism will prosper. That is what has happened in at least three crucial ways. First, in spite of the Protestant ethic, in the United States and Europe commitment to religion weakens materialism.[59] And over the long term, religious commitment has declined, even in the United States, leaving the field relatively more open to materialism. 'Religiosity is related to life satisfaction at all age levels but especially among the young and the over 65s.'[60] Moreover, economic insecurity and the decline of religion interact, for 'religion seems to play a significant role in adapting to adversity.'"[61] As a confirmed agnostic, Dessie found this alliance with religion in opposition to materialism a bit strange, but he reconciled the conflict by endorsing religious beliefs in the sacredness of human beings while rejecting the metaphysics of the supernatural.

"Strange bedfellows," said Adam, reading Dessie's thoughts and forgetting that Shakespeare had said that misery produced "strange bedfellows," whereas cheerful Dessie showed no signs of the misery he revealed at the beginning of this Spanakopita. "I think we are on familiar turf here, for the OED defines materialism as 'devotion to material needs and desires to the neglect of spiritual matters.' But aren't you going to say something about Sir Henry Maine's thesis that the movement 'from status to contract' was a move from family status to commercial relations?"

The Family Contribution

"Second, commitment to family life seems to impede materialism," said Dessie without a break. "That is, both market work for mothers and fathers' absence from the family encourage materialism in children."[62] The increase in market work by mothers of small children is well known (and often lamented),[63] and father absence is epidemic. In reverse, where family satisfaction is high, materialism is low. Cross-culturally, the Dieners found not only that wealthier nations were less materialistic than poor nations but that in those same richer nations 'family satisfaction was high and correlated with life satisfaction. . . . This set of findings,' report the authors, 'supports the idea of a postindustrial society in which attention turns from the acquisition of material goods to self-development and other pursuits.'"[64] Despite his gratitude, Dessie thought the inference a little premature. He felt more comfortable with a U.S. study that, as he told Adam, "showed that for adolescents 'their mother's materialism level and their mother's report of the family communication style alone could reliably predict her child's level of materialism.'[65] It is good news, however, that 'the higher the level of the mother's education, the less materialistic will she be,'"[66] continued Dessie, "for mothers are increasingly well educated."

"So (1) materialism declines with the increase in women's education and rises because of the disintegration of the family, and (2) materialism rises when religion declines—because religion is an alternative source of value—and materialism also rises when religious authority endorses materialism as in the Protestant ethic," said Adam. "No wonder Engels, Spencer, and Keynes got their prophecies wrong."

"The pattern makes sense: higher education for mothers introduces children to nonmaterial values at earlier ages; disintegration of the family (which is *more* likely when the mother is less well educated) creates the insecurity where materialism thrives; religiosity tends to offer a set of values alternative to those offered by materialism, but religiosity of this spiritual kind has nothing to do with the materialistic Protestant ethic that Weber thought was an origin of capitalism. ('Gain all you can. Save all you can. Give all you can.')[67] Engels and Keynes got their prophecies wrong because they paid no attention to the causal forces of noneconomic matters."

"And Spencer had to prove his special version of historical direction toward individualism," said Adam, helping to answer his own question.

The Community Contribution

"Along with the family and religion, communities have declined, this time because of the pressure of urbanization and the market," said Dessie. "As Tönnies, in response to Maine, made clear, community, or gemeinschaft, was once a major source of meaning and value but has lost its power to associations of contracting parties.[68] Polanyi also made this clear:

> The outstanding discovery of recent historical and anthropological research is that man's economy, as a rule, is submerged in his social relationships. He does not act so as to safeguard his individual interest in the possession of material goods; he acts so as to safeguard his social standing, his claims, his social assets. He values material goods only in so far as they serve [these] ends.[69]

In Polanyi's view, social standing and social assets are among the benefits that material goods buy. But communities also offer companionship and social support, ethical norms and social guidance. When communities decline, these other goods decline, and the fruits of materialism are left as the sole standard for social standing. If, as the evidence shows, the fruits of materialism are in themselves unsatisfying, people have lost some of their most treasured sources of well-being." Dessie saw that one link in his argument was missing and went on to point out that "both satisfaction with 'the place that you live in' and actual visiting with neighbors have substantially declined since World War II."[70]

"There you have it," said Adam, relieved that Dessie was not finding fault with the market.

"Not quite," said Dessie, wound up. "As you might expect from the evidence on the effects of insecurity on materialism, social violence and war are also associated with materialism.[71] Furthermore, the kind of social demoralization reflected in anomie (normlessness and cynicism) is congenial to materialism,[72] and some people think anomie has also risen in our time." Dessie paused and added, "Materialism has also been implicated in teenage suicide,[73] which has been rising in recent decades, though that rise has somewhat abated recently."

"Family, religion, community as alternatives to materialism," murmured Adam. "You are saying that when these institutions decline, materialism rises. To use your language, they are 'functional equivalents' of seeking satisfaction through the market." Adam seemed curiously lost in meditation on these subversive blows to the value of the market as *the* liberating and enriching force of civilization. With something like wistfulness, he asked, "Does that mean that your beloved humanism cannot arrive until family, religion, and community are restored?"

"Not quite," said Dessie, impressed by Adam's change in mood. "In my optimistic moments, I believe that the longing for better-integrated families, for the ethical messages of religion (which may travel piggyback on the longing for metaphysical reassurance—it can't be helped), and the palpable desire to restore some aspects of community will erode the materialist impulse. But scanning the social indicators offers little reassurance, nor does the belief that in the long run people will seek to maximize their utilities give me much hope, since this belief relies on choices made in darkness."

"From your point of view, that's pretty bleak," said Adam sympathetically. "In my profession, we tend to relieve such disappointments by talking about the 'long run'—or we did until Keynes scotched that phrase."

The Long Run

*T*hank you," responded Dessie more cheerfully. "In the long run, all cultural transitions are the products of conflicts among the mixed forces of a culture—in this case, of materialism and humanism. You saw that in the figures showing high school and college freshmen struggling to find the right balance between materialism and humanism. Give them time.

After all, Pitirim Sorokin found that in the oscillation between sensate and ideational themes the ideational was hardly challenged for twelve hundred years, from about 300 B.C. to about 1500 A.D.[74] And Sorokin's contesting themes were nowhere nearly as close to parity as the conflicting themes we saw in our data on American youth."

Adam thought of economic long-wave (Kondratief) cycles and, turning to the crucial question, asked, "So what causes a major cultural revolution when it does come?"

"As I mentioned in Spanakopita 5, I see an analogy with A. L. Kroeber's idea of long-term 'culture configurations,' like those marking the Babylonian, Grecian, and medieval Christian periods. Kroeber says that each such culture explores its own unique cultural theme until it is exhausted and repeated without innovation, making way for a different and novel theme.[75] The great outcry against the consumer culture suggests that it is being repeated too often and too insistently.[76] Time for the next step in a journey of a thousand miles."

Adam, who had thought of an idea that would exonerate the market and market economics, was back at Dessie again. "You know," he said, "there is more to cultural persistence than Kroeber's repetition of patterns you mentioned. Cultural persistence is the norm for good reasons. Whatever it is that makes a dominant culture successful also makes it resist change. And the greater the success, the more the resistance.[77] Moreover, if we changed our institutions and values every time a persuasive prophet came along, we would have even more unstable societies—and more posttraumatic stress disorder."

"The trajectory of progress is certainly not linear," said Dessie ruminatively, "and perhaps not curvilinear either. Perhaps, like the oligopoly curve, it is 'kinky.'" He laughed, but without much humor.

Time was getting short, so Adam turned to the heart of the matter. "You have two fairly persuasive but conflicting sets of data: one showing that increased income in rich countries does not increase happiness, the other showing that in these same rich countries people, especially the educated young, continue to pursue money as though their happiness depended on it. You cannot repeal the law of diminishing returns that governs the first set of data. Rather, the pair of findings suggests that people's subjective reality is different from one version of 'objective reality,' or at least the reality reflected in your data. You build your hopes for change on this so-called objective reality that most people do not see or share or believe in."

"That's the point," said Dessie with enthusiasm. "If you will excuse the term, we are *educators*, and it is our job to correct public misinterpretations of the social world. How can we spend our time better than exposing falsehood and presenting the versions of the truth that seem to us to be convincing. And if, in the process, we happen to make people happier and, well, perhaps"—he hesitated but then rushed ahead—"perhaps even 'better,' what greater calling is there?" He beamed his beatific smile at Adam and everyone else in the vicinity.

"Go to it," said Adam, adding "as long as we can afford it."

Dessie's smile faded. "Can we afford to send forth another generation of American children who are richer, fatter, and a little dumber than northern European and Japanese children?" he asked, his voice breaking.

Here Adam extended an olive branch over the spinach pie. "Dear Dessie," he said, "You made that point about vision eight weeks ago. Who knows? Some visions are true. Adam Smith, John Locke, and others have been here before you, and, well, the shadows of St. Paul and Muhammed put even your substantial, globular shadow in the shade. It is early June and the vacation sun is shining. I'll see you in September. That will be $8.75."

Notes

1. PROLOGUE

1. Francis Fukuyama, *The End of History and the Last Man* (New York: Free Press, 1992).

2. James F. Engel, Roger D. Blackwell, and David T. Kollat, *Consumer Behavior,* 3d ed. (Hinsdale, Ill.: Dryden Press, 1978), 3.

3. Stanley Diamond, *In Search of the Primitive* (New Brunswick, N.J.: Transaction Books, 1974), 11.

4. Erich Fromm, *The Revolution of Hope* (New York: Rinehart, 1968), 1, 28. Along lines similar to Dessie's, Fromm then advises a more "humanistic" form of consumption (120). For a rejoinder to this and other criticisms of consumption, see George Katona, *Psychological Economics* (New York: Elsevier, 1975), 376.

5. Alexis de Tocqueville, *Democracy in America,* ed. Phillips Bradley (1840; New York: Knopf, 1945), 2:136–37.

6. Jean-Paul Sartre, *Existentialism and Human Emotion* (New York: Wisdom Library, 1957).

7. Burt Alpert, *Inversions: A Study of Warped Consciousness* (Ann Arbor, Mich.: Edwards Brothers, 1973), 1–2.

8. Solomon Fabricant, "Productivity and Economic Growth," in *Technology and Social Change,* ed. Eli Ginzberg (New York: Columbia University Press, 1964),108–20.

9. Fukuyama, *End of History,* 349.

10. Karl Marx, *Grundrisse: Introduction to the Critique of Political Economy,* trans. M. Nicolaus (1859; Harmondsworth: Penguin, 1973).

11. Bruce Mazlish, *The Meaning of Karl Marx* (New York: Oxford University Press, 1984), 25.

12. See Bruno S. Frey and Alois Stutzer, *Happiness and Economics: How the Economy and Institutions Affect Well-Being* (Princeton: Princeton University Press, 2002).

13. David A. Crocker and Toby Linden, eds., *Ethics of Consumption: The Good Life, Justice, and Global Stewardship* (Lanham, Md.: Rowman and Littlefield, 1997). See also publications of the Global Development and Environment Institute at Tufts University, the International Society for Quality of Life Studies, the Karl Polanyi Institute of Political Economy, and the Center for a New American Dream and such periodicals as the *Journal of Macromarketing* and *Socio-Economic Review.*

14. "If I have ever seen further, it is by standing on the shoulders of giants" (Isaac Newton to Robert Hooke, February 3, 1675).

15. Vaclav Havel, "The End of the Modern Era," *New York Times,* March 1, 1992, E15.

16. Donella H. Meadows, Dennis L. Meadows, Jørgen Randers, and William W. Behrens III, *The Limits to Growth* (New York: Potomac/Earth Island, 1972).

17. R. F. Fortune, *The Sorcerers of Dobu: The Social Anthropology of the Dobu Islanders of the Western Pacific,* rev. ed. (London: Routledge and Kegan Paul, 1963).

18. For example, among the Manus, the system of debt imposed on newly marrieds was onerous for a lifetime, and the system was maintained by elders who profited from their juniors' debts (Margaret Mead, *New Lives for Old* [New York: Morrow, 1956]).

19. E. R. Dodds, *The Greeks and the Irrational* (Boston: Beacon, 1957); Edward Gibbon, *History of the Decline and Fall of the Roman Empire* (New York: Harcourt, Brace, 1960); Archie Brown, ed., *Contemporary Russian Politics: A Reader* (Oxford: Oxford University Press, 2001).

20. United Nations Development Programme, *Human Development Report 1998* (New York: Oxford University Press, 1998).

21. Frank M. Andrews and Stephen B. Withey, *Social Indicators of Well-Being: Americans' Perceptions of Life Quality* (New York: Plenum, 1976); Angus Campbell, Philip E. Converse, and Willard L. Rodgers, *The Quality of American Life: Perceptions, Evaluations, and Satisfactions* (New York: Russell Sage, 1976); Ed Diener and E. M. Suh, eds., *Culture and Subjective Well-Being* (Cambridge: MIT Press, 2000); Ruut Veenhoven, *Happiness in Nations: Subjective Appreciation of Life in 56 Nations, 1946–1992* (Rotterdam: Erasmus University, RISBO Press, 1993).

22. Tibor Scitovsky, *The Joyless Economy: An Inquiry into Human Satisfaction and Consumer Dissatisfaction* (New York: Oxford University Press, 1977).

23. Adam Smith, *An Inquiry into the Nature and Causes of the Wealth of Nations,* ed. Edwin Cannan (1776; New York: Modern Library/Random House, 1937), 14.

24. Daniel Bell, *The Coming of Post-Industrial Society* (New York: Basic Books, 1973).

25. Ronald Inglehart, *The Silent Revolution* (Princeton: Princeton University Press, 1972).

26. Ronald Inglehart, *Modernization and Postmodernization: Cultural, Economic, and Political Change in Forty-three Societies* (Princeton: Princeton University Press, 1997).

27. Fukuyama, *End of History.*

28. Ed Diener and Robert Biswas-Diener, "Will Money Increase Subjective Well-Being? A Literature Review and Guide to Needed Research," *Social Indicators Research* 57 (2002): 161–62.

29. Robert E. Lane, *The Loss of Happiness in Market Democracies* (New Haven: Yale University Press, 2000).

30. Inglehart, *Silent Revolution;* Ronald Inglehart, *Culture Shift in Advanced Industrial Society* (Princeton: Princeton University Press, 1990).

31. John Maynard Keynes, "Economic Possibilities for Our Grandchildren," in *Essays in Persuasion,* vol. 9 of *Collected Works of John Maynard Keynes* (1930; London: Macmillan for the Royal Economic Society, 1972), 321–34.

32. Bell, *Coming of Post-Industrial Society,* 20.

33. Kenneth Boulding, *The Image* (Ann Arbor: University of Michigan Press, 1956), 82.

34. Robert E. Lane, "Self-Reliance and Empathy: The Enemies of Poverty—and of the Poor," *Political Psychology* 22 (2001): 473–92.

35. Theodore W. Schultz, *Investing in People: The Economics of Population Quality* (Berkeley: University of California Press, 1981).

36. Amartya Sen, *Development as Freedom* (New York: Knopf, 1999).

37. Inglehart, *Modernization and Postmodernization.*

38. United Nations Development Programme, *Human Development Report 1998.*

39. Sigmund Freud, *Civilization and Its Discontents,* trans. J. Riviere (London: Hogarth, 1951), 144.

40. Immanuel Kant, *Fundamental Principles of the Metaphysic of Morals,* trans. T. K. Abbott (Indianapolis: Bobbs-Merrill, 1949).

41. Keynes, "Economic Possibilities for Our Grandchildren," 332.

42. See Melvin J. Lerner, *The Belief in a Just World: A Fundamental Delusion* (New York: Plenum, 1980).

43. Lee Ross calls this dispositional attribution "the 'fundamental attribution error'"; see his "The Intuitive Psychologist and His Shortcomings," in *Advances in Experimental Psychology,* ed. L. Berkowitz (New York: Academic Press, 1977), 10:173–220.

44. Max Weber, *The Protestant Ethic and the Spirit of Capitalism* (articles first published 1904–6), trans. T. Parsons (New York: Scribner's, 1958), 182.

45. Marsha L. Richins and Scott Dawson, "A Consumer Values Orientation for Materialism and Its Measurement: Scale Development and Validation," *Journal of Consumer Research* 19 (1992): 304.

46. Arthur C. Pigou, *The Economics of Welfare,* 4th ed. (1932; London: Macmillan, 1948), xi.

47. Perez Zagorin, "On Humanism Past and Present," *Daedalus* 132 (2003): 87.

48. Lewis Austin, *Saints and Samurai* (New Haven: Yale University Press, 1975).

49. John Kenneth Galbraith, *The Affluent Society* (1958; Harmondsworth:

190   Penguin, 1970), 279, citing Bertrand Russell, *The Conquest of Happiness* (London: Allen and Unwin, 1930), 248.

50. Galbraith, *Affluent Society,* 279.

51. Avner Ben-Ner, "Changing Values and Preferences in Communal Organizations: Economic Evidence from the Experience of the Israeli Kibbutz," in *Participatory and Self-Managed Firms: Evaluating Economic Performance,* ed. D. Jones and J. Svejnar (Lexington, Mass.: Lexington/Heath, 1982).

52. Keynes, "Economic Possibilities for Our Grandchildren," 332.

53. Karl Polanyi, *The Great Transformation* (New York: Rinehart, 1944).

54. T. S. Ashton, *The Industrial Revolution, 1760–1830* (London: Oxford University Press, 1948).

55. Ann M. Beutel and Margaret Mooney Marini, "Gender and Values," *American Sociological Review* 60 (1995): 436–48; Wendy M. Rahn and John E. Transue, "Social Trust and Value Change: The Decline of Social Capital in American Youth, 1976–1995," *Political Psychology* 19 (1998): 559, 560.

56. Floyd W. Rudmin, "German and Canadian Data on Motivations for Ownership: Was Pythagoras Right?" *Advances in Consumer Research* 17 (1990): 176–81.

2. WHAT SHOULD WE BE DOING?

1. Charles Stevenson, *Facts and Values: Studies in Ethical Analysis* (New Haven: Yale University Press, 1963).

2. Charles E. Osgood, G. J. Suci, and P. H. Tannenbaum, *The Measurement of Meaning* (Urbana: University of Illinois Press, 1957).

3. Robert B. Zajonc, "Feeling and Thinking: Preferences Need No Inferences," *American Psychologist* 35 (1980): 151–75. A later and fuller treatment of this problem of two models of judgment is available in Daniel Kahneman, "A Perspective on Judgment and Choice: Mapping Bounded Rationality," *American Psychologist* 58 (2003): 697–720.

4. Marie Jahoda points out that even the commonplace idea of mental health implied "that [certain] psychological attributes are 'good.'" But she goes on to ask, "Good for what? Good in terms of middle class ethics? Good for democracy? For the *status quo?* For the individual's happiness?" and so forth (*Current Concepts of Positive Mental Health* [New York: Basic Books, 1958], 77).

5. Tjalling C. Koopmans, *Three Essays on the State of Economic Science* (New York: McGraw-Hill, 1957), 169.

6. Roy Harrod, *Sociology, Morals, and Mystery* (London: Macmillan, 1971), 64.

7. Dean Keith Simonton, *Genius, Creativity, and Leadership: Historiometric Inquiries* (Cambridge: Harvard University Press, 1984), 141.

8. I. M. D. Little, *A Critique of Welfare Economics,* 2d ed. (Oxford: Oxford University Press, 1957).

9. See Baruch Fischoff, "Value Elicitation: Is There Anything There?" in *The Origin of Values,* ed. Michael Hechter, Lynn Nadel, and Richard E. Michod (New York: Aldine de Gruyter, 1993), 187–214; Gregory R. Maio and James M. Olson, "Values as Truisms: Evidence and Implications," *Journal of Personality and Social Psychology* 74 (1998): 294–311.

10. Engel, Blackwell, and Kollat, *Consumer Behavior,* 592.

11. Little, *Critique of Welfare Economics,* 31.

12. Kent C. Berridge, "Pleasure, Pain, Desire, and Dread: Hidden Core Processes of Emotion," in *Well-Being: The Foundations of Hedonic Psychology,* ed. Daniel Kahneman, Ed Diener, and Norbert Schwarz (New York: Russell Sage Foundation, 1999), 525–56. Other relevant experiments reported in this account are based on work done by Daniel Kahneman; see Kahneman and Carol Varey, "Notes on the Psychology of Utility," in *Interpersonal Comparisons of Well-Being,* ed. Jon Elster and John H. Roemer (New York: Cambridge University Press, 1991), 127–63.

13. Desiderius Erasmus, *In Praise of Folly and Letter to Martin Dorp* (1515), trans. Betty Radice (Harmondsworth: Penguin, 1971), 204.

14. "Think where man's glory most begins and ends, / And say my glory was I had such friends" W. B. Yeats, "The Municipal Gallery Revisited, ll. 54–55, in *Variorum Edition of Poems of W. B. Yeats,* edited by Peter Allt and Russell K. Alspach (New York: Macmillan, 1957).

15. "Enjoyment of beauty—aesthetic, puts us beyond many troubles. . . . Its derivation from the realms of sexual sensation is all that seems certain" (Freud, *Civilization and Its Discontents,* 39).

16. Karl Marx and Friedrich Engels, *Manifesto of the Communist Party* (1848; New York: International, 1932), 31.

17. Margaret J. Radin, "Justice and the Market Domain," in *Markets and Justice: Nomos XXXI,* ed. John W. Chapman and J. Roland Pennock (New York: New York University Press, 1989), 165–97.

18. Martha C. Nussbaum, "Human Functioning and Social Justice: In Defense of Aristotelian Essentialism," *Political Theory* 20 (1992): 202–46.

19. Albert O. Hirschman, "Rival Interpretations of Market Society: Civilizing, Destructive, or Feeble?" *Journal of Economic Literature* 20 (1982): 1463–84.

20. Fischoff, "Value Elicitation."

21. Joseph A. Schumpeter, *Capitalism, Socialism, and Democracy,* 3d ed. (London: Allen and Unwin, 1950), 123.

22. Abraham H. Maslow, *Motivation and Personality,* 2d ed. (New York: Harper and Row, 1970), 35.

23. Alfred Marshall, *Principles of Economics,* 8th ed. (London: Macmillan, 1938), 16–17; emphasis added.

24. Ludwig von Mises, *Epistemological Problems of Economics,* trans. G. Reisman (Princeton: Van Nostrand, 1960), 61.

25. Koopmans, *Three Essays,* 169.

26. Milton Friedman, *Capitalism and Freedom* (Chicago: University of Chicago Press, 1962), 9.

27. Quoted in Robert L. Heilbroner, *The Nature and Logic of Capitalism* (New York: Norton, 1986), 109.

28. Cited in Ernest van den Haag, *Capitalism: Sources of Hostility* (New Rochelle, N.Y.: Epoch/Heritage, 1979).

29. Erik Erikson, "The Golden Rule and the Cycle of Life," in *The Study of Lives: Essays on Personality in Honor of Henry A. Murray,* ed. Robert White (New York: Atherton, 1963), 422–23.

30. Mark R. Lepper and David Greene, eds., *The Hidden Costs of Rewards:*

192   *New Perspectives on the Psychology of Human Motivation* (Hillsdale, N.J.: Wiley/Erlbaum, 1978).

31. E. L. Deci and R. M. Ryan, *Intrinsic Motivation and Self-Determination in Human Behavior* (New York: Plenum, 1985).

32. Osgood, Suci, and Tannenbaum, *Measurement of Meaning.*

33. Zajonc, "Feeling and Thinking."

34. Melvin J. Lerner, "The Justice Motive in Human Relations," in *The Justice Motive in Social Behavior: Adapting to Times of Scarcity and Change,* ed. Melvin J. Lerner and Sally C. Lerner (New York: Plenum, 1981), 20.

35. P. W. Bridgman, "Operational Analysis," *Philosophy of Science* 5 (1938): 114–31.

36. W. David Ross, *The Right and the Good* (Oxford: Clarendon, 1930), 140–41.

37. Paul A. Samuelson and William D. Nordhaus, *Economics,* 12th ed. (New York: McGraw-Hill, 1985), 24.

38. Charles Fried, *The Anatomy of Values* (Cambridge: Harvard University Press, 1970).

39. Icek Ajzen and Martin Fishbein, *Understanding Attitudes and Predicting Social Behavior* (Englewood Cliffs, N.J.: Prentice-Hall, 1980).

40. George J. Stigler and Gary S. Becker, "De Gustibus Non Est Disputandum," *American Economic Review* 67 (1977): 76–90.

41. Kenneth Boulding, "Economics as a Moral Science," *American Economic Review* 59 (1969): 4. Preferences are considered "outside the purview of economists' analytical apparatus" (Martha S. Hill and F. Thomas Juster, "Constraints and Complementarities in Time Use," in *Time, Goods, and Well-Being,* ed. F. Thomas Juster and Frank Stafford [Ann Arbor: Institute for Social Research of the University of Michigan, 1985], 443).

42. See, e.g., Immanuel Kant. "What Is Enlightenment?" in *The Enlightenment,* ed. Peter Gay (New York: Simon and Schuster, 1973), 385.

43. Stuart Hampshire, *Freedom of the Individual,* rev. ed. (Princeton: Princeton University Press, 1975).

44. Isaiah Berlin, "Two Concepts of Liberty," in Berlin, *Four Essays on Liberty* (London: Oxford University Press, 1969), 138.

45. In addition to H. Simon, "A Behavioral Model of Rational Choice," *Quarterly Journal of Economics* 69 (1955): 99–118; repr., Simon, *Models of Bounded Rationality* (Cambridge: MIT Press, 1982), vol. 2, chap. 7.2, see S. E. Taylor, "The Interface of Cognitive and Social Psychology," in *Cognition, Social Behavior, and the Environment,* ed. J. H. Harvey (Hillsdale, N.J.: Erlbaum, 1981).

46. Jonathan D. Brown and Keith A. Dutton, "Truth and Consequences: The Costs and Benefits of Accurate Self-Knowledge," *Personality and Social Psychology Bulletin* 21 (1995): 1288–96. Access to feelings varies among cultures as well as among individuals (R. W. Levenson, P. Ekman, K. Heider, and W. V. Friesen, "Emotion and Autonomic Nervous System Activity in the Minangkabau of West Sumatra," *Journal of Personality and Social Psychology* 62 [1992]: 977–88).

47. Daryl J. Bem, "Self-Perception Theory," in *Advances in Experimental Social Psychology,* ed. Berkowitz, 6:1–62.

48. Karl-Erik Wärneryd, "Social Influence on Economic Behavior," in

Handbook of Economic Psychology, ed. W. Fred van Raaij, Gery M. Van Veldhoven, and Karl-Erik Wärneryd (Dordrecht: Kluwer, 1988), 207–48.

49. John Kenneth Galbraith, *The New Industrial State,* 2d ed. (New York: New American Library/Mentor, 1972); see also Neil Fligstein, *The Transformation of Corporate Control* (Cambridge: Harvard University Press, 1990).

50. Daryl J. Bem and David C. Funder, "Predicting More of the People More of the Time: Assessing the Personality of Situations," *Psychological Review* 85 (1978): 485–501. This statement by Adam surprised Dessie because he knew that analysis of variance was not the economist's preferred mode of analysis.

51. Milton Rokeach, *The Nature of Human Values* (New York: Free Press, 1973).

52. Harry G. Frankfurt, "Freedom of the Will and the Concept of a Person," *Journal of Philosophy* 68 (1971): 5–20.

53. Klaus R. Scherer, Herald G. Walbott, and Angela B. Summerfield, eds., *Experiencing Emotion: A Cross-Cultural Study* (Cambridge: Cambridge University Press, 1986).

54. R. E. Pitts and A. G. Woodside, eds., *Personal Values and Consumer Psychology* (Lexington, Mass.: Heath, 1984).

55. Hechter, Nadel, and Michod, *Origin of Values.*

56. Susan Moller Okin, *Women in Western Political Thought* (Princeton: Princeton University Press, 1979); Alison M. Jaggar, *Feminist Politics and Human Nature* (Totowa, N.J.: Rowman and Allenheld, 1983).

57. Lewis A. Coser, *Greedy Institutions* (New York: Free Press, 1974).

58. Polanyi, *Great Transformation.*

59. Here Adam is referring to points made by Robert E. Lane, "Moral Blame and Causal Explanation," *Journal of Applied Philosophy* 17 (2000): 45–58.

60. Margaret J. Lundberg, *The Incomplete Adult: Social Class Constraints on Personality Development* (Westport, Conn.: Greenwood, 1974).

61. Herbert A. Simon, "The Architecture of Complexity," in *General Systems,* ed. L. Bertalanffy and A. Rapoport (Ann Arbor, Mich.: Society for General Systems Research, 1965), 10:63–76.

62. In Spanakopita 9, "After the End of History."

63. Martin E. P. Seligman, *Helplessness: On Depression, Development, and Death* (San Francisco: Freeman, 1973).

64. Jean Piaget and Barbara Inhelder, *The Psychology of the Child,* trans. H. Weaver (1966; New York: Basic Books, 1969).

65. Herbert M. Lefcourt, *Locus of Control: Current Trends in Theory and Research* (Hillsdale, N.J.: Erlbaum/Wiley, 1976). See also Spanakopita 6.

66. Lee Ross, "Intuitive Psychologist and His Shortcomings," 174–220.

67. Ellen J. Langer, *The Psychology of Control* (Beverly Hills, Calif.: Sage, 1983).

68. W. E. Henley, "Invictus" (1888), in *Modern British Poetry,* ed. Louis Untermeyer (New York: Harcourt, Brace, and Howe, 1920).

69. Lerner, *Belief in a Just World.*

3. WHAT'S WRONG WITH MATERIALISM?

1. See Frederick A. Lange, *The History of Materialism,* trans. E. C. Thomas, 3d ed. (1865; London: Routledge and Kegan Paul, 1925).

2. Tom Bottomore, ed., *A Dictionary of Marxist Thought* (Cambridge: Harvard University Press, 1983), 402.

3. Edward O. Wilson, *Sociobiology: The New Synthesis* (Cambridge: Harvard University Press, 1975); Edward O. Wilson, *Consilience: The Unity of Knowledge* (Boston: Little, Brown, 1998).

4. Karl Marx and Friedrich Engels, *Manifesto of the Communist Party* (1848), repr., *Essential Works of Marxism,* ed. Arthur P. Mendel (New York: Bantam, 1963), 31.

5. John R. Hicks, *A Theory of Economic History* (Oxford: Oxford University Press, 1959).

6. Joseph A. Schumpeter, *History of Economic Analysis,* ed. Elizabeth Boody Schumpeter (New York: Oxford University Press, 1954), 124.

7. Eugene Kamenka, lecture on Marxism, Australian National University, Canberra, March 6, 1985.

8. Karl Marx, "The German Ideology," in *Marx and Engels: Basic Writings on Economics and Politics,* ed. Lewis Feuer (New York: Doubleday/Anchor, 1959), 247.

9. Of an enormous literature on consumerism, covered in half a dozen journals, Robert Lane summarizes a small part in "The Road Not Taken: Friendship, Consumerism, and Happiness," in *Ethics of Consumption,* ed. Crocker and Linden, 218–48.

10. See discussion of effect of working with things in Melvin L. Kohn and Carmi Schooler, *Work and Personality: An Inquiry into the Impact of Social Stratification* (Norwood, N.J.: Ablex, 1983), 64. Focus on things of course influences consumption as well. Certain kinds of nonmaterialists spend on experiences rather than on things (Miriam Tatzel, "Money Dispositions, Material Values, and Price-Related Behavior: An Integration" [unpublished paper, State University of New York, 2001]). Similarly, Russell Belk and associates have found that some kinds of materialists must "make experiences tangible through souvenirs and photographs" (Guliz Ger and Russell W. Belk, "Cross-Cultural Differences in Materialism," *Journal of Economic Psychology* 17 [1996]: 55).

11. Mihalyi Csikszentmihalyi and Eugene Rochberg-Hilton, *The Meaning of Things: Domestic Symbols and the Self* (New York: Cambridge University Press, 1981).

12. Russell W. Belk, "Attachment to Possessions," *Human Behavior and Environment: Advances in Theory and Research* 12 (1992): 37–62.

13. Richins and Dawson, "Consumer Values Orientation," 308–9. Attitudes toward money also make a difference. Those who are "loose with money" and nonmaterialistic spend on experiences rather than on things and seem to be mentally healthier than others (Tatzell, "Money Dispositions").

14. Russell W. Belk, "Materialism: Trait Aspects of Living in a Material World," *Journal of Consumer Research* 12 (1985): 265–80.

15. Aaron C. Ahuvia and Nancy Wong, *Three Types of Materialism: Their Relationship and Origins,* working paper (Ann Arbor: University of Michigan Business School, 1998).

16. See Maslow, *Motivation and Personality.*

17. F. de Saussure, *Cours de linguistique generale* (Paris: Payot, 1971).

18. Susan Fournier and Marsha L. Richins, "Some Theoretical and Popular

Notions Concerning Materialism," *Journal of Social Behavior and Personality* 6 (1991): 403.

19. Richins and Dawson, "Consumer Values Orientation," 312–13.

20. Belk, "Materialism."

21. Richins and Dawson, "Consumer Values Orientation," 304, 308.

22. Ibid., 311.

23. Emile Durkheim, *Suicide,* trans. J. A. Spaulding and G. Simpson (1897; Glencoe, Ill.: Free Press, 1951), 256.

24. Richins and Dawson, "Consumer Values Orientation," 308.

25. R. H. Frank, *Luxury Fever: Why Money Fails to Satisfy in an Era of Excess* (New York: Free Press, 1999).

26. Richins and Dawson, "Consumer Values Orientation," 313. But materialists are not less happy than nonmaterialists in Singapore (Kau Ah Keng, Kwon Jung, Tan Soo Jiuan, and Jochen Wirtz, "The Influence of Materialistic Inclinations on Values, Life Satisfaction, and Aspirations: An Empirical Analysis," *Social Indicators Research* 49 [2000]: 317–33).

27. "In a sample of adult subjects (Study 1), the relative importance and efficacy of extrinsic aspirations for financial success, an appealing appearance, and social recognition were associated with lower vitality and self-actualization and more physical symptoms" (Tim Kasser and Richard Ryan, "Further Examining the American Dream: Differential Correlates of Intrinsic and Extrinsic Goals," *Personality and Social Psychology Bulletin* 22 [1996]: 280).

28. Diener and Biswas-Diener, "Will Money Increase Subjective Well-Being?" 119–69.

29. Newell D. Wright and Val Larsen, "Materialism and Life Satisfaction: A Meta-Analysis," *Journal of Consumer Satisfaction, Dissatisfaction, and Complaining Behavior* 6 (1993): 158–65.

30. Abhishek Srivastava, Edwin A. Locke, and Kathryn M. Bartol, "Money and Subjective Well-Being: It's Not the Money, It's the Motive," *Journal of Personality and Social Psychology* 80 (2001): 959–71.

31. Frank Knight, *The Ethics of Competition and Other Essays* (New York: Kelley, 1935), 66.

32. Ed Diener, Marissa Diener, and Carol Diener, "Factors Predicting the Subjective Well-Being of Nations," *Journal of Personality and Social Psychology* 69 (1995): 860.

33. Tim Kasser and Richard M. Ryan, "A Dark Side of the American Dream: Correlates of Financial Success as a Central Life Aspiration," *Journal of Personality and Social Psychology* 65 (1993): 417, 419; Tim Kasser, *The High Price of Materialism* (Cambridge: MIT Press, 2002).

34. Leo Srole, "Social Integration and Certain Corollaries," *American Sociological Review* 21 (1956): 709–16.

35. Joseph A. Schumpeter, *The Theory of Economic Development: An Inquiry into Profits, Capital, Credits, Interest, and the Business Cycle,* trans. R. Opie, 2d ed. (1911; Cambridge: Harvard University Press, 1936).

36. Robert W. White, "Exploring the Origins of Competence," *APA Monitor,* April 1976, 40–45.

37. Jane Loevinger, *Ego Development* (San Francisco: Jossey-Bass, 1976).

38. Tocqueville, *Democracy in America,* 2:129; emphasis added.

39. "When . . . social conditions differ but little, the slightest privileges are of some importance; as every man sees around himself a million people enjoying precisely similar or analogous advantages, his pride becomes craving and jealous, he clings to mere trifles and doggedly defends them" (ibid., 226).

40. Robert E. Lane, "The Fear of Equality," *American Political Science Review* 53 (1959): 35–51.

41. Thomas Ashby Wills, "Downward Comparison Principles in Social Psychology," *Journal of Personality and Social Psychology* 90 (1981): 245–71.

42. Gallup poll, May 17–20, 1990, reported in James K. Glassman, "For Most People, Real Wealth Doesn't Come in a Wallet," *Washington Post,* October 22, 1993, B1, B2.

43. Russell W. Belk, "Three Scales to Measure Constructs Related to Materialism: Reliability, Validity, and Relationship to Measures of Happiness," *Advances in Consumer Research* 11 (1984): 291–97; Jonathan E. Schroeder and Sanjiv S. Dugal, "Psychological Correlates of the Materialism Construct," *Journal of Social Behavior and Personality* 10 (1995): 243–53; Richins and Dawson, "Consumer Values Orientation," 313.

44. Keynes, "Economic Possibilities for Our Grandchildren," 321–34.

45. David Hume, *A Treatise of Human Nature,* 2 vols. (1738; London: Dent, 1911).

46. Ralph Waldo Emerson, "Nominalist and Realist," in *The Complete Essays and Other Writings of Ralph Waldo Emerson* (New York: Modern Library/Random House, 1940), 439.

47. Ralph Waldo Emerson, "Self-Reliance," in *Essays of Ralph Waldo Emerson,* ed. Irwin Edman (New York: Crowell, 1951), 148–49.

48. M. Joseph Sirgy, "Materialism and Quality of Life," *Social Indicators Research* 43 (1998): 227–60.

49. Mario Mikulincer and Israel Orbach, "Attachment Styles and Repressive Defensiveness: The Accessibility and Architecture of Affective Memories," *Journal of Personality and Social Psychology* 68 (1995): 917–26.

50. Scherer, Walbott, and Summerfield, *Experiencing Emotion.*

51. James M. Hunt, Jerome B. Kernan, and Deborah J. Mitchell, "Materialism as Social Cognition: People, Possessions, and Perception," *Journal of Consumer Psychology* 5 (1996): 65.

52. Joseph Luft, "Monetary Value and the Perception of Persons," *Journal of Social Psychology* 46 (1957): 245–51.

53. Helga Dittmar and Lucy Pepper, "To Have Is to Be: Materialism and Person Perception in Working-Class and Middle-Class British Adolescents," *Journal of Economic Psychology* 15 (1994): 233–51.

54. Geoffrey Gorer, *The American People: A Study in National Character* (New York: Norton, 1948), 175.

55. J. J. La Gaipa and H. D. Wood, "Friendship in Disturbed Adolescents," in *Personal Relationships,* vol. 3, *Personal Relationships in Disorder,* ed. S. Duck and R. Gilmour (London: Academic Press, 1981), reported in Michael Argyle, *Cooperation: The Basis of Sociability* (London: Routledge, 1991), 166.

56. Rudmin, "German and Canadian Data," 176–81.

57. Some of the physiology explaining this sex difference is supplied by the

female hormone oxytocin, which stimulates sociability and orchestrates maternal responses; see Natalie Angier, "Illuminating How Bodies Are Built for Sociability," *New York Times,* April 30, 1996, C1, C11.

58. Robert D. Putnam, "Bowling Alone: America's Declining Social Capital," *Journal of Democracy* 6 (1995): 65–78.

59. Francis Fukuyama, *Trust: The Social Virtues and the Creation of Prosperity* (New York: Free Press, 1995).

60. Rahn and Transue, "Social Trust and Value Change," 545–65.

61. Alex Inkeles and Larry Diamond, "Personal Development and National Development: A Cross-Cultural Perspective," in *Quality of Life: Comparative Studies,* ed. Alexander Szalai and Frank M. Andrews (Beverly Hills, Calif.: Sage, 1980), 79.

62. Deirdre N. McCloskey, *The Vices of Economists—The Virtues of the Bourgeoisie* (Amsterdam: Amsterdam University Press, 1996), 96.

63. See, e.g., Frey and Stutzer, *Happiness and Economics;* Bruno S. Frey, "Institutions and Morale: The Crowding Out Effect," in *Economics, Values, and Organization,* ed. Avner Ben-Ner and Louis Putterman (New York: Cambridge University Press, 1998), 437–60; Bruno S. Frey, *Not Just for the Money: An Economic Theory of Personal Motivation* (Cheltenham, U.K.: Elgar, 1997); Ernst Fehr and Simon Gächter, "How Effective Are Trust- and Reciprocity-Based Incentives?" in *Economics, Values, and Organization,* ed. Ben-Ner and Putterman, 337–63; Ernest Fehr and Simon Gachter, "Altruistic Punishment in Humans," *Nature,* January 10, 2002, reported in Natalie Angier. "The Urge to Punish Cheats: It Isn't Merely Vengeance," *New York Times,* January 22, 2002, F1, F6.

64. Lange, *History of Materialism,* 243–44.

65. Robert E. Goodin, *Political Theory and Public Policy* (Chicago: University of Chicago Press, 1982), 116–21.

66. Richins and Dawson, "Consumer Values Orientation," 312.

67. For the Americans, Dennis W. Brogan says, "Wealth, material success, happiness in this world *is* the Kingdom of God" (*The American Character* [New York: Vintage, 1956], 81).

68. Floris W. Wood, ed., *An American Profile—Opinions and Behavior, 1972–1989* (Detroit: Gale, 1990), 982. Dessie knew that these materialist-religious Americans gave more in charity than the more secular Europeans, but in a timid fashion, he suppressed that idea; see Helmut K. Anheier, Lester Salamon, and Edith Archambault, "Participating Citizens: U.S.-Europe Comparisons in Volunteer Action," *Public Perspective* 5 (March–April 1994): 16–17, 34.

69. Jacques Maritain, quoted by George Santayana, "Americanism," *Virginia Quarterly Review* 31 (winter 1955): 1.

70. George J. Stigler, "Economics or Ethics?" In *Tanner Lectures on Human Values,* ed. S. McMurrin (Cambridge: Cambridge University Press, 1981), 2:176.

71. Frey, "Institutions and Morale."

72. Ibid., 448–54.

73. W. Upton, *Altruism, Attribution, and Intrinsic Motivation in the Recruitment of Blood Donors* (Ph.D. diss., Cornell University, 1973), reported in

198   John Condry and James Chambers, "Intrinsic Motivation and the Process of Learning," in *Hidden Costs of Rewards,* ed. Lepper and Greene, 71.

74. Dale T. Miller and Rebecca K. Rattner, "The Disparity between the Actual and Assumed Power of Self-Interest," *Journal of Personality and Social Psychology* 74 (1998): 53–62.

75. Adam Smith, *Inquiry into the Nature and Causes,* 14.

76. Adam Smith, *The Theory of Moral Sentiments,* ed. D. D. Rafael and A. L. Macfie (1759; Oxford: Clarendon, 1976), 50.

77. Robert H. Frank, "Rethinking Rational Choice," in *Beyond the Marketplace: Rethinking Economy and Society,* ed. Roger Friedland and A. F. Robertson (New York: Aldine de Gruyter, 1990), 53–87.

78. Howard Margolis, *Selfishness, Altruism, and Rationality: A Theory of Social Choice* (Cambridge: Cambridge University Press, 1982).

79. P. Lynn and J. D. Smith, *Voluntary Action Research* (London: Volunteer Center, 1991), reported in Michael Argyle, "Causes and Correlates of Happiness," in *Well-Being,* ed. Kahneman, Diener, and Schwarz, table 2.

80. C. Daniel Batson and Rebecca A. Gray, "Religious Orientation and Helping Behavior: Responding to One's Own or to the Victim's Needs," *Journal of Personality and Social Psychology* 40 (1981): 511–20.

81. Marshall had said that although economists were primarily interested in material rewards, they were "also interested in man's highest nature and affections . . . stimulated by a noble emulation more than by any love of wealth for its own sake" (*Principles of Economics,* 14).

82. See, e.g., Frederick Herzberg, *Work and the Nature of Man* (1966; New York: Mentor/New American Library, 1973); Edward E. Lawler III, *Motivation in Work Organizations* (Monterey, Calif.: Brooks/Cole, 1973); Victor H. Vroom, *Work and Motivation* (New York: Wiley, 1964).

83. Lepper and Greene, *Hidden Costs of Rewards.*

84. Deci and Ryan, *Intrinsic Motivation and Self-Determination.*

85. George J. Stigler, *The Economist as Preacher and Other Essays* (Chicago: University of Chicago Press, 1992), does not report the effect of payment on economists' behavior but says that they cultivate ideas that find a market (32–33), producing what people desire (63), and preach what society wants to hear (13).

86. Gerald Marwell and Ruth Ames, "Economists Free Ride. Does Anyone Else?" *Journal of Public Economics* 15 (1981): 259–310. Adam apparently was not familiar with contrary evidence in T. D. Stanley and Ume Tran, "Economics Students Need Not Be Greedy: Fairness and the Ultimatum Game," *Journal of Socio-Economics* 27 (1998): 657–64; Amanda Bennett, "Economics Students Aren't Selfish; They're Just Not Entirely Honest," *Wall Street Journal,* January 18, 1995, B1.

87. E. A. Locke, D. B. Feren, V. M. McCaleb, K. N. Shaw, and A. T. Denny, "The Relative Effectiveness of Four Methods of Motivating Employee Performance," In *Changes in Working Life,* ed. K. D. Duncan, M. M. Gruenberg, and D. Wallis (Chichester, U.K.: Wiley, 1980), 379.

88. Hannah Arendt, *The Human Condition* (Chicago: University of Chicago Press, 1958); Erich Fromm, *The Sane Society* (New York: Rinehart, 1968).

89. Karl Marx, "The Power of Money in Bourgeois Society" (1844), in *Eco-*

nomic and Philosophical Manuscripts of 1844, ed. Dirk Struik, trans. M. Milligan (New York: International, 1964), 167.

90. Ibid., 169.

91. Scitovsky, *Joyless Economy.*

92. Robert E. Lane, *The Market Experience* (New York: Cambridge University Press, 1991), 516–19.

93. Karl Polanyi, "Our Obsolete Market Mentality," in *Primitive, Archaic, and Modern Economies* (Boston: Beacon, 1971), 70.

94. Kasser and Ryan, "Further Examining the American Dream," 280–87.

95. Veenhoven, *Happiness in Nations,* 76.

96. Gary S. Becker, *The Economic Approach to Human Behavior* (Chicago: University of Chicago Press, 1976).

97. See, e.g., Joan Huber and Glenna Spitze, *Sex Stratification: Children, Housework, and Jobs* (New York: Academic Press, 1983).

4. HUMANISM: THE VALUE OF PERSONS

1. Pigou, *Economics of Welfare,* ix.

2. Marcel Proust, "Cities of the Plain," in *Remembrance of Things Past* (New York: Random House, 1932), 2:191–92.

3. Boulding, *The Image,* 82.

4. Klaus R. Scherer, "Emotion Experiences across European Cultures: A Summary Statement," in *Experiencing Emotion,* ed. Scherer, Wallbott, and Summerfield, 176.

5. Juster and Stafford, *Time, Goods, and Well-Being.*

6. F. Thomas Juster, "Preferences for Work and Leisure," in ibid., 336.

7. "The thrust of my argument is that investment in population quality and in knowledge in large part determines the future prospects of mankind" (Schultz, *Investing in People,* xi).

8. Michael Young, *The Rise of the Meritocracy, 1870–2033* (1958; Harmondsworth: Penguin, 1961).

9. Reported in Shlomo Maitel, "The Pursuit of Happiness: If We're So Rich, Why Aren't More of Us Satisfied?" *Barron's,* May 1, 2000, 70.

10. Adam Smith, *Inquiry into the Nature and Causes,* 70–71.

11. Andrews and Withey, *Social Indicators,* 306, 332.

12. Juster, "Preferences for Work and Leisure," 333–51.

13. Okin, *Women in Western Political Thought,* 298–302.

14. Lane, *Loss of Happiness.*

15. Andrews and Withey, *Social Indicators,* 124; Campbell, Converse, and Rodgers, *Quality of American Life,* 76.

16. Campbell, Converse, and Rodgers, *Quality of American Life,* 380.

17. Ruut Veenhoven, *Conditions of Happiness: Summary Print* (1984; Dordrecht: Reidel, 1989), 25.

18. Ed Diener and Marissa Diener, "Cross-Cultural Correlates of Life Satisfaction and Self-Esteem," *Journal of Personality and Social Psychology* 68 (1995): 655.

19. Albert Bandura, *Social Learning Theory* (Englewood Cliffs, N.J.: Prentice-Hall, 1977).

20. Immanuel Kant, *Grounding the Metaphysics of Morals,* in *Ethical Philosophy,* trans. James W. Ellington (1785; Indianapolis: Hackett, 1993), 34.

21. Argyle, *Cooperation,* 166.

22. Diogenes Laertius, "'The Stoics': from Diogenes Laertius" (c. 230 A.D.), in *Lives of Eminent Philosophers,* trans. R. D. Hicks, repr., *Value and Obligation: Systematic Readings in Ethics,* ed. Richard B. Brandt (New York: Harcourt, Brace, and World, 1961), 87–92.

23. G. E. Moore, *Principia Ethica* (Cambridge: Cambridge University Press, 1903).

24. Thomas Aquinas, *Treatise on Law: Summa Theologica, Questions 90–97.* South Bend, Ind.: Gateway, n.d.

25. Aristotle, *The Ethics of Aristotle: The Nicomachean Ethics,* trans. J. A. K. Thompson (c. 330 B.C.; Harmondsworth: Penguin, 1956), 330.

26. Catherine E. Ross, "Religion and Psychological Distress," *Journal for the Scientific Study of Religion* 29 (1990): 236–45.

27. Immanuel Kant, preface to *The Fundamental Principles of the Metaphysic of Morals,* ed. and trans. T. K. Abbott, published as *Kant's Theory of Ethics,* 6th ed. (London: Longmans, Green, 1909); repr., T. M. Greene, ed., *Kant: Selections* (New York: Scribner's, 1920), 268–374.

28. Henry Sidgewick, *The Methods of Ethics,* 7th ed. (London: Macmillan, 1907), Book I.ix, sec. 4.

29. A generation later, intuitionist philosopher W. David Ross said, "Contemplate any imaginary universe from which you suppose [human] mind entirely absent, and you will fail to find anything in it that you can call good in itself" (*Right and the Good,* 140).

30. Karl Popper, *Unended Quest: An Intellectual Autobiography* (London: Fontana/Collins, 1976).

31. Kenneth Burke, *A Grammar of Motives* (1949; Berkeley: University of California Press, 1969).

32. See Ian Shapiro, "Gross Concepts in Political Argument," *Political Theory* 17 (1989): 51–76.

33. Kurt Baier, "What Is Value? An Analysis of the Concept," In *Values and the Future,* ed. Kurt Baier and Nicholas Rescher (New York: Free Press, 1969), 33–67.

34. Harry C. Triandis, *Individualism and Collectivism* (Boulder, Colo.: Westview Press, 1995).

35. Peter Laslett, *The World We Have Lost,* 2d ed. (New York: Scribner's, 1971).

36. Steven Lukes, *Individualism* (Oxford: Blackwell, 1973).

37. Benito Mussolini, *La Dottrina del Fascismo* (1932), repr., *The Social and Political Doctrines of Contemporary Europe,* ed. Michael Oakeshott (New York: Macmillan, 1942), 166.

38. Lukes, *Individualism,* 51.

39. Valuing individuals because of their contribution to other individuals was suggested by Neva Goodwin, but she is not responsible for my variation on her suggestion.

40. Diener and Diener, "Cross-Cultural Correlates," 660.

41. Eunkook Suh, Ed Diener, Shifehiro Oishi, and Harry C. Triandis, "The

Shifting Basis of Life Satisfaction Judgments across Cultures: Emotions versus Norms," *Journal of Personality and Social Psychology* 74 (1998): 482–93.

42. Thorstein Veblen, "Why Is Economics Not an Evolutionary Science?" in *The Portable Veblen,* ed. Max Lerner (New York: Viking, 1948), 232. Harry Girvetz, *The Evolution of Liberalism* (New York: Collier, 1963), 36–39, says that one of the main principles of Manchester liberalism is "quietism," the idea that for most people action must be induced, that they are passive until stimulated to action, that work, therefore, is only the response to the offer of pay. Citing Malthus's concept of "indolent" man, Girvetz traces the origin of this quietism back to Locke's and Condillac's associational psychology stating that people learned not by a creative act but by passively observing associations between events within their fields of observation.

43. George Katona, Burkhard Strumpel, and Ernest Zahn, *Aspirations and Affluence: Comparative Studies in the United States and Western Europe* (New York: McGraw-Hill, 1971), 12, 31.

44. Robert E. Lane, "Procedural Goods in a Democracy: How One Is Treated vs. What One Gets," *Social Justice Research* 2 (1988): 177–92.

45. Tom R. Tyler and R. Folger, "Distributional and Procedural Aspects of Satisfaction with Citizen-Police Encounters," *Basic Applied Psychology* 1 (1980): 281–92.

46. Morris Rosenberg and Roberta G. Simmons, *Black and White Self-Esteem: The Urban School Child* (Washington, D.C.,: American Sociological Association, 1971).

47. Charles Horton Cooley, *Human Nature and the Social Order* (New York: Scribner's, 1912), 152.

48. California State Department of Education, *Toward a State of Esteem: The Final Report of the California Task Force to Promote Self-Esteem and Personal and Social Responsibility* (Sacramento: California State Department of Education Bureau of Publications, 1990); Robyn M. Dawes, "The Social Usefulness of Self-Esteem: A Skeptical View," *Harvard Mental Health Letter* 15 (October 1998): 4–5.

49. E. A. Lind and T. R. Tyler, *The Social Psychology of Procedural Justice* (New York: Plenum, 1988).

50. Compton Advertising, *National Survey of the U.S. Economic System: A Study of Public Understanding and Attitudes* (New York: Compton, 1975).

51. Kohn and Schooler, *Work and Personality.*

52. Milton Friedman, *Capitalism and Freedom.*

53. "Bossed to Death?" *Harvard Mental Health Letter* 19 (February 2003): 8, reporting on Benjamin C. Amick, Peggy McDonough, Hong Chang, William H. Rogers, Carl F. Pieper, and Greg Duncan, "Relationship between All-Cause Mortality and Cumulative Working Life Course for Psychosocial and Physical Exposures in the United States Labor Market from 1968 to 1992," *Psychosomatic Medicine* 64 (2002): 370–81.

54. Robert Blauner, *Alienation and Freedom* (Chicago: University of Chicago Press, 1964); Duncan Gallie, Michael White, Yuan Cheng, and Mark Tomlinson, *Restructuring the Employment Relationship* (Oxford: Clarendon, 1998).

55. Lane, *Market Experience.*

56. See Robert P. Abelson, "The Psychological Status of the Script Concept," *American Psychologist* 36 (1981): 715–29.

57. Robert D. Putnam, "Social Capital and Public Affairs," *Bulletin: The American Academy of Arts and Sciences* 47 (May 1994): 5–19.

5. THE HUMANIST-MATERIALIST AXIS

1. Veenhoven, *Happiness in Nations,* 50; Ed Diener and Shigehiro Oishi, "Money and Happiness: Income and Subjective Well-Being across Nations," in *Culture and Subjective Well-Being,* ed. Diener and Suh, 185–218; Diener, Diener, and Diener, "Factors Predicting the Subjective Well-Being of Nations," 851–64.

2. Ed Diener, Carol L. Gohm, Eunkook Suh, and Shigehiro Oishi, "Similarity of the Relations between Marital Status and Well-Being across Cultures," *Journal of Cross-Cultural Psychology* 31 (2000): 419–36; Diener and Diener, "Cross-Cultural Correlates," 653–63.

3. Schumpeter, *History of Economic Analysis,* 1058.

4. Angus Campbell, *The Sense of Well-Being in America* (New York: McGraw-Hill, 1981).

5. Triandis, *Individualism and Collectivism;* Geert Hofstede, *Culture's Consequences: International Differences in Work-Related Values,* abridged ed. (Beverly Hills, Calif.: Sage, 1984).

6. Diener and Diener, "Cross-Cultural Correlates."

7. Joseph A. Vandello and Dov Cohen, "Patterns of Individualism and Collectivism across the United States," *Journal of Personality and Social Psychology* 77 (1999): 279–92.

8. Henry Sumner Maine, *Ancient Law* (1861; London: Oxford University Press, 1931); Thomas Hill Green, *Lectures on the Principles of Political Obligation* (London: Longmans, Green, 1911); Lukes, *Individualism.*

9. Ferdinand Tönnies, *Community and Society,* trans. C. P. Loomis (1897; New York: Harper Torchbook, 1963); Robert N. Bellah, Richard Madsen, William M. Sullivan, Ann Swidler, and Steven M. Tipton, *Habits of the Heart: Individualism and Commitment in American Life* (Berkeley: University of California Press, 1985); Philip Selznick, *The Moral Commonwealth: Social Theory and the Promise of Community* (Berkeley: University of California Press, 1992); Amitai Etzioni, *The Spirit of Community: Rights, Responsibilities, and the Communitarian Agenda* (New York: Simon and Schuster/Touchstone, 1993).

10. Rachel Carson, *Silent Spring* (Boston: Houghton Mifflin, 1962); E. F. Schumacher, *Small Is Beautiful: Economics as If People Mattered* (New York: Harper/Colophon, 1973).

11. Inglehart, *Culture Shift.*

12. Inglehart, *Modernization and Postmodernization,* 108.

13. Lewis Mumford, *The Transformations of Man* (New York: Harper Torchbook, 1972); Jacques Ellul, *The Technological Society,* trans. J. Wilkinson (1954; London: Cape, 1965); David Keith Landes, *The Unbound Prometheus: Technological Change and Industrial Development in Western Europe from 1750 to Today* (London: Cambridge University Press, 1969).

14. Inglehart, *Modernization and Postmodernization,* 108.

15. Ernest Gellner, *Nations and Nationalism* (Ithaca: Cornell University Press, 1983).

16. Lee Ross, "Intuitive Psychologist and His Shortcomings," 173–220.

17. "Man's attitude to the world must be radically changed [to release such human forces as] an elementary sense of justice, the ability to see things as others do, a sense of transcendent responsibility" (Havel, "End of the Modern Era," E15).

18. Max Weber, *Protestant Ethic and the Spirit of Capitalism;* Richard H. Tawney, *Religion and the Rise of Capitalism* (1926; New York: Penguin, 1947).

19. See, e.g., Daniel Bell, *The End of Ideology* (New York: Free Press, 1960).

20. For a discussion of the role of the preference for the similar and the familiar, see Lane, "Self-Reliance and Empathy," 473–92. See also research showing that egalitarians use stereotypes in spite of themselves: Gordon B. Moskowitz, Peter M. Gollwitzer, Wolfgang Wasel, and Berndt Schaal, "Preconscious Control of Stereotype Activation through Chronic Egalitarian Bias," *Journal of Personality and Social Psychology* 77 (1999): 167–84. Research by Alan J. Lambert and Robert S. Wyer shows that "when subjects believed a group to be heterogeneous, they based their liking for a particular group member on their liking for the group as a whole, independently of and in addition to the target's behavior, regardless of the target's typicality" ("Stereotypes and Social Judgment: The Effects of Typicality and Group Heterogeneity," *Journal of Personality and Social Psychology* 59 [1990]: 664).

21. Jon Huer, *The Wages of Sin: America's Dilemma of Profit against Humanity* (New York: Praeger, 1991).

22. Vern L. Bengsten, "Generation and Family Effects in Value Socialization," *American Sociological Review* 40 (1975): 358–71.

23. Shalom H. Schwartz, "Individualism-Collectivism: Critique and Proposed Refinements," *Journal of Cross-Cultural Psychology* 22 (1990): 139–57.

24. Shalom H. Schwartz and Galit Sagie, "Value Consensus and Importance: A Cross-National Study," *Journal of Cross-Cultural Psychology* 31 (2000): 468.

25. Donald R. Kinder and David O. Sears, "Political Opinion and Political Action," in *Handbook of Social Psychology,* ed. Gardner Lindzey and Elliott Aronson, 3d ed. (Hillsdale, N.J.: Erlbaum, 1985), 659–74.

26. "The essence of the argument here is that those values and ethics that effectively served our ancestors, whose genes we carry and that are inevitably associated with our ontogeny, remain in some fashion encoded in our cognitive and behavioral apparatus" (Lionel Tiger, "Morality Recapitulates Phylogeny," in *Origin of Values,* ed. Hechter, Nadel, and Michod, 291).

27. Adam's little joke could have prompted Dessie to reply with a selection from Steven Pinker's *The Blank Slate: The Modern Denial of Human Nature* (New York: Viking 2002). Pinker claims that, among others, the following are innate dispositions: primacy of family ties, making nepotism and inheritance appealing; a propensity to share based on reciprocity where nonrelatives are concerned (within the family, it is free); a drive for dominance and a willingness to use violence to attain goals; ethnocentrism and other forms of group-against-group hostility; self-serving biases that deceive people into thinking they are freer,

wiser, and more honest than they are; a moral sense, biased toward kin and friends, and linked to ideas of purity, beauty, and rank; an intuitive psychology, used to understand others by imputing to them a mind with beliefs and desires; and an intuitive economics, used in exchange of goods and calculated favors (220–21, 294).

28. Richard Dawkins, *The Selfish Gene,* new ed. (New York: Oxford University Press, 1989).

29. Natalie Angier, "What Makes a Parent Put Up with It All?" *New York Times,* November 2, 1993, C1, C14.

30. John Stuart Mill, *On Liberty, Representative Government, and the Subjection of Women: Three Essays,* with an introduction by Millicent Garrett Fawcett (London: Oxford University Press, 1912; repr., 1969).

31. John H. Flavell, "Cognitive Development: Children's Knowledge about the Mind," *Annual Review of Psychology* 50 (1999): 21–45.

32. Hugh McIntosh, "New Technologies Advance Study of Autism," *APA Monitor* 29 (November 1998): 14.

33. "While the sexes do not appear to differ appreciably on data versus ideas, they routinely differ by a full standard deviation on people versus things (females tend to gravitate toward the former, males toward the latter)" (David Lubinski, "Scientific and Social Significance of Assessing Individual Differences: 'Sinking Shafts at a Few Critical Points,'" *Annual Review of Psychology* 51 [2000]: 421).

34. Rahn and Transue, "Social Trust and Value Change," 559.

35. A. Tesser and C. Leonie, "Cognitive Schemas and Thought as Determinants of Attitude Change," *Journal of Experimental Psychology* 13 (1977): 340–56.

36. T. Likona, "A Cognitive Developmental Approach to Interpersonal Relations," in *Foundations of Interpersonal Attraction,* ed. Ted L. Huston (New York: Academic Press, 1974), 34–50.

37. David O. Sears, "The Person-Positivity Bias," *Journal of Personality and Social Psychology* 44 (1983): 233.

38. Scherer, "Emotion Experiences across European Cultures," 176.

39. Diane G. Symbaluk, C. Donald Heth, Judy Cameron, and W. David Pierce, "Social Modeling, Monetary Incentives, and Pain Endurance," *Personality and Social Psychology Bulletin* 23 (1997): 258–69.

40. Richard Nisbett and Lee Ross, *Human Inference: Strategies and Shortcomings of Social Judgment* (Englewood Cliffs, N.J.: Prentice-Hall, 1980), 52.

41. For further discussion, see Lane, *Market Experience,* 563–68.

42. Lita Furby, "Possessions: Toward a Theory of Their Meaning and Function throughout the Life Cycle," in *Life-Span Development and Behavior,* ed. P. B. Baltes (New York: Academic Press, 1978), 304–5.

43. Somewhere Margaret Mead suggests that when toddlers begin to reach for things that do not belong to them, they are told "That is not yours."

44. White, "Exploring the Origins of Competence."

45. Ernest Beaglehole, *Property: A Study in Social Psychology* (London: Allen and Unwin, 1931).

46. Stephen E. G. Lea, Roger M. Tarpy, and Paul Webley, *The Individual in the Economy* (Cambridge: Cambridge University Press, 1987), 165.

47. Lawrence D. Becker, "The Moral Basis of Property Rights." In *Property: Nomos XXII*, ed. J. R. Pennock and J. W. Chapman (New York: New York University Press, 1980), 201.

48. William James, *Psychology: The Briefer Course* (1892; New York: Harper, 1961). James thought that possessiveness was instinctual. To support that view, recent research is relevant on the "endowment effect," people's tendency to assign higher values to objects they own than to the same objects not owned.

49. Frans B. M. de Waal, "Sex Differences in Chimpanzee (and Human) Behavior: A Matter of Social Values," in *Origin of Values,* ed. Hechter, Nadel, and Michod, 283–303.

50. Okin, *Women in Western Political Thought,* 299–300.

51. Mary Douglas, *Natural Symbols* (New York: Pantheon/Random House, 1970).

52. Simonton says that sensate cultures are more likely to cultivate science (*Genius, Creativity, and Leadership,* 139).

53. C. P. Snow, *The Two Cultures and the Scientific Revolution* (New York: Cambridge University Press, 1959).

54. Simonton, *Genius, Creativity, and Leadership,* 133.

55. A. L. Kroeber, *Configurations of Culture Growth* (Berkeley: University of California Press, 1944).

56. Ed Diener and Carol Diener, "The Wealth of Nations Revisited: Income and Quality of Life," *Social Indicators Research* 36 (1995): 275–86.

57. Simonton, *Genius, Creativity, and Leadership,* 142.

58. Thomas S. Eliot, *Christianity and Culture: The Idea of a Christian Society and Notes toward the Definition of Culture* (New York: Harcourt, Brace, Jovanovich, 1968).

59. Simonton, *Genius, Creativity, and Leadership,* 145.

60. Fernand Braudel, *Capitalism and Material Wealth, 1400–1800,* trans. M. Kochan (London: Weidenfeld and Nicolson, 1967), xiii.

61. See, e.g., Daniel Miller, *Material Culture and Mass Consumption* (New York: Blackwell, 1987); Grant McCracken, *Culture and Consumption: New Approaches to the Symbolic Character of Goods and Activities* (Bloomington: Indiana University Press, 1988); Mary Douglas and Baron Isherwood, *The World of Goods: Towards An Anthropology of Consumption* (Harmondsworth: Penguin, 1980). John P. Robinson reports on recent changes in the use of leisure time: "Rather than marked increase in self-growth and personally expressive leisure activities (such as participation in the creative arts, culture, education, or physical fitness), we find instead increased time being spent in sleep, in resting, in personal care, and in automobile travel" ("Changes in Time Use: An Historical Overview," in *Time, Goods, and Well-Being,* ed. Juster and Stafford, 311).

62. Arendt, *Human Condition,* 100. In 1865, another German, Frederick Lange, held that the acquisitiveness of capitalist materialism "chokes true science" (*History of Materialism,* 243).

63. Stanley Aronowitz, *False Promises: The Shaping of Working Class Consciousness* (New York: McGraw-Hill, 1973), 15.

64. Alfred Weber, "The Sociology of Culture," in *Social Thought from Lore to Science,* ed. Howard Becker and Harry Elmer Barnes, 3d ed. (New York: Dover, 1961), 2:772–75.

65. Simonton, *Genius, Creativity, and Leadership,* 145.

66. Everett E. Hagen, *On the Theory of Social Change: How Economic Growth Begins* (Homewood, Ill.: Dorsey, 1962).

67. Arnold J. Toynbee, *A Study of History: Abridgment of Vols. I–VI* (New York: Oxford University Press, 1947).

68. Simonton, *Genius, Creativity, and Leadership,* 158.

69. Norwood Russell Hanson, *Patterns of Discovery* (Cambridge: Cambridge University Press, 1958).

70. Thomas Paine, *Common Sense* (1776), repr., *The Political Works of Thomas Paine* (Chicago: Belford, Clarke, 1879), 7.

71. David Hume, "Of Independence of Parliament," in *Essays: Moral, Political, and Literary,* (1742; Oxford: Oxford University Press, 1963), 1:117–18, quoted in Frey, *Not Just for the Money,* 43.

72. Adam was mimicking Charles Schultze's phrase to describe the market economy but, in honor of Dessie, used the earlier version. See *Gosson's Schoole of Abuse,* in *The Cambridge History of English and American Literature,* vol. 6, *The Drama to 1642, Part Two,* ed. A. W. Ward, A. R. Waller, W. P. Trent, J. Erskine, S. P. Sherman, and C. van Doren (Cambridge: Cambridge University Press, 1909–21).

73. Derek Parfit, "Prudence, Morality and the Prisoner's Dilemma," in *Proceedings of the British Academy* (Oxford: Oxford University Press, 1981), 554.

74. Donald Granberg and Sören Holmberg, *The Political System Matters: Social Psychology and Voting Behavior in Sweden and the United States* (New York: Cambridge University Press, 1989).

75. See Inglehart, *Modernization and Postmodernization.*

76. Lawrence Harrison, *Underdevelopment is a State of Mind* (Lanham, Md.: University Press of America, 1986).

77. "We are moreover able to show, for the first time, that good political institutions do indeed raise happiness" (Frey and Stutzer, *Happiness and Economics,* 150).

78. John Orbell, Langche Zeng, and Matthew Mulford, "Individual Experience and the Fragmentation of Societies," *American Sociological Review* 61 (1996): 1018–32.

79. George E. Vaillant, "The 'Normal Boy' in Later Life: How Adaptation Fosters Growth," *Harvard Magazine* 80 (1977): 46–51, 60–61; Jonathan D. Brown and Dutton, "Truth and Consequences," 1288–96.

80. Eshkol Rafaeli-Mor and Jennifer Steinberg, "Self-Complexity and Well-Being: A Review and Research Synthesis," *Personality and Social Psychology Review* 6 (2002): 31–58.

81. Amos Tversky and Daniel Kahneman, "The Framing of Decisions and the Psychology of Choice," *Science* 211 (January 30, 1981): 453–58.

82. Norbert Elias, *The History of Manners,* vol. 1 of *The Civilizing Process,* trans. Edmund Jephcott (1939; New York: Pantheon, 1982).

83. Robert A. Wicklund, "Objective Self-Awareness," in *Advances in Experimental Social Psychology,* ed. Berkowitz, 8:233–75.

84. Ivana Markova, "Medical Ethics: A Branch of Societal Psychology," in *Societal Psychology,* ed. Hilda T. Himmelweit and George Gaskell (Newbury Park, Calif.: Sage, 1990), 112–37.

85. Patricia W. Linville, "Self-Complexity as a Cognitive Buffer against

Stress-Related Illness and Depression," *Journal of Personality and Social Psychology* 52 (1987): 663–67.

86. Mihalyi Csikszentmihalyi and T. J. Figurski, "Self-Awareness and Aversive Experience in Everyday Life," *Journal of Personality* 50 (1982): 15–24.

87. C. Daniel Batson, Jim Fultz, Patricia Schoenrade, and Alan Paduano, "Critical Self-Reflection and Self-Perceived Altruism: When Self-Reward Fails," *Journal of Personality and Social Psychology* 53 (1987): 594–602.

88. Timothy D. Wilson and Jonathan W. Schooler, "Thinking Too Much: Introspection Can Reduce the Quality of Preferences and Decisions," *Journal of Personality and Social Psychology* 60 (1991): 181–92.

89. Norma Haan, *Coping and Defending: Processes of Self-Environment Organization* (New York: Academic Press, 1977), 80.

6. DIMINISHING RETURNS TO HAPPINESS

1. Ed Diener and Carol Diener, "Most People Are Happy," *Psychological Science* 7 (1996): 181–90.

2. "For most people, happiness is the main, if not the only, ultimate objective of life" (Yew-Kwang Ng, "Happiness Surveys: Some Comparability Issues and an Exploratory Survey Based on Just Perceivable Increments," *Social Indicators Research* 38 [1996]: 1).

3. "Thus the pleasures of which we can say without doubt are good are . . . the pleasures of moral beings that are deserved" (W. David Ross, *Right and the Good*, 138). See also Nicholas Rescher, *Introduction to Value Theory* (Englewood Cliffs, N.J.: Prentice-Hall, 1969), 54.

4. Immanuel Kant, preface to *The Foundations of the Metaphysics of Morals*, trans. L. W. Beck. (Indianapolis: Bobbs-Merrill, 1959), 12.

5. Deirdre McCloskey was probably right about economists' aversion to ethics talk. She said, "I have been suggesting all along in this book that ethics, character, identity are necessary for science and for an economy. . . . If you are an economist, though, you are going to resist" (*Vices of Economists,* 125).

6. Russell Hardin, *Morality within Limits of Reason* (Chicago: University of Chicago Press, 1988), xvii.

7. Robert Nozick, *Anarchy, State, and Utopia* (New York: Basic Books, 1974).

8. Jeremy Bentham, "The Rationale of Punishment," in *Jeremy Bentham's Economic Writings,* vol. 1 of *Works,* ed. W. Stark (1830; London: Royal Economic Society by Allen and Unwin, 1954), 468.

9. See, e.g., Drucilla K. Barker and Susan K. Feiner, *Liberating Economics: Feminist Perspectives* (Ann Arbor: University of Michigan Press, 2004).

10. See, e.g., Nicholas Rescher, *Distributive Justice: A Constructive Critique of the Utilitarian Theory of Distribution* (Indianapolis: Bobbs-Merrill, 1966), 54.

11. Boulding, "Economics as a Moral Science," 7.

12. Baruch Spinoza, *Ethics Demonstrated in Geometrical Order* (1677), trans. W. H. White (1883), rev. A. Hutchinson (1899), repr., in abridged form, in *The European Philosophers: From Descartes to Nietzsche,* ed. Monroe C. Beardsley (New York: Random House Modern Library, 1960), 197, 209.

13. Kant, preface, in *Kant: Selections,* ed. Greene, 277.

14. Alice M. Isen, "Positive Affect, Cognitive Processes, and Social Behavior," in *Advances in Experimental Social Psychology,* ed. Berkowitz, 20:203–53.

15. Veenhoven, *Conditions of Happiness,* 29.

16. Robert R. McCrae and Paul T. Costa Jr., "Adding *Liebe und Arbeit:* The Full Five-Factor Model and Well-Being," *Personality and Social Psychology Bulletin* 17 (1991): 227–32.

17. See Amitai Etzioni, *The Moral Dimension: Toward a New Economics* (New York: Free Press, 1988).

18. Aristotle, *Aristotle's Ethics for English Readers, Rendered from the Greek of the Nicomachean Ethics,* trans. H. Rackham (Oxford: Blackwell, 1943), repr., *Value and Obligation,* ed. Brandt, 59.

19. John Stuart Mill, "Utilitarianism," in *Utilitarianism, Liberty, and Representative Government* (1861; London: Dent, 1910).

20. Peter Schizgal, "On the Neural Computation of Utility: Implications from Studies of Brain Stimulation Reward," in *Well-Being,* ed. Kahneman, Diener, and Schwarz, 500–524.

21. R. J. Davidson and N. A. Fox, "Asymmetrical Brain Activity Discriminates between Positive versus Negative Affective Stimuli in Human Infants," *Science* 218 (1982): 1235–37; see also Pam Bellum, "Looking for Happiness? It May Be Very Near," *New York Times,* July 14, 1999, B7.

22. J. S. Morris, C. D. Frith, D. I. Perrett, D. Rowland, A. W. Young, A. K. Calder, and R. J. Dolan, "A Differential Neural Response in the Human Amygdala to Fearful and Happy Facial Expressions," *Nature* 383 (October 31, 1996): 812–16.

23. David M. Buss, "The Evolution of Happiness," *American Psychologist* 55 (2000): 15–23.

24. Robert M. Sapolsky, "The Physiology and Pathophysiology of Unhappiness," in *Well-Being,* ed. Kahneman, Diener, and Schwarz, 453–69.

25. Veenhoven, *Happiness in Nations,* 14.

26. Robert Wright, *The Moral Animal: Evolutionary Psychology and Everyday Life* (New York: Vintage/Random House, 1994), 211, 298.

27. Buss, "Evolution of Happiness," 15; emphasis added.

28. Erica Goode, "Viewing Depression as Tool for Survival," *New York Times,* February 1, 2000, F7.

29. Buss, "Evolution of Happiness," 15.

30. Ibid.

31. Natalie Angier, "Status Isn't Everything, at Least for Monkeys," *New York Times,* April 18, 1995, C1.

32. Amartya Sen, *Ethics and Economics* (Oxford: Blackwell, 1987), 55.

33. Leon Festinger, *A Theory of Cognitive Dissonance* (Stanford, Calif.: Stanford University Press, 1957).

34. James, *Psychology.*

35. Thomas Schelling, *Choice and Consequence* (Cambridge: Harvard University Press, 1984), 113.

36. Kahneman and Varey, "Notes on the Psychology of Utility," 136.

37. Ibid., 130–33.

38. Gordon Allport, "The Historical Background of Social Psychology," in *The Handbook of Social Psychology,* ed. Gardner Lindsay and Elliot Aronson (New York: Random House, 1985), 1:18.

39. Albert O. Hirschman, *The Passions and the Interests: Political Arguments for Capitalism before Its Triumph* (Princeton: Princeton University Press, 1977).

40. See Peter Singer, *Practical Ethics,* 2d ed. (Cambridge: Cambridge University Press, 1993); J. J. C. Smart and Bernard Williams, eds., *Utilitarianism, For and Against* (Cambridge: Cambridge University Press, 1973).

41. Amartya Sen and Bernard Williams, introduction, in *Utilitarianism and Beyond,* ed. Sen and Williams (Cambridge: Cambridge University Press, 1982), 7.

42. Ibid., 4, 5–6. "The neoclassical economic agent is not a thinking, creative chooser in any meaningful sense. She is simply a preference system with a limited endowment, who faces a given set of market prices" (Peter Earl, *The Economic Imagination: Towards a Behavioral Analysis of Choice* [Armonk, N.Y.: Sharpe, 1983], 56).

43. Amartya Sen, "Utilitarianism and Welfarism," *Journal of Philosophy* 76 (1979): 463–88.

44. Mill, "Utilitarianism," 32.

45. Ruut Veenhoven, ed. *How Harmful Is Happiness?* (1984; Rotterdam: University Pers Rotterdam, 1989).

46. George J. Stigler, "The Adoption of the Marginal Utility Theory," in *The Economist as Preacher and Other Essays,* 72–85.

47. Ed Diener and Richard E. Lucas, "Personality and Subjective Well-Being," in *Well-Being,* ed. Kahneman, Diener, and Schwarz, 213–29.

48. See, e.g., M. Joseph Sirgy, *Quality of Life Studies and Social Indicators Research: An Annotated Bibliography of Selected Works (1984–1998)* (Blacksburg, Va.: International Society of Quality of Life Studies, 1998).

49. Frey and Stutzer, *Happiness and Economics.*

50. David G. Myers and Ed Diener, "The New Scientific Pursuit of Happiness," *Harvard Mental Health Letter* 14 (August 1997): 4–7.

51. Ibid., 6–7.

52. Daniel Goleman, "The Secret of Long Life? Be Dour and Dependable," *New York Times,* November 9, 1993, C3. Based on Terman's study of California boys and girls of about eleven in the 1920s. These data were analyzed by Howard S. Friedman, a psychologist at University of California, Riverside. The news story is based on an article by Friedman, "Does Childhood Personality Predict Longevity?" *Journal of Personality and Social Psychology* 65 (1993): 176–85.

53. Alice M. Isen, "Feeling Happy, Thinking Clearly," *APA Monitor* 19, no. 4 (1988): 6; see also Isen, "Positive Affect, Cognitive Processes, and Social Behavior," 203–53.

54. George W. Brown and Tirril Harris, *Social Origins of Depression: A Study of Psychiatric Disorder* (London: Tavistock/Cambridge University Press, 1978), 283.

55. Jack E. Hokanson and Andrew C. Butler, "Cluster Analysis of Depressed College Students' Social Behaviors," *Journal of Personality and Social Psychology* 62 (1992): 273–80; Juliet Harper and Elizabeth M. Kelly, "Anti-Social Behaviour as a Mask for Depression in Year 5 and 6 Boys," *Mental Health in Australia* 1 (1985): 14–19.

56. John S. Gillis, "Effects of Life Stress and Dysphoria on Complex Judgments," *Psychological Reports* 72 (1993): 1355–63.

57. Kenneth K. Miya, "Autonomy and Depression," *Clinical Social Work Journal* 4 (1976): 260–68.

58. Nancy E. Meyer, Dennis G. Dyck, and Ron J. Petrinack, "Cognitive Appraisal and Attributional Correlates of Depressive Symptoms in Children," *Journal of Abnormal Child Psychology* 17 (1989): 325–36.

59. Richard C. Fowler, Barry I. Liskow, and Vasantkumar L. Tanna, "Alcoholism, Depression, and Life Events," *Journal of Affective Disorders* 22 (1980): 127–35.

60. Charles P. Cummings, Charles K. Prokop, and Ruth Cosgrove, "Dysphoria: The Cause or the Result of Addiction?" *Psychiatric Hospital* 16 (1985): 131–34.

61. Bernard Lubin, Marvin Zuckerman, Linda M. Breytspraak, and Neil C. Bull, "Affects, Demographic Variables, and Health," *Journal of Clinical Psychology* 44 (1988): 131–41.

62. Veenhoven, *Happiness in Nations,* 50; $p > .01$.

63. Diener, Diener, and Diener, "Factors Predicting the Subjective Well-Being," 859; $p > .001$.

64. Reported in Maitel, "Pursuit of Happiness," 70.

65. Diener and Biswas-Diener, "Will Money Increase Subjective Well-Being?" 119–69.

66. Myers and Diener, "New Scientific Pursuit of Happiness," 6.

67. Isen, "Feeling Happy, Thinking Clearly," 7.

68. Andreas Knapp and Margaret S. Clark, "Some Detrimental Effects of Negative Mood on Individuals' Ability to Solve Resource Dilemmas," *Personality and Social Psychology Bulletin* 17 (1991): 678–88.

69. Michael Argyle and Maryanne Martin, "The Psychological Causes of Happiness," in *Subjective Well-Being: An Interdisciplinary Perspective,* ed. Fritz Strack, Michael Argyle, and Norbert Schwarz (Oxford: Pergamon, 1991), 93.

70. Joseph P. Forgas, "On Feeling Good and Being Rude: Affective Influences on Language Use and Request Formulations," *Journal of Personality and Social Psychology* 76 (1999): 930.

71. Isaac M. Lipkus, Claudia Dahlbert, and Ilene D. Siegler, "The Importance of Distinguishing the Belief in a Just World for the Self versus for Others: Implications for Psychological Well-Being," *Personality and Social Psychology Bulletin* 22 (1996): 666–77.

72. Ibid., 674.

73. In the 1970s, it seems that educated but not less educated African-Americans were able to distinguish between their own responsibility and their less fortunate associates' responsibility for their fates; see Gerald Gurin and Patricia Gurin, "Personal Efficacy and the Ideology of Individual Responsibility," in *Economic Means for Human Needs,* ed. Burkhard Strumpel (Ann Arbor, Mich.: Institute for Social Research, 1976), 137–40.

74. Rafaeli-Mor and Steinberg, "Self-Complexity and Well-Being."

75. Gerald Gurin, Joseph Veroff, and Sheila Feld, *Americans View Their Mental Health* (New York: Basic Books, 1960).

76. Argyle and Martin, "Psychological Causes of Happiness," 93.

77. Jaihyun Park and Mahzarin R. Banaji, "Mood and Heuristics: The

Influence of Happy and Sad States on Sensitivity and Bias in Stereotyping," *Journal of Personality and Social Psychology* 78 (2000): 1005, 1019.

78. Veenhoven, *Conditions of Happiness*, 27.

79. R. M. Schwartz and G. I. Garamoni, "Cognitive Balance and Psychopathology: Evaluation of an Information Processing Model of Positive and Negative States of Mind," *Clinical Psychological Review* 9 (1989): 271–94.

80. R. M. Schwartz, "Consider the Simple Screw: Cognitive Science, Quality Improvement, and Psychotherapy," *Journal of Consulting and Clinical Psychology* 65 (1997): 970–83.

81. Elisha Tarlow Friedman, Roberta M. Schwartz, and David A. F. Haaga, "Are the Very Happy Too Happy?" *Journal of Happiness Studies* 3 (2002): 355.

82. Isen, "Positive Affect, Cognitive Processes, and Social Behavior," 203–53.

83. Ed Diener, Ed Sandvik, and William Pavot, "Happiness Is the Frequency, Not the Intensity, of Positive versus Negative Affect," in *Subjective Well-Being*, ed. Strack, Argyle, and Schwarz, 123. Also, a German study found that "norm-oriented" people are happier than others (Hermann Brandstatter, "Emotions in Everyday Life Situations. Time Sampling of Subjective Experience," in *Subjective Well-Being*, ed. Strack, Argyle, and Schwarz, 189–90.

84. Veenhoven, *Conditions of Happiness*, 29.

85. Benjamin Radcliff, "Politics, Markets, and Life Satisfaction: The Political Economy of Human Happiness," *American Political Science Review* 95 (2001): 939–52.

86. Bert Klandermans, "Does Happiness Soothe Political Protest? The Complex Relation between Discontent and Political Unrest," in *How Harmful Is Happiness?* ed. Veenhoven, 61–78.

87. Ruut Veenhoven, "The Utility of Happiness," *Social Indicators Research* 20 (1988): 333–54.

88. Veenhoven, *Conditions of Happiness*, 30.

89. Wicklund, "Objective Self-Awareness."

90. Daniel Kahneman, Peter P. Wakker, and Rakesh Sarin, "Back to Bentham? Explorations of Experienced Utility," *Quarterly Journal of Economics* 112 (1997): 375–405.

91. Lane, *Loss of Happiness*, pt. 5.

92. Jeremy Bentham, *An Introduction to the Principles of Morals and Legislation* (1780), in *A Bentham Reader*, ed. Mary Peter Mack (New York: Pegasus, 1969), 97.

93. John Stuart Mill, *Autobiography* (Oxford: Oxford University Press, 1969), 86; see also Jon Elster, *Sour Grapes: Studies in the Subversion of Rationality* (Cambridge: Cambridge University Press, 1983), 91.

94. Schumpeter, *History of Economic Analysis*, 1058.

95. Dessie did not fully agree that there was a balancing process such that for each gain in one good there was an equivalent loss in the other. He knew that some physiological psychologists thought there was an "opponent process" such that for each pain there was an equivalent pleasure—and vice versa—but he did not believe it, partly because further research had not supported it. The opponent-process thesis is set forth in Richard L. Solomon, "The Opponent-Process

212   Theory of Motivation: The Costs of Pleasure and the Benefits of Pain," *American Psychologist* 35 [1980]: 691–712.

7. BETTER PEOPLE

1. Robert E. Lane, *The Liberties of Wit: Humanism, Criticism, and the Civic Mind* (1961; Hamden, Conn.: Archon, 1970).

2. Karl R. Popper, *Conjectures and Refutations: The Growth of Scientific Knowledge* (London: Routledge and Kegan Paul, 1963), 380–83.

3. Max Weber, "Science as a Vocation," in *From Max Weber: Essays in Sociology,* ed. H. H. Gerth and C. Wright Mills (New York: Oxford University Press, 1946), 137.

4. Cardinal Wolsey, *Henry VIII,* act 3, scene 2, line 352.

5. Adam apparently did not know about the (failed) California experiments (California State Department of Education, *Toward a State of Esteem*); nor had he read Robert E. Lane, "Government and Self-Esteem," *Political Theory* 10 (1982): 5–31.

6. Janet Polivy and C. Peter Herman, "If at First You Don't Succeed: False Hopes of Self-Change," *American Psychologist* 57 (2002): 677–89.

7. Walter Mischel, "Processes in Delay of Gratification," *Advances in Experimental Social Psychology* 7 (1974): 249–92.

8. Aristotle, *Nicomachean Ethics,* in *Value and Obligation,* ed. Brandt, 67.

9. Wilhelm von Humboldt, *The Sphere and Duties of Government,* trans. J. Coulthard (1791; London: Trubner, 1854).

10. Antoine-Nicolas de Condorcet, "Sketch of the Progress of the Human Mind" (1794), in *The Enlightenment: A Comprehensive Anthology,* ed. Peter Gay (New York: Simon and Schuster, 1973), 804. In *De l'esprit,* Helvetius says that all men are capable of rising to the highest level; see John B. Bury, *The Idea of Progress* (1920; New York: Dover, 1955), 166.

11. Condorcet, "Sketch," 805.

12. Herbert Spencer, *Social Statics; or, The Conditions Essential to Human Happiness* (New York: Appleton, 1878), 482.

13. Marx and Engels, *Manifesto* (1932 ed.), 31. But then, Engels may have later stolen from Spencer in prophesying that socialism "guarantees to [everyone] the completely unrestricted development and exercise of their physical and mental faculties—this possibility now exists for the first time, but it does exist" (Friedrich Engels, "Socialism: Utopian and Scientific" [1890], in *Karl Marx: Selected Works,* ed. V. Adoratsky [New York: International Publishers, n.d.], 185).

14. Erich Fromm, *Escape from Freedom* (New York: Rinehart, 1941), 288–89.

15. United Nations Development Programme, *Human Development Report 1991* (New York: Oxford University Press, 1991), 10. A little later, that same agency reports on a "growing recognition of the need for a people-centered policy focus in national development. . . . The concept of human development provides an alternative to the view of development equated exclusively with economic growth. [This concept] sees economic growth and consumption not as

ends in themselves but as means to achieve human development" (United Nations Development Programme, *Human Development Report 1998,* 16).

16. Maslow, *Motivation and Personality,* 35–46.

17. M. A. Wahba and L. G. Bridewell, "Maslow Reconsidered: A Review of Research on the Need Hierarchy," *Organizational Behavior and Human Performance* 15 (1976): 210–40; Edward E. Lawler III and J. Lloyd Suttle, "A Causal Correlational Test of the Need Hierarchy Concept," in *Motivation and Work Behavior,* ed. Richard M. Steers and Lyman W. Porter (New York: McGraw-Hill, 1975).

18. Inglehart, *Silent Revolution.*

19. International Society of Quality of Life Studies (sirgy@mail.vt.edu).

20. Gordon W. Allport, *Becoming* (1955; New Haven: Yale University Press, 1960); Carl R. Rogers, *On Becoming a Person* (Boston: Houghton Mifflin, 1961); Maslow, *Motivation and Personality.*

21. Mill, *Subjection of Women,* 452, quoted in Okin, *Women in Western Political Thought,* 222.

22. Loevinger, *Ego Development.* For an evaluation of this measure, see Stuart Hauser, "Loevinger's Model and Measure of Ego Development: A Critical Review," *Psychological Bulletin* 83 (1976): 928–55; Ravenna Nelson and Paul Wink, "Two Conceptions of Maturity Examined in the Findings of a Longitudinal Study," *Journal of Personality and Social Psychology* 53 (1987): 531–41.

23. Schultz, *Investing in People.*

24. Piaget and Inhelder, *Psychology of the Child;* Jean Piaget, *The Origins of Intelligence in the Child,* trans. M. Cook (New York: Norton, 1977).

25. I am grateful to Dana Ward for guiding me through the Piagetian literature. At the same time, I wish to exculpate him for my interpretation and gross abbreviation of his careful exegesis.

26. Wicklund, "Objective Self-Awareness," 235.

27. Daniel Goleman, "Fear of Death Intensifies Moral Code, Scientists Find," *New York Times,* December 5, 1989, C1.

28. P. R. Dasen, "Cross-Cultural Piagetian Research: A Summary," *Journal of Cross-Cultural Psychology* 3 (1972): 23–39.

29. Ibid.

30. Christopher Jencks, Marshall Smith, Henry Acland, Mary Jo Bane, David Cohen, Herbert Gintis, Barbara Heyns, and Stephan Michelson, *Inequality: A Reassessment of the Effect of Family and Schooling in America* (New York: Harper Colophon, 1972), 180. The best estimates are that IQ explains 5–10 percent of the occupational status differences between the top fifth and bottom fifth of the status hierarchy. Differences in home environment account for another 10–20 percent. And differences in educational achievement (beyond what is accounted for by cognitive skill) account for another 40–50 percent.

31. Christopher Jencks, Susan Bartlett, Mary Corcoran, *Who Gets Ahead? The Determinants of Economic Success in America* (New York: Basic Books, 1979), 222, 307–8.

32. Ibid., 219.

33. Jencks et al., *Inequality,* 225.

34. Ibid., 192.

35. Ibid., 198.

36. J. McVicker Hunt and Girvin E. Kirk, "Social Aspects of Intelligence: Evidence and Issues," in *Intelligence: Genetic and Environmental Influences,* ed. Robert Cancro (New York: Grune and Stratton, 1971), 270.

37. Reported in ibid., 275.

38. J. McVicker Hunt, "Psychological Development," *Annual Review of Psychology* 30 (1979): 111.

39. Philip E. Vernon, *Intelligence and Cultural Environment* (London: Methuen, 1969), 218.

40. James R. Flynn, "Massive IQ Gains in Fourteen Nations: What IQ Tests Really Measure," *Psychological Bulletin* 101 (1987): 171–91.

41. Schumpeter, *Capitalism, Socialism, and Democracy,* 258.

42. Lane, *Market Experience,* 141–45.

43. "High growth rates do not automatically translate into higher levels of human development. And firm policy is required to forge a closer link between economic growth and human development" (United Nations Development Programme, *Human Development Report 1991,* 1). See also M. Joseph Sirgy, "Consumption and Quality of Life: A Review and Critique of the Work of the United Nations Development Programme," *SINET,* May 1999, 6–7.

44. Giovanni Andrea Cornia and Sheldon Danziger, eds., *Child Poverty and Deprivation in the Industrialized Countries* (New York: Clarendon, 1997).

45. Quoted in Victoria Brittain, "Poor Countries Shame U.S. in Care of Children," *Guardian* [London], June 22, 1994, 24. Grant based his remarks on UNICEF, *The Progress of Nations: The Nations of the World Ranked According to Their Achievements in Child Health, Nutrition, Education, Family Planning, and Progress of Women* (New York: United Nations, 1993).

46. Byron Kolb and Ian Q. Whishaw, "Brain Plasticity and Behavior," *Annual Review of Psychology* 49 (1998): 47.

47. Ibid., 55.

48. John W. Berry, *Human Ecology and Cognitive Style* (Beverly Hills, Calif.: Sage/Halsted, 1976), 48, 219; Herbert A. Barry, Irwin L. Childs, and Margaret K. Bacon, "Relation of Child Training to Subsistence Economy," *American Anthropologist* 61 (1959): 52–53.

49. "The net effect [of the weakness of genetic and family background predictors] is to reduce the association between test scores and economic success to a rather modest level" (Jencks et al., *Inequality,* 57).

50. Giambattista Vico held that men were governed by "ferocity, avarice, and ambition," and the literature on mass publics featured this view of the passions; see, e.g., Gustave Le Bon, *The Crowd* (1895; London: T. Fisher Unwin, 1920); William McDougall, *The Group Mind* (Cambridge: Cambridge University Press, 1920); José Ortega y Gasset, *The Revolt of the Masses* (1930; New York: Norton, 1932).

51. Hirschman, *Passions and the Interests.*

52. Schumpeter, *Capitalism, Socialism, and Democracy,* 122, 123.

53. Kohn and Schooler, *Work and Personality.*

54. See, e.g., Jacob Jacoby, Robert W. Chestnut, and William A. Fisher, "A Behavioral Process Approach to Information Acquisition in Nondurable Purchasing," *Journal of Marketing Research* 15 (1978): 532–44.

55. David O. Sears, "Passion and the Science of Politics" (presidential address delivered at the fourth annual meeting of the Society for the Advancement of Socio-Economics, Irvine, Calif., March 28, 1992).

56. C. Daniel Batson, Laura L. Shaw, and Kathryn C. Oleson, "Differentiating Affect, Mood, and Emotion: Toward Functionally Based Conceptual Distinctions," in *Emotion, Review of Personality, and Social Psychology,* ed. Margaret S. Clark (Newbury Park, Calif.: Sage, 1992), 13:294–326.

57. "By rapidly influencing activation level and producing prepared responses, [emotions] increase the likelihood of success when plans go awry." Good mood improves the metabolic system. Communication to others who are able to help also adds to fitness (William N. Morris, "A Functional Analysis of the Role of Mood in Affective Systems," in *Emotion, Review of Personality, and Social Psychology,* ed. Clark, 263).

58. Lane, *Market Experience,* 58–78.

59. Ibid., 58.

60. John Maynard Keynes, *A General Theory of Employment, Interest, and Money* (London: Macmillan, 1936), 161.

61. Knight, *Ethics of Competition,* 50.

62. See Michael Lewis and Jeannette M. Haviland-Jones, eds., *Handbook of Emotions,* 2d ed. (New York: Guilford, 2000).

63. Ed Diener and Eunkook Mark Suh, "National Differences in Subjective Well-Being," in *Well-Being,* ed. Kahneman, Diener, and Schwarz, 434–50.

64. Fortune, *Sorcerers of Dobu;* Oscar Lewis, *Life in a Mexican Village* (Urbana: University of Illinois Press, 1963).

65. Ronald Inglehart, "Changing Values in Japan and the West," *Comparative Political Studies* 14 (1982): 445–79.

66. Scherer, "Emotion Experiences across European Cultures," 189.

67. Suh et al., "Shifting Basis."

68. Deborah Stipek, Bernard Weiner, and Kexing Li, "Testing Some Attribution-Emotion Relations in the People's Republic of China," *Journal of Personality and Social Psychology* 56 (1989): 109–16; Jens B. Assendorpf and Gertrud Nunner-Winkler, "Children's Moral Motive Strength and Temporal Inhibition Reduce Their Immoral Behavior in Real Moral Conflicts," *Child Development* 63 (1992): 1223–35.

69. Li-Jun Ji, Kaiping Peng, and Richard E. Nisbett, "Culture, Control, and Perceptions of Relationships in the Environment," *Journal of Personality and Social Psychology* 78 (2000): 943–55.

70. Cheryl L. Rusting and Susan Nolen-Hoeksema, "Regulating Responses to Anger: Effects of Rumination and Distraction on Angry Mood," *Journal of Personality and Social Psychology* 74 (1998): 790–803.

71. "There appears to be a positive relation between regulation and sympathy/empathy, especially in childhood, and a consistent negative relation between personal distress and regulation in adulthood" (Nancy Eisenberg, "Emotion, Regulation, and Moral Development," *Annual Review of Psychology* 51 [2000]: 675).

72. Grazyna Kochanska, Katherine C. Coy, Terri L. Tjebkes, and Susan J. Husarek, "Individual Differences in Emotionality in Infancy," *Child Development* 69 (1998): 375–90.

73. June Price Tangney, "Situational Determinants of Shame and Guilt in Young Adulthood," *Personality and Social Psychology Bulletin* 18 (1992): 199–206.

74. Scherer, "Emotion Experiences across European Cultures," 180.

75. "Aging and Personality," *Harvard Mental Health Letter* 17 (September 2000): 7; based on Robert R. McCrae, Paul T. Costa Jr., Margarida Pedroso de Lima, Antonio Simoes, Fritz Ostendorf, Alois Angleitner, Iris Marusic, Denis Bratko, Gian Vittorio Caprara, Claudio Barbaranelli, Joon-Ho Chae, and Ralph L. Piedmont, "Age Differences in Personality across the Adult Life Span: Parallels in Five Cultures," *Developmental Psychology* 35 (1999): 466–77.

76. Daniel Goleman, "To 3Rs Some Schools Add Emotional Skills," *New York Times,* March 10, 1994, C1. The program has been adopted by other school systems, including those in the Bronx and Seattle.

77. Daniel Goleman, *Working with Emotional Intelligence* (New York: Bantam, 1998), 317.

78. Ibid.

79. Joseph V. Ciarrochi, Amy Y. Chan, and Peter C. Caputi, "A Critical Evaluation of the Emotional Intelligence Construct," *Personality and Individual Differences* 28 (2000): 539–61.

80. Ibid.

81. See Peter Salovey, Brian T. Bedell, Jerusha B. Detweiler, and John D. Mayer, "Current Directions in Emotional Intelligence Research," in *Handbook of Emotions,* ed. Michael Lewis and Haviland-Jones, 504–20.

82. Goleman, *Working with Emotional Intelligence,* 12. Goleman's account was based on Thomas M. Achenbach and Catherine T. Howell, "Are American Children's Problems Getting Worse? A Thirteen-Year Comparison," *Journal of the American Academy of Child and Adolescent Psychiatry* 32 (1993): 1145–54.

83. Barbara Bergman, *Saving Our Children from Poverty: What the United States Can Learn from France* (New York: Russell Sage Foundation, 1998).

84. Joseph Veroff, Elizabeth Douvan, and Richard Kulka, *The Inner Americans: A Self-Portrait from 1957 to 1976* (New York: Basic Books, 1981), 531.

85. Juster, "Preferences for Work and Leisure," 333–51.

86. Daniel Yankelovich, Hans Zetterberg, Burkhard Strümpel, and Michael Shanks, *The World at Work: An International Report on Jobs, Productivity, and Human Values* (New York: Octagon, 1985), 284.

87. Katona, *Psychological Economics,* 237.

88. Fred Hirsch, *Social Limits to Growth* (Cambridge: Harvard University Press, 1976), 12. "Capitalism exhibits a pronounced proclivity toward undermining the moral foundations on which any society, including the capitalist variety, must rest" (Hirschman, "Rival Interpretations," 1466).

89. Quoted in Etzioni, *Moral Dimension,* 40.

90. Joan Robinson, *Economic Philosophy* (Harmondsworth: Penguin, 1964), 48.

91. Nussbaum, "Human Functioning and Social Justice," 205.

92. Kurt Baier, *The Moral Point of View: A Rational Basis for Ethics* (Ithaca: Cornell University Press, 1958). Hume seems to have some similar formulation, but Dessie did not know where.

93. Lawrence Kohlberg and Robert A. Ryncarz, "Beyond Justice Reasoning: Moral Development and Consideration of a Seventh Stage," in *Higher Stages*

of Human Development: Perspectives on Adult Growth, ed. Charles N. Alexander and Ellen J. Langer (Oxford: Oxford University Press, 1990), 193.

94. Ibid., 194.

95. Ibid.

96. Ibid., 205.

97. Carol Gilligan, John Michael Murphy, and Mark B. Tappan, "Moral Development beyond Adolescence," in *Higher Stages of Human Development,* ed. Alexander and Langer, 209; see also Carol Gilligan, Janie Victoria Ward, and Jill McLean Taylor, eds., *Mapping the Moral Domain* (Cambridge: Harvard University Press, 1989).

98. Gilligan, Murphy, and Tappan, "Moral Development beyond Adolescence," 224.

99. Zajonc, "Feeling and Thinking."

100. Valerie Stander and Larry Jensen, "The Relationship of Value Orientation to Moral Cognition: Gender and Cultural Differences in the United States and China Explored," *Journal of Cross-Cultural Psychology* 24 (1993): 42–52. The authors express surprise that the Confucian code does not elicit higher caring responses in China than the American market code in the United States.

101. Lane, *Loss of Happiness.*

102. Martin Morse Wooster, "Can Character Be Taught?" *American Enterprise* 1 (November–December 1990): 51.

103. Eisenberg, "Emotion, Regulation, and Moral Development," 685.

104. William Damon, "The Development of Justice and Self-Interest during Childhood," in *Justice Motive in Social Behavior,* ed. Lerner and Lerner, 57–72.

105. Nancy Eisenberg, Rita Schell, Jeannette Pasternack, Randy Lennon, Rob Beller, and Robin N. Mathy, "Prosocial Development in Middle Childhood: A Longitudinal Study," *Developmental Psychology* 23 (1987): 712–18.

106. Veenhoven, *Conditions of Happiness,* 54. In Europe, suicide rates are inversely related to average measures of subjective well-being (Ronald Inglehart and Jacques-René Rabier, "Aspirations Adapt to Situations—But Why Are the Belgians So Much Happier Than the French? A Cross-Cultural Analysis of the Subjective Quality of Life," in *Research on the Quality of Life,* ed. Frank M. Andrews [Ann Arbor, Mich.: Institute for Social Research, 1986], 51).

107. Laboratory of Comparative Human Cognition, "What's Cultural about Cross-Cultural Cognitive Psychology?" *Annual Review of Psychology* 30 (1979): 153.

108. Alex Inkeles, *Exploring Individual Modernity* (New York: Columbia University Press, 1983), 313.

109. Milton Rokeach and Sandra J. Ball-Rokeach, "Stability and Change in American Value Priorities, 1968–1981," *American Psychologist* 44 (1989): 783.

110. Mark Miringoff and Margue-Luisa Miringoff, *The Social Health of the Nation: How America Is Really Doing* (New York: Oxford University Press, 1999).

8. GETTING RICH THE RIGHT WAY

1. "The feverish haste of acquisition and pleasure . . . may serve to make achievements for the future when the fruits of a higher culture [will be] accessible to the widest circle" (Lange, *History of Materialism,* 238).

2. Fukuyama, *End of History.*

3. Keynes, "Economic Possibilities for Our Grandchildren," 329.

4. C. Droge, M. Agrawal, and R. Mackoy, "The Consumption Culture and Its Critiques: A Framework for Analysis," *Journal of Macromarketing* 13 (1993): 32–45.

5. Charles Wolf Jr., *Markets or Governments: Choosing between Imperfect Alternatives* (Cambridge: MIT Press, 1988), 146–47.

6. Ibid.

7. Jan Ott, "Freedom and the Achievement of Happiness," in *Challenges to Democracy: Ideas, Involvements, and Institutions: The PSA Yearbook 2000,* ed. Keith Dowding, James Hughes, and Helen Margetts (London: Palgrave, 2000), 48.

8. Inglehart, *Modernization and Postmodernization.*

9. Lane, "Self-Reliance and Empathy," 473–92.

10. Robert E. Lane, " 'Losing Touch' in a Democracy: Demands vs. Needs," in *Élitism, Populism, and European Politics,* ed. Jack Hayward (Oxford: Clarendon, 1996), 33–66.

11. United Nations Development Programme, *Human Development Report 1998,* 20.

12. Sen, *Development as Freedom.*

13. Victoria Brittain and Kevin Whitney, "A Continent Driven to Economic Suicide," *Guardian* [London], July 20, 1994, 11; Gary M. Woller, "Economic Reform in Latin America and Prospects for Distributive Justice: The Market, Neoliberal Theory, and the State" (paper presented at the fifth annual meeting of the Society for the Advancement of Socio-Economics, New York, March 26–28, 1993).

14. Thomas L. Friedman, "Africa's Economies: Reforms Pay Off," *New York Times,* March 13, 1994, 18; Vinod Thomas, Mansoor Dailami, Ashok Dhareshwar, Daniel Kaufmann, Nalin Kishor, Raimon Lopez, and Van Wang, *The Quality of Growth* (Washington, D.C.: International Bank for Reconstruction and Development/World Bank, 2000); James D. Wolfensohn, *People First: 1997 Paul G. Hoffman Lecture* (New York: United Nations Development Programme, Office of Development Studies, 1997).

15. John Walsh, "A Plenipotentiary for Human Intelligence," *Science* 214 (November 6, 1981): 640–41. But, disturbed by a political upheaval, alas, the minister of intelligence lost his job a few years later.

16. In the United States, the net return on human capital has exceeded that of conventional capital since 1930 (Jeffrey G. Williamson and Peter H. Lindert, *American Inequality: A Macroeconomic History* [New York: Academic Press, 1980], 59–60).

17. Keynes, "Economic Possibilities for Our Grandchildren," 329.

18. Landes, *Unbound Prometheus,* repr., *Industrial Man,* ed. Tom Burns (Harmondsworth: Penguin, 78).

19. Philip E. Tetlock, Orie V. Kristel, S. Beth Elson, Melanie C. Green, and Jennifer S. Lerner, "The Psychology of the Unthinkable: Taboo Trade-Offs, Forbidden Base Rates, and Heretical Counterfactuals," *Journal of Personality and Social Psychology* 78 (2000): 854.

20. Bronislaw Malinowski, *Magic, Science, and Religion* (New York: Doubleday/Anchor, 1955).

21. Ruth W. Lidz, Theodore Lidz, and G. Burton-Bradley, "Cargo Cultism: A Psychosocial Study of Melanesian Millenarianism," *Journal of Nervous and Mental Disease* 157 (1973): 370–88.

22. Maine, *Ancient Law,* 131.

23. Ferdinand Tönnies, *Community and Society* [Gemeinschaft und Gesellschaft], trans. C. P. Loomis (1887; East Lansing: Michigan State University Press, 1957).

24. H. M. Parsons, "What Happened at Hawthorne? New Evidence Suggests the Hawthorne Effect Resulted from Operant Reinforcement," *Science* 181 (March 8, 1974): 922–32.

25. F. J. Roethlisberger, *Management and Morale* (Cambridge: Harvard University Press, 1941), 52, 53.

26. Tocqueville, *Democracy in America,* 2:98.

27. Triandis, *Individualism and Collectivism.*

28. Alan Macfarlane, *The Origins of English Individualism: The Family, Property, and Social Transition* (New York: Cambridge University Press, 1978); Alan Macfarlane, *The Culture of Capitalism* (Cambridge: Blackwell, 1987).

29. Lane, *Loss of Happiness,* 113–19.

30. See, e.g., Sandra Wallman, introduction to *Social Anthropology of Work,* ed. Wallman (London: Academic, 1979), 17.

31. Robert E. Lane, "Individualism and the Market Society," in *Liberal Democracy: Nomos XXV,* ed. Roland Pennock and John W. Chapman (New York: New York University Press, 1983), 374–407.

32. Compton Advertising, *National Survey of the U.S. Economic System.* Nevertheless, people do feel "tied down" in their general lives; see Campbell, Converse, and Rodgers, *Quality of American Life,* 38. Perhaps this contrast between people's free-answer questions and their responses to a semantic differential measure results from the differences in method—or perhaps it results from the feeling that they are more "tied down" by family and other obligations than by the economy.

33. Harris survey reported in Seymour Martin Lipset and William Schneider, *The Confidence Gap: Business, Labor, and Government in the Public Mind* (New York: Free Press, 1983), 286.

34. Richard DeCharms, *Personal Causation* (New York: Academic Press, 1968), 269.

35. Seligman, *Helplessness.*

36. Ellen J. Langer, "The Illusion of Control," *Journal of Personality and Social Psychology* 32 (1975): 311–28.

37. Polanyi, *Great Transformation.*

38. Amartya Sen, *Commodities and Capabilities* (Amsterdam: North-Holland, 1985).

39. Aquinas, the greatest of the schoolmen, was certainly cognitively developed, but without understanding the relationships between evidence and theory, hypothesis and proof, physics and metaphysics, his work could not advance our understanding of the way the world works; see Otton Neurath, Rudolf Carnap,

and Charles Morris, eds., *International Encyclopedia of Unified Science* (Chicago: University of Chicago Press, 1955), vol. 1, nos. 1–5.

40. Quoted in Guido de Ruggiero, *The History of European Liberalism,* trans. R. G. Collingwood (London: Oxford University Press, 1927), 126.

41. Etzioni, *Moral Dimension,* 250; Hirsch, *Social Limits to Growth,* 12; Hirschman, "Rival Interpretations," 1466.

42. Spencer, *Social Statics,* 482.

43. Fromm, *Escape,* 288–89.

44. Charles A. Beard, *An Economic Interpretation of the Constitution of the United States* (New York: Macmillan, 1948).

45. Simonton, *Genius, Creativity, and Leadership,* 140.

46. See Nathan J. Bender's review of Sorokin's *The Basic Trends of Our Times* (1964) and *The Crisis of Our Age* (1969), "Value Systems in a Changing Culture," *Journal of Religion and Health* 12 (1973): 259–77.

47. Simonton, *Genius, Creativity, and Leadership,* 156.

48. See Alison M. Jaggar and Iris M. Young, eds., *Companion to Feminist Philosophy* (Malden, Mass.: Blackwell, 1998).

49. George M. Guthrie, "A Social Psychological Analysis of Modernization in the Philippines," *Journal of Cross-Cultural Psychology* 8 (1977): 177–206.

50. Oscar Lewis, *Life in a Mexican Village.*

51. Robert Redfield, *A Village That Chose Progress: Chan Kom Revisited* (Chicago: University of Chicago Press, 1950).

52. Kenneth Boulding, "The Basis of Value Judgments in Economics," in *Human Values and Economic Policy,* ed. Sidney Hook (New York: New York University Press, 1967), 68; Neva R. Goodwin, "Economic Meanings of Trust and Responsibility," in *As If the Future Mattered: Translating Social and Economic Theory into Human Behavior,* ed. Neva R. Goodwin (Ann Arbor: University of Michigan Press, 1996), 45–82.

53. Putnam, "Social Capital and Public Affairs."

54. Inkeles and Diamond, "Personal Development and National Development," 97.

55. Edward F. Denison, *Accounting for United States Economic Growth, 1929–1969* (Washington, D.C.: Brookings Institution, 1974).

56. Marx and Engels, *Manifesto* (1932 ed.), 12.

57. Inglehart, *Modernization and Postmodernization,* 101.

58. Rahn and Transue, "Social Trust and Value Change," 560.

59. Herbert Hyman, *Political Socialization* (Glencoe, Ill.: Free Press, 1959); Herbert H. Hyman, Charles R. Wright, and John Shelton Reed, *The Enduring Effects of Education* (Chicago: University of Chicago Press, 1975).

60. Eric L. Dey, Alexander W. Astin, and William S. Korn, *The American Freshman: Twenty-five Year Trends* (Los Angeles: Higher Education Research Institute, UCLA, 1991); Alexander W. Astin et al., *The American Freshman: National Norms for Fall 1991* (and similar volumes through 1995).

61. Galbraith, *Affluent Society,* 252.

62. Kohn and Schooler, *Work and Personality,* 64 n. 8.

63. U.S. Bureau of Labor Statistics, *Monthly Labor Review,* November 1993, repr., U.S. Bureau of the Census, *Statistical Abstract of the United States: 1995* (Washington, D.C.: U.S. Government Printing Office, 1995), table 650,

"Civilian Employment in Occupations with the Largest Job Growth: 1922 to 2005," 414.

64. In a December 2003 private communication, Paul Streeten told me that the BLS is now predicting the fastest growth among low-skill service jobs, which are often in public service and invulnerable to computer replacement and to competition from overseas.

65. Dessie might have added another occupational cycle: from crafts through assembly line to automation, a cycle that dealt not with learning but with job satisfaction; see Blauner, *Alienation and Freedom*.

66. Harry Braverman, *Labor and Monopoly Capital: The Degradation of Work in the Twentieth Century* (New York: Monthly Review Press, 1974).

67. Adam Smith, *Inquiry into the Nature and Causes,* 734–35. Smith was not alone; Ferguson (quoted in Marx, *Capital*) and Steuart and Montesquieu joined the chorus, although the latter were more likely to criticize the effects of commerce than of industry. Marx (*Capital*) criticized Smith for minimizing the effects of the division of labor on the worker. See Karl Marx, *Capital,* ed. G. D. H. Cole, trans. Eden Paul and Cedar Paul (1867; New York: Dutton Everyman, 1974), 383.

68. William Form, "On the Degradation of Skills," *Annual Review of Sociology* 13 (1987): 29–47; Eva Mueller, *Technological Advance in an Expanding Economy* (Ann Arbor, Mich.: Institute for Social Research, 1969).

69. Inkeles and Diamond, "Personal Development and National Development," 104. Alex Inkeles, *National Character: A Psycho-Social Perspective* (New Brunswick, N.J.: Transaction, 1997), 206, also says that the most important contribution to his measure of individual modernity is education, followed by factory experience.

70. Jeylan T. Mortimer and Jon Lorence, "Work Experience and Occupational Value Socialization: A Longitudinal Study," *American Journal of Sociology* 84 (1979): 1361–85.

71. Leonard J. Pearlin and Melvin L. Kohn, "Social Class, Occupation, and Parental Values: A Cross-Cultural Study," *American Sociological Review* 31 (1966): 466–79.

72. George E. Vaillant and Caroline O. Vaillant, "Natural History of Male Psychological Health: Work as a Predictor of Positive Mental Health," *American Journal of Psychiatry* 138 (1981): 1433–40. But see Ellen Greenberger and Lawrence Steinberg, *When Teenagers Work: The Psychological and Social Costs of Adolescent Employment* (New York: Basic Books, 1986).

73. Paul F. Wernimont and Susan Fitzpatrick, "The Meaning of Money," *Journal of Applied Psychology* 50 (1972): 218–26.

74. Denison, *Accounting for United States Economic Growth,* 132.

75. Inglehart, *Modernization and Postmodernization*. For reports on the value of government jobs, see Christopher Jencks, Lauri Perman, and Lee Rainwater, "What Is a Good Job? A New Measure of Labor-Market Success," *American Journal of Sociology* 93 (1988): 1322–57.

76. Charles Lewis Taylor, ed., *Why Governments Grow: Measuring Public Sector Size* (Beverly Hills, Calif.: Sage, 1983).

77. Juliet B. Schor, *The Overworked American: The Unexpected Decline of Leisure* (New York: Basic Books, 1991), 117.

1. A. E. Houseman, "XL," in *A Shropshire Lad* (New York: Henry Holt, 1924), repr., *The Collected Poems of A. E. Houseman* (New York: Henry Holt, 1940), 58.
2. Inkeles, *Exploring Individual Modernity,* 322.
3. Engels, "Socialism: Utopian and Scientific," 186.
4. Spencer, *Social Statics,* 482.
5. Keynes, "Economic Possibilities for Our Grandchildren," 325, 328.
6. Pitirim A. Sorokin, *The Crisis of Our Age: The Social and Cultural Outlook* (New York: Dutton, 1941).
7. Daniel Bell, *The Cultural Contradictions of Capitalism* (New York: Basic Books, 1976), 84.
8. Lange, *History of Materialism,* 244.
9. Max Weber, *Protestant Ethic and the Spirit of Capitalism,* 181.
10. Maslow, *Motivation and Personality.*
11. Inglehart, *Modernization and Postmodernization,* 108. Inglehart's first book on postmaterialism in Europe was *The Silent Revolution.*
12. Dessie apparently did not know that postmaterialists in the United States were no different from materialists in their support for abortion or their attitudes toward homosexuals (Edward G. Carmines and Geoffrey C. Layman, "Value Priorities, Partisanship, and Electoral Choice: The Neglected Case of the United States," *Political Behavior* 19[1997]: 283–316).
13. Warren W. Davis and Christian Davenport, "Assessing the Validity of the Postmaterialism Index," *American Political Science Review* 93 (1999): 649–64.
14. Ronald Inglehart and Wayne E. Baker, "Modernization, Cultural Change, and the Persistence of Traditional Culture," *American Sociological Review* 65 (2000): 19–51.
15. A methodological review of Inglehart's analysis suggested skepticism about the socialization theory. The authors report, "The differences between the impact and process of 'modernisation' as opposed to 'postmodernisation' are not clearly discernible" (Roger Jowell, John Curtice, Allison Park, Lindsay Brook, Katarina Thomson, and Caroline Bryson, eds., *British and European Social Attitudes: How Britain Differs* [London: Ashgate, 1998], summarized in *SINET* 60 [1999]: 1–6).
16. Inglehart and Baker, "Modernization," 87–89.
17. Ibid., 90.
18. Okin, *Women in Western Political Thought,* 294.
19. Harold D. Clarke, Allan Kornberg, Chris McIntyre, Patra Bauer Kaase, and Max Kaase, "The Effect of Economic Priorities on the Measurement of Value Change: New Experimental Evidence," *American Political Science Review* 93 (1999): 637–47; Randall MacIntosh, "Global Attitude Measurement: An Assessment of the World Values Survey Postmaterialism Scale," *American Sociological Review* 63 (1998): 452–64. Ahuvia and Wong report that "life satisfaction for *post*materialists is actually more dependent on satisfaction with income than it was for materialists. In sum, this research has provided reason to doubt the primary theoretical mechanism proposed by Inglehart to explain his findings" (*Three Types of Materialism,* 15).

20. Rahn and Transue, "Social Trust and Value Change," 554. In search of a silver lining, Dessie could take a little comfort from the fact that the particular measures of materialism used here seemed to be statistically different from (load on a different factor than) other measures with economic content.

21. Schor, *Overworked American,* 116.

22. Other data cast doubt on even this minimal concession. Thus, the percentage of a cross-national European sample agreeing to the need for "less emphasis on money" dropped by just 1 percentage point (from 68 to 67 percent) from 1981 to 1990 (Sheena Ashford and Noel Timms, *What Europe Thinks: A Study of Western European Values* [Aldershot, U.K.: Dartmouth, 1992], 134–36).

23. Elinor Scarborough, "Materialist-Postmaterialist Value Orientations," in *The Impact of Values: Beliefs in Government,* ed. Jan W. Van Deth and Elinor Scarborough (Oxford: Oxford University Press, 1995), 4:138.

24. Ibid., 155.

25. Rahn and Transue, "Social Trust and Value Change," 555.

26. Dieter Fuchs and Hans-Dieter Klingeman, "Citizens and the State: A Relationship Transformed," in *Citizens and the State: Beliefs in Government,* ed. Hans-Dieter Klingeman and Dieter Fuchs (Oxford: Oxford University Press, 1995), 1:439.

27. Polanyi, *Great Transformation.*

28. Oliver Goldsmith goes on to note that the loss of a "bold peasantry, their country's pride, / When once destroyed, can never be supplied." From "The Deserted Village," ll. 55–56 (1770), in *English Poetry II: From Collins to Fitzgerald.* Vol. 41 of : *The Harvard Classics,* ed. C. W. Eliot (New York: P. F. Collier & Son, 1909–14).

29. Hicks, *Theory of Economic History.*

30. Jean F. Revel, *Without Marx or Jesus* (New York: Delta, 1971), 162. Revel was not alone in this interpretation. At the time, Jürgen Habermas and Charles Reich concurred, and as late as 1992, William Strauss and Neil Howe could say that as a result of observing their parents, members of "this [current] generation may increasingly seek happiness in nonmaterial, spiritual activities and in human relationships" (*Generations: The History of America's Future from 1584 to 2069*). Nor is this just intuitive social science. The Harwood Group reports a survey in which 72 percent of respondents said they had more possessions than their parents but only 49 percent thought they were happier than their parents (*Public Perspective* 9 [February–March 1998]: 13).

31. Knight, *Ethics of Competition,* 66.

32. Myrna M. Weissman and 17 others. "Cross-National Epidemiology of Major Depression and Bipolar Disorder," *Journal of the American Medical Association* 275 (July 24–26, 1996): 293–99.

33. "Generalized Anxiety Disorder: Toxic Worry," *Harvard Mental Health Letter* 19 (January 2003): 1.

34. Hirschman, *Passions and the Interests.*

35. Kahneman, Diener, and Schwarz, *Well-Being.*

36. Lane, *Loss of Happiness,* 231–48. John Mirowski and Catherine E. Ross point out, "Of all the beliefs about self and society that might increase or reduce distress, one's sense of control over one's own life may be the most important"

224   (*Social Causes of Psychological Distress* [New York: Aldine de Gruyter, 1989], 131).

37. C. Wright Mills, *The Sociological Imagination* (New York: Oxford University, 1967), 186, 188.

38. Aristotle, *Nicomachean Ethics,* in *Value and Obligation,* ed. Brandt, 59.

39. Immanuel Kant, *On the Old Saw: That May Be Right in Theory but It Won't Work in Practice* (Philadelphia: University of Pennsylvania Press, 1974), 63.

40. Michael E. Porter, "Capital Choices: National Systems of Investment," in *As If the Future Mattered,* ed. Goodwin, 15–44.

41. Michael T. Jacobs, *Short-Term America: The Causes and Cures of Our Business Myopia* (Boston: Harvard Business School Press, 1991).

42. "In the ordinary run of often repeated decisions the individual is subject to the salutary and rationalizing influence of favorable and unfavorable experience. He is also under the influence of relatively simple and unproblematic motives and interests which are but occasionally interfered with by excitement" (Schumpeter, *Capitalism, Socialism, and Democracy,* 158).

43. Andrews and Withey, *Social Indicators,* 115, 135.

44. Jonathan Freedman, *Happy People* (New York: Harcourt, Brace, 1980), 41.

45. Daniel Kahneman, "Assessment of Individual Well-Being: A Bottom-Up Approach" (paper presented at the Conference on Enjoyment and Suffering, Princeton University, October 31–November 3, 1996).

46. Howard L. Fromkin, "Effects of Experimentally Aroused Feelings of Undistinctiveness Upon Valuation of Scarce and Novel Experiences," *Journal of Personality and Social Psychology* 16 (1970): 521–29.

47. John P. Robinson, "Changes in Time Use," 311.

48. Schor, *Overworked American.*

49. Campbell, Converse, and Rodgers, *Quality of American Life,* 270.

50. Donald M. Cohen, *Beyond Rhetoric: A New American Agenda for Children and Families* (Washington, D.C.: U.S. Government Printing Office, 1991).

51. Scott T. Yabiku, William G. Axinn, and Arland Thornton, "Family Integration and Children's Self-Esteem," *American Journal of Sociology* 104 (1999): 1494–1524.

52. Durkheim, *Suicide,* 378.

53. Louis Uchitelle, "The Rise of the Losing Class," *New York Times,* November 20, 1994, sec. 4, p. 1; based on Robert Reich, polls by Michigan Consumer Surveys, Chicago NORC, Louis Harris Polls, and others.

54. Roper Starch Worldwide, May 15–22, 1993, reported in *American Enterprise,* November–December 1994, 98.

55. Ronald Inglehart, "Post-Materialism in an Environment of Insecurity," *American Political Science Review* 75 (1981): 880–900.

56. Jowell et al., *British and European Social Attitudes.* European trends on the continent are different, as reported in Spanakopita 3. In flat contradiction to Frederick Lange (see Spanakopita 3), modern religion and materialism are quite able to accommodate each other.

57. Rahn and Transue, "Social Trust and Value Change."

58. See Lane, *Market Experience,* 553–56.

59. Priscilla A. La Barbera and Zeynep Guerhan, "The Role of Materialism, Religiosity, and Demographics in Subjective Well-Being," *Psychology and Marketing* 14 (1997): 71–97; Jerry W. Lee, Gail T. Rice, and V. Bailey Gillespie, "Family Worship Patterns and Their Correlation with Adolescent Behavior and Beliefs," *Journal for the Scientific Study of Religion* 36 (1997): 372–81. Rahn and Transue, "Social Trust and Value Change," 560, report that religious commitment was the most important variable in influencing materialism.

60. James R. Peacock and Margaret M. Poloma, "Religiosity and Life Satisfaction across the Life Course," *Social Indicators Research* 48 (1999): 321.

61. Inglehart and Rabier, "Aspirations Adapt to Situations," 17.

62. Rahn and Transue, "Social Trust and Value Change," 560.

63. Before the feminists land with both feet on Dessie, he would like to point out that he is aware of the research showing that the children of working mothers are often as happy and healthy as others. See, e.g., Elena Dockett and Maryse H. Richards, "Maternal Employment and the Quality of Experience for Young Adolescents of Single Mothers," *Journal of Family Psychology* 9 (1995): 418–32.

64. Diener and Diener, "Cross-Cultural Correlates," 661.

65. Eirini Flouri, "An Integrated Model of Consumer Materialism: Can Economic Socialization and Maternal Values Predict Materialistic Attitudes in Adolescents?" *Journal of Socio-Economics* 28 (2000): 707.

66. Rahn and Transue, "Social Trust and Value Change," 559, 560.

67. John Wesley, "The Use of Money," in *John Wesley's Fifty-Three Sermons,* ed. Edward H. Sugden (Nashville, Tenn.: Abingdon, 1983), 632–46.

68. Tönnies, *Community and Society* (1957 ed.).

69. Polanyi, *Great Transformation,* 46.

70. Lane, *Loss of Happiness,* figures 2.5, 6.1.

71. Simonton, *Genius, Creativity, and Leadership,* 176.

72. Srole, "Social Integration and Certain Corollaries."

73. Brian Barry, "Suicide: The Ultimate Escape," *Death Studies* 13 (1989): 185–90.

74. Sorokin, *Crisis of Our Age,* 133–36.

75. Kroeber, *Configurations of Culture Growth.*

76. See, e.g., Michael E. Sobel, *Lifestyle and Social Structure* (New York: Academic Press, 1981); see also reports of the Karl Polanyi Institute of Political Economy (Concordia University); articles in *Journal of Macromarketing, Journal of Socio-Economics, Social Indicators Research, Journal of Consumer Research,* and so on.

77. Lane, *Loss of Happiness,* 130.